METROPOLITAN PHILADELPHIA

April, '07

Enjoy

Steve

METROPOLITAN PORTRAITS

Metropolitan Portraits explores the contemporary metropolis in its

diverse blend of past and present. Each volume describes a North

American urban region in terms of historical experience, spatial

configuration, culture, and contemporary issues. Books in the

series are intended to promote discussion and understanding of

metropolitan North America at the start of the twenty-first century.

JUDITH A. MARTIN, SERIES EDITOR

METROPOLITAN

PHILADELPHIA

Living with the Presence of the Past

STEVEN CONN

University of Pennsylvania Press | Philadelphia

10 9 8 7 6 5 4 3 2 1

Published by

University of Pennsylvania Press

Philadelphia, Pennsylvania 19104-4112

Library of Congress Cataloging-in-Publication Data

Conn, Steven.

Metropolitan Philadelphia : living with the presence of the past / Steven Conn.

p. cm. — (Metropolitan portraits)

Includes bibliographical references and index.

ISBN-13: 978-0-8122-1943-2 (alk. paper)

ISBN-10: 0-8122-1943-0 (pbk. : alk. paper)

1. Philadelphia Region (Pa.)—Civilization. 2. Philadelphia Region (Pa.)—Social conditions. 3. Philadelphia Region (Pa.)—History. 4. Human geography—Pennsylvania—Philadelphia Region. 5. Middle class—Pennsylvania—Philadelphia Region. I. Title. II. Series.

F158.3.C66   2006

974.8'11—dc22

2005058484

For my parents, Terry and Peter.
Philip Larkin was wrong.

CONTENTS

The Naked City

There are a million stories in the naked city.

That line closes the 1948 classic film noir *The Naked City*.[1] The film, drenched in shadow and filled with the grit and swelter of a hot city summer, is a crime story set in New York. The movie, innovatively filmed in the city itself, out in the open, without stage sets, also purports to be, as the narrator explains, a story about the city. Its closing line, uttered by that same narrator over scenes of the city at night, has always struck me as the most astute characterization of any city: a great city is, at one level, a vast accumulation of its individual stories—some extraordinary, some quite quotidian, each different, and every one undeniable.

We can imagine, if you like, that these stories exist in two directions—horizontally across the city at any given moment, and vertically through time. These two axes are equally important, for just as the city belongs to those who occupy it from day to day, their stories carry on a conversation with the stories—histories— of those who have been there before. Part of what makes any great city great is this ongoing, effortless dialogue between past and present. That conversation contributes to the unique sense of place every real city has.

If there are millions of stories in the naked city, then there have been almost a million stories—and histories—written about the naked city. Historians who have turned their attention to the city have found political cities, places where great men gathered to do great deeds, and they have found cities teeming with radical women and men who came together to challenge those allegedly great men. They have found immigrant cities that functioned as beacons for millions looking for better opportunities, and cities that in many cases turned out to be squalid, oppressive, xenophobic places, places that made a mockery of American high ideals. They have found economic cities, bustling ports, and thrumming factory towns, and they have found artistic cities, places where writers, painters, architects, and institution builders drew their inspiration and made their mark. They have found cities on the rise in all these respects, and cities in decline. And of course, all these histories are at once right and incomplete. As the most complex and interesting thing human beings have ever created, the city is probably impossible to capture in its totality in any single book.

As one of the older American cities, Philadelphia has a longer history than most other places. But even more than that, it has also generated an enormous literature about that history. Sam Bass Warner, writing his own book about Philadelphia, noted that Philadelphia had become "a leading center of urban history."[2] That was in 1987, and in the subsequent years the shelves have grown even heavier with volumes about Philadelphia, making my task even more daunting. So I should be clear at the outset. This book does not even aim to be a comprehensive account or a full history. I certainly can't claim to have read all that has been written about Philadelphia and its region. Rather, my purpose is to consider Philadelphia as part of a larger metropolitan region, to examine how the region has evolved over time, and to hint at what might face the city and region in the future.

Philadelphia, and all American cities for that matter, have always existed in the center of larger regions, but by and large we haven't understood them that way. When we look at regions in the eighteenth and nineteenth centuries, our model is usually that of center (city) and periphery (hinterland), town and country. Given the way metropolitan regions have developed since the Second World War, however, that model no longer works. Like other older American cities, Philadelphia's population and economic prowess have both decreased even as the size and economic prosperity of the region has grown. Which, then, is center and which is periphery?

As we work toward a new model to understand regional dynamics, we see, generally speaking, our cities pitted in an antagonistic, largely racial struggle with their surrounding suburbs. In this view, white suburbs have proliferated since the end of World War II like parasites feeding off the shrinking, increasingly black body of deindustrializing cities. Philadelphia's story, then, is the same as Pittsburgh's, Detroit's, Chicago's, and St. Louis's. George Clinton, the intergalactic funk musician, summarized this version of the state of metropolitan America in the 1970s as succinctly as anyone when he riffed about "chocolate cities and vanilla suburbs."

I am, I confess, largely sympathetic to this view. There is no end of examples illustrating how Philadelphia's suburbs have siphoned resources, population, jobs, and more from the city, all the while taking advantage of the city in many ways. City schools are underfunded by the state, as is the city's public transit system. Since the eighteenth century, Philadelphia has led the country in medical research and training, establishing the nation's first hospital and first medical school among other things. Today, the city's medical centers groan under the burden of caring for a disproportionate number of the region's poor and uninsured. Suburbanites in great numbers from both Pennsylvania and New Jersey treat the city as their playground, using it for everything from art and high culture to drugs and prostitution, while simultaneously,

Fig. 1. The Philadelphia region imagined in a map of 1777. The orderly grid contrasts with the irregular roads that connected the city with towns such as Lancaster and Baltimore. Courtesy of the Library Company of Philadelphia.

often angrily, disavowing the notion that they share any responsibility for the city's considerable problems.[3]

Yet, as much as this gets the big picture right, it doesn't capture the fine grain of metropolitan realities, especially in Greater Philadelphia. More so than Greater Boston or Greater Chicago, I suspect, the Greater Philadelphia region has always had pockets of racial and class diversity. It contains several small urban centers and towns of considerable age, each with its own identity and each connected to the urban center in certain ways and independent from it in others.

In the eighteenth century, Philadelphia itself had the largest, most influential black community of any city in the nation; in the nineteenth century black communities grew elsewhere—in South Jersey and in West Chester, Pennsylvania for example. Later, West Chester would nurture both Horace Pippin, an African American painter, and Bayard Rustin, the African American who was the tactical genius behind the civil rights movement.[4] Coatesville's black community included Essie Mae Washington-Williams's aunt. Washington-Williams, the daughter of the savage racist Strom Thurmond and his black housekeeper, was raised by her aunt in that African American community. In the 1950s Bucks County became the site of the second Levitt and Sons development. It was all white, and when a black family tried to move in, its members were greeted with racist hostility. And at the same time, five miles down the road from Levittown, Concord Park was developed to be an intentionally integrated suburban subdevelopment. By all accounts it worked wonderfully well.

Race and racism are undeniably at the root of much of the visceral hatred some suburbanites feel toward the increasingly black and brown city. When John Street, Philadelphia's second black mayor, tried to make a speech at the opening of the Philadelphia Phillies' new baseball park in the spring of 2004, he was booed for nearly five minutes. The vast majority of fans who come to root for the Phils are whites from the suburbs. Here again: another example of suburbanites using the city for their own fun, in this case treating with contempt the mayor who helped use city funds to pay for the very stadium in which they were sitting. (Of course, Philadelphia fans would boo their own mothers if they struck out with runners in scoring position, so in the end maybe this episode didn't have much to do with race.)

But for others the emotions are probably more complicated. According to *Philadelphia Inquirer* editor Chris Satullo, what many suburbanites feel toward the city is "an angry love": "People who grew up in certain city neighborhoods and moved out to the suburbs literally can't go home again. It hurts too much. When they do, they find their old neighborhood has fallen apart, their old house is derelict. They react irrationally. When they try to make some sort of sense of the situation, they wind up blaming the people who live there now."[5]

I can confirm that assessment if only anecdotally. Some years ago, I wrote a newspaper essay about Levittown and about the postwar suburbs generally. In it, I argued that fear—especially the racially based fear of blacks by whites—drove much of the flight to the suburbs, particularly in the 1950s and 1960s. I got lots of hate mail about that piece, most of it confirming my premise in the first place, spewing as much of it did about dark-skinned people. One letter, however, caught me by the throat. "You do not know whereof you speak," it defiantly began, and the rest is worth quoting at some length, "until you have lived with the sound of police sirens every night—until you can recite the names of the shopkeepers in your area who have been robbed, stabbed, shot, and killed—until you have received a call from the hospital that your son has been badly beaten . . . until you live through the terrible day when a friend of your son, with whom he had eaten lunch, had been robbed and killed. He was 15 years old and only a child." The writer—anonymous, so I don't know whether male or female, black or white—went on: "That is when we decided to leave—it broke my heart to leave the house where my children grew up—the neighborhood where I grew up. It still hurts to think about." Anger and love in equal measure, because, as Neil Young sang, only love can break your heart.

These antagonisms, and the consequences that flow from them, are real. Yet despite that hostility, it has also become increasingly clear that the cities and their regions are now linked in ways that make them dependent on each other. Cities still provide most of the institutional infrastructure for regions— everything from hospitals and universities to art museums and symphonies—while many of the patrons of those institutions reside in suburbs. Suburbanites worry about the sprawl they themselves have created—no region in the country sprawled more than Greater Philadelphia during the 1990s—while cities struggle to attract new residents to older neighborhoods. Inner ring suburbs have begun to experience decline and abandonment while downtowns—Philadelphia's Center City exemplary among them—have boomed, becoming home to a growing number of young couples and empty nesters.

Indeed, as an editorial in the *Philadelphia Inquirer* astutely put it, "blight and sprawl are intimately linked." They feed one another: "Urban blight fuels middle-class flight which fuels sprawl which chews up government resources which worsens blight which propels sprawl ever outward." In fact, Greater Philadelphia served as the case that the Brookings Institution used to study the relationship between blight and sprawl. Its report described in grim detail the challenges the Philadelphia region faces as it confronts urban decay and the disappearance of farm land and open space.[6] That grim detail might be best summarized in two words: Toll Brothers. The Horsham, Montgomery County-based corporation is the nation's premier purveyor of luxury sprawl. It,

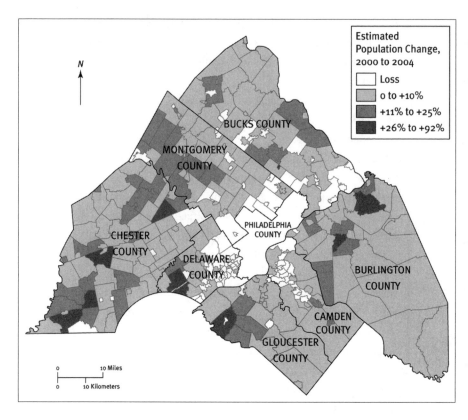

Fig. 2. The core of Greater Philadelphia, the city and the surrounding suburban areas, has lost population while the edge continues to grow. Data from the *Philadelphia Inquirer*.

along with a number of imitators, has transformed the landscape of metropolitan Philadelphia more quickly and more dramatically probably than at any time since European settlers arrived.

And yet, Greater Philadelphia has a legacy of sensible town planning, mass transit, mixed-income housing, and a front-porch, stoop-sitting culture that could make "smart growth" work perhaps better than anywhere else in the country. It is no accident surely that Tom Hylton, one of the nation's leading crusaders for smart growth, has done much of his work in and is based in Pottstown.[7] If blight and sprawl have been born of the same causes, and if they create many of the frictions in the region, then the solutions to those problems will lie in regional cooperation. Even politicians, whose political livelihoods depend on cultivating intense localism, are waking up to this. The Brookings report prompted the creation of the Philadelphia Regional Network of the National Environmental Leadership Program.

Few metropolitan regions have genuinely effective regional cooperation. But the need for it is even more true and more urgent for Greater Philadelphia than for almost any other metropolitan region. While the city of Philadelphia has suffered a great deal in the last fifty years, the Commonwealth of Pennsylvania has not fared much better. The industries that made it an economic power—coal, steel, railroads—have disappeared almost entirely. Its population is now the second oldest in the nation, and during the 1990s its economy did not boom the way economies of other states did. Greater Philadelphia was the only area in the state with any real economic dynamism, but Greater Philadelphia added jobs and population at a much slower rate than most other metropolitan regions. During the period 1989–99 employment grew 20 percent nationally, but only 7 percent in the Delaware Valley. Greater Pittsburgh, in contrast, didn't really grow at all during the 1990s, and that city finds itself teetering on the brink of financial collapse. Coming out of the second Bush recession, and as I write it isn't clear that it is proving much of a recovery, Greater Philadelphia saw a very slight rise in employment figures while the state as a whole continued to lose jobs.[8]

Put more simply, Philadelphia needs a healthy region in order to survive, and its suburbs need a healthy city in order to prosper. And as Greater Philadelphia goes, so goes the entire state of Pennsylvania. The stakes for thinking regionally are high indeed.

Having said that, however, I have only raised an additional set of questions. The city at least has a fixed line drawn around its boundary, but when we consider the region it isn't clear where those boundaries are. The problem begins with the very name of the area itself, or rather the lack thereof: Metropolitan Philadelphia, as in the title of this book? The Delaware Valley, though strictly speaking it isn't much of a valley, and the name itself ignores the region's other major river? The tri-state area? Greater Philadelphia? None of these seems quite satisfactory,[9] and I shall probably use them all in the course of this book.

Looked at demographically, Philadelphia is, as I write, vying with the urban agglomeration known as Phoenix to be the nation's fifth-largest city, and it is the fourth-largest metropolitan region. It is generally considered to include the five counties of southeastern Pennsylvania—Philadelphia, Bucks, Montgomery, Delaware, and Chester (though the latter until recently would probably not have been thought of as part of the region)—Burlington, Camden, and Gloucester counties in South Jersey, and New Castle County, Delaware, the top, rounded part of which includes the city of Wilmington.

In the world of vernacular architecture, however, the region is, or was once, much larger. Vernacular architecture refers to building done without formal planning or trained architects—it is folk architecture, reflecting people's particular cultural heritage. (We talk of vernacular architecture generally in the eighteenth and

PROLOGUE

nineteenth centuries. In the twentieth century, the architecture of houses, shopping areas, farms, and so on has largely been homogenized and turned into a mass-produced commodity.) As the pioneering folklorist Henry Glassie has documented and demonstrated, in the eighteenth century the Delaware Valley generated a unique vernacular that combined English and German building traditions. This Germano-Georgian style spread, by Glassie's reckoning, north and west and can be found throughout fully two-thirds of the state of Pennsylvania and into northern Maryland as well.[10]

If we map the region by its transportation routes, then we notice that the vestiges of the colonial-era road system remain, their very names a reminder of how the region was once connected: Lancaster Avenue still links the center of Philadelphia with the small city of Lancaster, and Chester Avenue still gets you to Chester. You will make it to Baltimore from Philadelphia, eventually, by following the route of Baltimore Avenue meandering south and west out of the city.

Thanks to the railroad development of the nineteenth century, one can take a commuter train run by the Southeastern Pennsylvania Transit Authority (SEPTA) from Center City Philadelphia as far north as Doylestown in central Bucks County and Trenton, New Jersey; as far south as Newark, Delaware; and as far west as Downingtown. By this measure, Trenton is part of Greater Philadelphia, but Princeton is not. Located halfway between Philadelphia and New York, that leafy, affluent university town has commuter service north to New York, but not south to Philadelphia.

Recreationally, the dimensions of Greater Philadelphia grow larger. In the latter half of the nineteenth century, Philadelphians journeyed, thanks to new railroad lines, to the Jersey Shore, where they escaped the muggy heat of the Philadelphia summer. In so doing, they built resort towns, from Atlantic City, with its spectacular boardwalk, to Cape May, with its Victorian gingerbread. For summer vacationers, Long Beach Island, north of Atlantic City, marked the boundary between Philadelphia and Brooklyn.[11] Those who wanted mountain air instead of sea breezes filled resorts in the Pocono Mountains, to the north of the city. Wealthy Philadelphians went even farther for their summer retreat, establishing outposts of Philadelphia in Maine.

In the geography of baseball, the Philadelphia region extends west to Reading and north to Scranton/Wilkes Barre, where the Phillies have farm teams, and as far south as Clearwater, Florida, which becomes a Philadelphia satellite for the months of spring training. Musically, there is another geography. While the Phils play baseball in South Philly during the summer, the Philadelphia Orchestra moves to Saratoga Springs, New York, and plays there. Meanwhile, music gets made more intimately at the Marlborough Music Festival in Vermont, an annual event founded by Philadelphians and still with many Philadelphia connections.

On the map of American regionalism, however, the region is shaped differently. Most people who live in Greater Philadelphia think of themselves, I suspect, as living in the center of the Northeast Corridor, the polite name given to what used to be called by some "Megalopolis," the largest urban concentration in the nation. As in the musical geography, our axis of cultural orientation is north-south. Philadelphians have more in common with New Yorkers, Bostonians, and Washingtonians than they do with people who live just west of the metropolitan area. Many Philadelphians believe the Midwest starts somewhere in Lancaster County, and in some ways they aren't wrong.

Regardless of where one draws an exact boundary around Greater Philadelphia, it is a remarkably varied area. Ecologically it takes in the Pocono Mountains and the Jersey Shore, running from deciduous forests to the Pine Barrens, from brackish saltwater marshes to clear trout streams. Its human creations include not only the major city of Philadelphia but also several smaller cities—Camden, Chester, Reading, Downington, Wilmington—that are, or were, vibrant urban centers in their own right, with their own sense of identity. It stretches from the Amish farms of Lancaster County, reminders of Philadelphia's role as a magnet for European religious dissenters, to the blueberry bushes and tomato fields of South Jersey, though both now are disappearing under the ever-spreading asphalt of suburban sprawl. It includes the bastions of Main Line blue bloods and working-class towns in Delaware County. It includes pockets of extraordinary wealth and some of the most crushing, desperate poverty in the nation.

At the birth of the republic, Philadelphia was the center of the nation's economy and of its politics. Two hundred years later it finds itself equidistant from both. And while there are certainly advantages to this location between Washington and New York, it has also meant living increasingly in their growing shadows. Philadelphia lost its supremacy in banking as a result of the fight President Andrew Jackson had with the Second Bank of the United States in the 1830s. Today, after more than a generation of mergers, acquisitions, and the like, most of the region's banking is done through institutions headquartered elsewhere. Commerce Bank, the largest bank headquartered in the area, has its home offices not in the city but in Cherry Hill, New Jersey, one of the first postwar suburbs. As the city and region struggle to fashion a new postindustrial economy from the rubble of the industrial one, Philadelphia's boosters have taken to calling the region "the buckle of the Money Belt," though it isn't clear how much staying power that catchy phrase will ultimately have.

In fact, Greater Philadelphia has never had a single economic identity in the way that New York became synonymous with Wall Street, that Chicago was the hog-butcher to the world, or that Detroit was the Motor City. In the eighteenth century, Philadelphia was the home of the finest craftsmen in the colonies, and its hinterland was their richest, most productive agricultural area. Early in the nineteenth century, the Philadelphia region led the nation in industrial development, from the anthracite coal fields north of the city, to the glass manufacturers in South Jersey, to the iron forges of Hopewell and other places to the west. Throughout the nineteenth century, the city was a leader in developing and applying industrial technologies. By the 1920s Philadelphia had become known as the Workshop of the World, a moniker which captured both the small scale of Philadelphia's production and the fact that no single industry dominated the economic scene. Indeed, by the 1920s Philadelphia and its surroundings probably had a diversity of industrial production greater than any city in the world—from railroad locomotives to lace to processed goat leather to hand-rolled cigars to refined sugar. Virtually anything made in a factory in the early twentieth century was probably made somewhere in Philadelphia.

That diversity has proved a mixed blessing to the region. When the industrial economy began its decline after the Second World War, the fall was not spectacular like the collapse of the steel industry in and around Pittsburgh, but it was no less inexorable. Philadelphia held on to its well-paying industrial jobs longer than many places did; they disappeared one small plant at a time. One consequence of this death of a thousand cuts was that Philadelphia's business and political leadership has only recently felt the need to plan and build for a postindustrial future. The process of deindustrialization resulted from a whole variety of national and international causes, almost all of which were beyond Philadelphia's—or any city's—ability to control. Philadelphia has weathered this economic storm better than some other places, such as Cleveland, Detroit, St. Louis, and Pittsburgh. Still, at the dawn of the twenty-first century, Greater Philadelphia has not yet entirely succeeded in replacing that older economy with something new. Only nineteen Fortune 500 companies have their headquarters in this area. (On the other hand, many would agree that large corporate headquarters do not a great city make. Wilmington is home to a disproportionate number of such operations, given how small the city is, but they have not transformed it into a particularly lively or interesting place.)

Pennsylvania's largest manufacturing sector is now pharmaceuticals, and it is centered in Greater Philadelphia. This is a legacy, in fact, of some of Philadelphia's pioneering nineteenth-century chemists—even on the cutting edge of the new biomedical economy, Philadelphia feels the hand of its history. Combined with the pharmaceutical corridor across the Delaware River in New Jersey, the region has grown to be the center of the nation's pharmaceutical industry—from the Juniata Park neighborhood in Philadelphia, where the small Mutual Pharmaceuticals makes two billion capsules of generic drugs, to Merck's 415-acre campus in Montgomery County, known as Vaccine Row, to Lititz, Lancaster County, where Pfizer produces eleven million gallons of Listerine every year. As I write this, the British pharmaceutical company Shire has announced that it will consolidate its North American operations into a new headquarters in Chester County.[12]

Recently the region has begun to market itself aggressively as a destination for tourists and conventions, those staples of the postindustrial economy. Persuading tourists to visit has proved more successful than convincing conventioneers. While the Philadelphia region saw increases in the number of tourists, even after September 11, conventioneers using Philadelphia's convention facility have found themselves confronted—and in many cases ripped off—by a set of hostile, thuggish unions that control all the work that goes on inside the building. Eventually the mayor and even the governor had to intervene to create some sort of labor detente. Whether or not this truce holds, the damage may already have been done. Fewer convention groups return to the Pennsylvania Convention Center than to any other major conven-

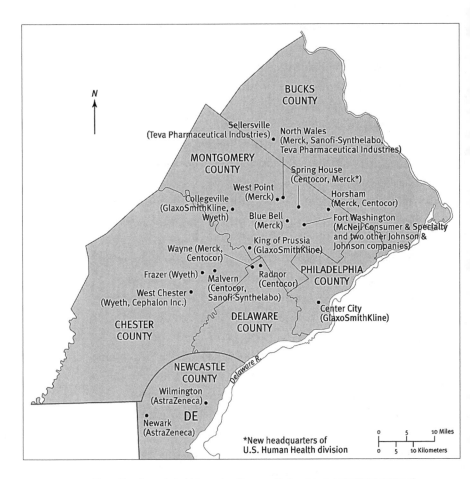

Fig. 3. The pharmo-industrial complex. Pharmaceuticals make up a significant portion of the region's economy. This map does not even show pharmaceutical operations in New Jersey. Data from the *Philadelphia Inquirer*.

tion center in the nation. For Chris Satullo, the labor fight at the Convention Center was a morality play for the entire region. "If we can't get this right," he said to me, "we won't be able to get anything right." Yet, the battle of the Convention Center strikes me as something less significant than some have made it. While the Convention Center surely contributes to the economic health of the city, it seems largely irrelevant to the amazing renaissance that has taken place in Center City. The thousands of new residents who have moved into the area have not been drawn by the Convention Center, nor does the city's lively cultural scene depend on conventioneers. Many city leaders see the Convention Center as the cornerstone of the city's postindustrial economy, and yet all sorts of good things are happening quite independently of it. Indeed, many state and regional leaders hope to expand the center even farther, quite oblivious, apparently, to the fact that the area just north of City Hall and just east of Broad Street, recently underutilized and shabby, is already springing back to life all on its own.

Jobs have followed people—or is it the other way around?—in a centrifugal move away from the city. The city itself continues to lose jobs (the result both of certain economic trends and of a political leadership that is uninterested in addressing structural problems that hinder economic growth), and its share of jobs in the region as a whole is shrinking even more dramatically. More city residents now commute to jobs in Montgomery County than the other way around, leading some planners to rethink the entire definition of the "reverse commute."[13] Service sector jobs—a vast, grab-bag category of employment that includes everything from hotel workers to computer professionals—have grown at a healthy rate but still probably not fast enough to make the region economically competitive with other areas.

Demographic data from the go-go 1990s reveal the relatively weak attractive power of the Philadelphia region's economy. During the height of that economic boom a smaller percentage of people left the area than they did New York, Chicago, Los Angeles, Washington, and Dallas. Migration from the Delaware Valley between 1995 and 2000 amounted to 8.6 percent of the total population, as compared to nearly 14 percent in San Francisco. But a smaller percentage of new residents arrived than in any of those places, meaning that Greater Philadelphia's population grew by only 3.6 percent during those years while San Francisco's jumped nearly 12 percent. As David Thornburgh of the Pennsylvania Economy League put it: "We really don't have an out-migration problem. We're lagging in population not because too many people are leaving, but because not enough people are coming."[14] These figures are mirrored in recent statistics on college graduates, one of the major "products" of the region. According to a study done by the Knowledge Industry Partnership, 86 percent of college graduates who grew up in Greater Philadelphia stay after they graduate from college. But only 29 percent of those who come from outside the Delaware Valley and graduate from Philadelphia-area colleges choose to stay.[15] Even in these statistics we find a double-edged sword, however. The region may not be the first place new graduates and others want to move to, but for those who do live in it, Philadelphia is a place where people sink deep roots.

It has become a truism widely accepted that immigrants play a vital role in the economies of metropolitan regions. During the 1990s, for example, much of New York's and Chicago's revitalizations came because of an enormous influx of foreigners—over a quarter million Chinese to New York City alone, according to one estimate. Historically, Philadelphia has always been a more "native" city than either New York or Chicago, and that has not changed significantly in more recent times. While it is true that virtually all immigrant groups are represented in the region, from Russian Jews to West Africans to Southeast Asians to Albanians,

Greater Philadelphia continues to be only a secondary immigrant destination. One hundred years ago, with the region's factories humming, Philadelphia's provincialism didn't matter much. Today, the price for provincialism is economic stagnation. The region's sense of economic insularity has been underscored recently by the regional competition over jobs. Part of Camden's revitalization plans involves the aggressive poaching of jobs from Philadelphia, offering generous—one might say ludicrous—tax breaks to lure employers across the river. Wilmington has done the same thing. Rather than imagining that the region might grow by adding to the total number of jobs, many political and economic leaders seem to see jobs as a zero-sum proposition. The best that can be hoped for, from their point of view, is to steal from another part of the region.

Regionalism faces political obstacles on several levels. Most obviously, the region encompasses three different states, which means dealing with three governors, three different state legislatures, and three different congressional delegations. Just as importantly, however, county-level government in Pennsylvania has been traditionally weak and ineffective. (Some of Philadelphia's problems are compounded because the city and its county are coterminus. The city thus has to pay for all municipal functions and for county-level functions as well.) Political life on the local level in the Delaware Valley thus tends to be organized around the township. While there is a certain quaintness to this, it has the effect of making larger-scale planning—about anything from transportation to land use to economic development—very difficult indeed.

All of this paints a bleak portrait of Greater Philadelphia. And yet, to make another literary allusion, it is also the best of times as well as the worst. Several recent developments suggest that, economically and demographically, the nearly half-century postindustrial decline, and the problems that swirled in its wake, probably bottomed out during the late 1970s and early 1980s. The population has stabilized at roughly 1.5 million, crime has been reduced, and the schools are now embarked on their most promising era of reform. The pendulum has begun to swing in the other direction. The region has an educational and medical infrastructure that is the envy of most other regions. Indeed, by one count, Philadelphia has the largest per capita concentration of colleges and universities in the country, and the second-largest concentration of health resources. One out of every six doctors in the nation spends some part of her or his training in Philadelphia, for example. Insofar as the new, "information" economy requires those kinds of institutions, Greater Philadelphia is poised to do well in the next century. In particular, the concentration of medical centers, pharmaceutical companies, and colleges is putting Philadelphia at the center of the biotech economy, which many have predicted will yield the next boom.

By the 1990s the bond market had lost confidence in Philadelphia's political leadership, and for better or worse, as the bond market goes, so goes the political future of any big city. That confidence was restored under the leadership of Mayor Ed Rendell, the most visible, dynamic, big-city mayor during the decade and dubbed "America's Mayor" by Vice President Al Gore. The budget is balanced, albeit precariously, and people no longer perceive the city to be on the verge of financial collapse. This is good news because a stable, revitalized city will be central to a newly vibrant region.

In fact, Rendell made fewer structural changes in the way the city does business than he is credited with. He did not restructure city contracts or finances significantly, he did not reign in the municipal unions, nor did he wrestle with the problems of city schools. He did have an almost perfect understanding of the poetics of governing, and more than anything else he made people, both inside and outside the region, feel good about the city again. That is no small claim. Whatever else they may be, cities are acts of faith, and Rendell restored that faith for a great many Philadelphians.

During the 1990s downtown Philadelphia experienced a stunning renaissance, which generated dozens of new restaurants and cultural venues. Unlike many downtown redevelopments, however, which simply turned downtown space into themed Romper Rooms for suburbanites (think St. Louis, Columbus, or Cleveland), the most significant piece of Philadelphia's rebirth was the number of people who live downtown. In a ten-year span, over 12,000 residential units were added to the housing stock in Center City, and now nearly 100,000 people reside in the 4.5-square-mile center of the city, making it the third-largest residential downtown in the country.[16] Central Philadelphia is now a more exciting, lively, vibrant place than at any time since Jefferson and Franklin were walking the streets.

The city also has the highest concentration of people who walk to work, according to the U.S. census, something that seems exactly right if you've ever walked around this most walkable of American cities. For those who don't, however, the region has a public transit infrastructure unequaled in all but a few places. Though SEPTA has been badly managed and underappreciated for years, public transit will prove indispensable as the era of cheap gas comes to a close.

If life in downtown has never been better, then life in the neighborhoods is getting there. Many city neighborhoods are improving—from Manayunk to Fishtown, from University City to Queen Village—and in others the sense of inevitable decline is fading. Lots have been cleaned and cleared, new school buildings are going up and real estate is hot all over, including places in North Philadelphia, once considered utterly hopeless. Measured against the bad old days of the 1970s, life is generally better for most Philadelphians, regardless of race or class. This is not to play Pollyanna about the city's very real problems, but it is to say that people throughout the region feel differently about the city than they did just a few decades ago. The importance of that emerging sense of confidence is hard to overestimate.

Indeed, one way to take the measure of this reversal of fortune is to listen to the growing anxiety expressed publicly by the region's suburban residents. Increasingly they are worried about environmental degradation, congestion, and social alienation. While real estate investment pours into former industrial neighborhoods in the city, news stories about "urban decay" are now generated from inner-ring suburbs and abandoned shopping centers.

Though much divides the city from its surrounding Pennsylvania suburbs, race and class most bitterly, the region did demonstrate the political potential it holds during the last three presidential elections. Traditionally, the city voted heavily Democratic, while the suburbs were a bastion of what the political scientist Patricia Craig, herself a product of the area, calls "Episcopalian Republicanism."[17] As the national and state Republican Party have careened further and further toward the radical right, however, those fiscally conservative, socially moderate Main Line Republicans have been persuaded to vote for Democrats. In 1992, and again in 1996, the city and the surrounding suburbs gave Bill Clinton such an overwhelming majority that it made the votes of the rest of the state largely irrelevant. The state narrowly went for Al Gore in 2000, again entirely because of the support he got in the five counties of Southeastern Pennsylvania. This city-suburb coalition came together once more to elect Ed Rendell—the former mayor of Philadelphia and Jewish to boot!—to the governorship in 2002. And in 2004, the same ad hoc political coalition gave Pennsylvania to John Kerry. At least at certain electoral moments, the city and surrounding counties have more in common than they used to.

To capitalize on all this, to put these pieces together, will require not simply greater political cooperation, more active and visionary leadership from the private sector, which has traditionally conducted itself very privately, and a broader willingness to share prosperity and burdens more equitably throughout the region; it will require a fundamental change of ethos. Satullo asks this rhetorical question: "What big economic development of the twentieth century has been good for the Philadelphia region?" Indeed, each new economic wave, from aerospace to computers, to the globalization of manufacturing, has largely been bad for Greater Philadelphia. This has contributed to an overriding conservatism in the region. Philadelphians are Olympic-class cynics and demonstrate a greater willingness to complain about the region than people almost anywhere else. Philadelphians seem to have learned this lesson in the latter half of the twentieth century: the status quo may not be great, but change will almost certainly be worse. The result of this, Satullo thinks, is that "Philadelphians just don't believe. Everything is in place here to make this region work," he continues, "but we have to break old rules and think in new ways."

That is surely right. But at the same time, such a statement does not give enough credit to the history of the Delaware Valley and its people. Philadelphia has sat at the heart of its region for over three hundred years now, and it has weathered an extraordinary number of social, political, and economic changes. Over those three hundred years, it has handled some of those changes well, others not so well, but one way or the other, it has survived them, adapting and reinventing itself while holding on to its sense of place and identity. There has been a great deal of water under its bridges in the last three hundred years.

In this book I will trace the contours of metropolitan Philadelphia by looking at just a few themes. These themes are my own estimation of what explains this region, what holds it together, and what makes it different from any other place. If I've made wise choices, then this book will both touch on familiar things, and, I hope, help people to think about this place in some new ways.

What follows are five thematic essays, each of which I hope stands on its own but which, taken together, capture what this region means. Chapter 1 looks at the utopian impulse that founded the city. William Penn brought both ideas about religious tolerance and a vision of city planning to his Philadelphia that made the city perhaps the most daring and remarkable of any of the utopian experiments Europeans founded in the New World. The Quakers may now be a tiny minority in the region, but I believe their utopian legacy lingers in a variety of ways. Chapter 1 examines what we mean when we call Philadelphia the Quaker City.

In Chapter 2 I look at the region's collective historical consciousness, the use it makes of its own past. Plenty of places express pride in their own history, but Greater Philadelphia's relationship with history is both longer and more complicated than that of any other place in the nation. Philadelphia's history—especially its connection to the founding of the nation—is, to borrow from the writer Nathaniel Popkin, both its trump card and the albatross around its neck, and this chapter tries to illuminate the way people in the region live with the ghosts of the past.

Philadelphia is often thought of popularly as a blue-collar town, a lunch-pail place where life is lived in tightly knit working-class enclaves. I argue in Chapter 3 that this isn't quite right. Rather, Greater Philadelphia was central to forming what we mean when we talk about the middle class in the United States. From the single-family home, to middle-brow summer recreation at the Jersey Shore and in the Poconos, Greater Philadelphia contributed to the emergence of an American middle class identity. It is also the place where the working class—artisans and factory workers—could first aspire to a middle-class life, and in this sense Greater Philadelphia has shaped our sense of ourselves as a middle-class nation.

Chapter 4 takes us back to the original lifelines of the region: the Delaware and Schuylkill Rivers. Here we trace the way the rivers have shaped the human activity of the region, how the rivers then largely disappeared from our daily awareness and daily lives, and how, in a postindustrial age, we are on the verge of rediscovering the two most significant natural features of the region. The rivers, which are not bothered by political, racial, or economic divisions, could well play a bigger role in tying the region all together.

The last chapter attempts to weave many of these themes together under the umbrella of culture. Philadelphia has been at the center of the nation's cultural life since the eighteenth century and in this chapter I examine certain institutions and certain artists to look at the way their visions of the region have been shaped by the connection to utopian impulses, to the area's history, and to a middle-class, middle-brow sensibility. Artists, after all, give us the images of places that we carry in our heads and I conclude this book by considering the images bequeathed to us by Philadelphia's artists.

A few issues recur throughout these chapters. I am interested in the particular way in which people in the Delaware Valley interact and live with the past; how they have interacted with the landscape; and how they have interacted with that set of principles and circumstances upon which the whole region was founded in the first place. If these essays are heavy with history, then forgive this historian's parochial interests. Still, I do believe that the Philadelphia region lives with a sense of its own past in a way few other places do, and it is that sense of history which contributes to its sense of place.

The themes I have chosen to examine in this book are not

usually of the sort that urban historians and urban studies scholars study. Much of their work continues to center on quantifiable questions—things that can be counted and analyzed numerically: jobs, housing, demographics, economics. Important as these issues are, they don't capture the totality of the lived experience of people in any metropolitan area. Life is more than the sum of its countable parts. I offer the chapters in this book as my attempt at a more cultural analysis of the region. "Culture" is a slippery analytic word. On the one hand, borrowing from the nineteenth-century critic Matthew Arnold, culture is a shorthand for "highbrow"—for fine art and serious literature, for the opera and the orchestra. On the other hand, we use the word the way anthropologists have, to mean the patterns and rituals, the traditions and beliefs of particular groups of people. The former certainly shapes the latter, and vice versa, and that intersection is what interests me most in this study. I believe that this realm of culture, fuzzy and hard to pin down as it may be, is just as important for us to understand as the world of hard data.

I have been acutely aware in writing this book that I have been shooting at a moving target. The dance I have tried to orchestrate between past and present is made that much more complicated by the fact that in a big, dynamic area like Greater Philadelphia, the present is changing all the time. Historians have a hard enough time getting the past right. I can only hope that the issues and themes on which I have chosen to focus will prove to be more enduring than much of what marches fleetingly across the stage of current events. My problem has been, to paraphrase a nineteenth-century writer, that, despite its age, Philadelphia did not sit still for this portrait.

There is a final way to conceive of the contours of metropolitan Philadelphia. At the level of how people conceive of themselves and their identity, the boundaries of Greater Philadelphia prove

Fig. 4. Somewhere in Thailand, Eagles fans gather. Courtesy of Alison Conn, Worldwide Photos.

almost unmappable. Large quantities of Tastykake, the local snack cake, are shipped regularly to lost and homesick Philadelphians around the country, particularly in Florida, Texas, and California. Several of those Philadelphians have established eateries specializing in Philadelphia foods: a meal at one of these places might start with scrapple, proceed to a main course of soft pretzels (with mustard) and cheesesteak sandwiches, and conclude with a Tastykake (and perhaps a coronary episode).[18] According to a recent report, one far-flung Philadelphian has set up a restaurant serving Philly cheesesteaks in Thailand.

And so a final caveat: in this book I shall call people in the region generally and generically "Philadelphians." In the end, perhaps the most important contribution the city makes to the region, and thus the biggest debt owed by the region to the city, is the most ineffable and immeasurable. To say "I'm from Philadelphia" gives people a sense of themselves. It means something, and whatever that something is, it is different from what it means to say "I'm from Chicago," or "I'm from Phoenix." I suspect that most people in the region, when they are asked by someone outside the Delaware Valley where they come from, identify themselves as Philadelphians. After all, whatever it may mean to say "I'm from Philadelphia," responding, "I'm from Horsham," or "I'm from Upper Dublin," doesn't really mean anything at all. For better or worse, in both anger and love, we are Philadelphians.

There are indeed a million stories in the naked city and just as many about it too. This one is simply mine.

Echoes of William Penn

It is fair to say, I think, that no other American city is still so thoroughly identified with its founder as Philadelphia is with William Penn. Bostonians might remember John Winthrop's connection to the founding of their city, and New Yorkers have named a high school after Peter Stuyvesant, but Philadelphians live and work, literally and figuratively, in the shadow of William Penn. His statue, all thirty-six feet and twenty-six tons of it, gazes upon his city from the top of City Hall tower, and his name is attached to everything, from the Penn City Elevator Company to the state itself. "If ever one man created a city," as historians Richard and Mary Maples Dunn have written, "William Penn founded Philadelphia."[1]

Penn came to the New World dreaming utopian dreams, and Philadelphia became the physical manifestation of those visions. This in and of itself is not particularly remarkable. The history of America in the seventeenth, eighteenth, and even nineteenth centuries can be written as a series of utopian experiments. Some were religiously based, even millennial, such as Puritan Boston (more dystopian in its orthodoxy and intolerance) and the Shaker communities; others were decidedly secular, such as Robert Owens's New Harmony in Indiana and John Humphrey Noyes's

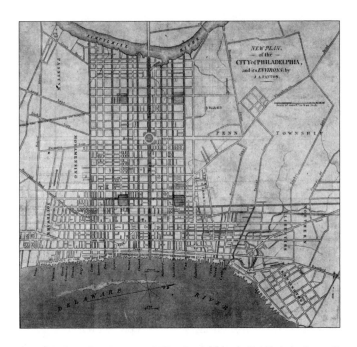

Fig. 5. The shape of utopia ca. 1811. William Penn's grid embodied his desire for a well-ordered society. After Penn laid out his grid, virtually every city in the United States adopted it. Courtesy of the Library Company of Philadelphia.

Oneida. Most have long since evaporated. Penn's utopian vision, by contrast, remains a palpable part of Philadelphia.

That vision, as it took form in the late seventeenth century, came in two parts. The first shaped the physical space of the city. Having witnessed plague in London in 1665 and the famously calamitous fire of 1666, Penn wanted his Philadelphia to be "a greene countrie towne, which will never be burnt, and allways be wholsome."[2] The way he proposed to achieve this was as simple as it was revolutionary: the grid.

While he held title to a very large tract of land, Penn set aside roughly two square miles for his "great towne." He then subdivided the space within those boundaries into a regular, orderly gridiron. Streets ran straight, north and south, east and west,

CHAPTER 1

intersecting at right angles. The two widest streets—now called Market and Broad—were more commodious than any street in seventeenth-century London. The grid made its public debut in London in 1683 in a plan titled "Portraiture of the City of Philadelphia," an advertisement designed to attract purchasers. That grid, and the city that was laid out from it, constituted the most dramatic act of urban planning in the West probably since the Romans. In an early act of Enlightenment rationality, Penn imposed abstract geometry on the American wilderness.

The grid had a purpose beyond a mere abstract, geometric exercise. Orderly space, Penn believed, would shape an orderly society. Rational space, rational people. Rectilinear geometry would be Penn's way of keeping the city's density low, or at least lower than the packed, crowded conditions typical of most European cities, and of creating spacious building lots with trees on them. The grid was the shape of utopia.

Penn embodied the second half of his utopian dream in the very name of the place: Philadelphia, city of brotherly love. The name comes from the city where, in the Book of Revelations, Jesus preached after his resurrection.[3] Penn, as most people know, was a member of the Society of Friends—a Quaker—and he intended his new city to be a physical manifestation of his Quaker principles. Most famously, Penn founded Philadelphia to be a place of religious tolerance, open to members of any religious sect. Quite unlike Boston, whose seventeenth-century purpose was to remain insulated and homogeneous in its brand of Calvinism, Penn wanted Philadelphia to become heterogeneous, and it quickly did so.

Like the grid, that religious freedom, which became a cornerstone of American rights under the Constitution almost exactly one hundred years later, was a revolutionary development. Quakerism itself grew in the religious ferment of the European seventeenth century, an age that witnessed warfare all over the continent as Europeans tore themselves apart over religious differences. Given that history, the very notion of religious tolerance in the 1680s must have struck some as heretical and others as downright mad.

Plan and principle came together in a few mutually reinforcing ways. As originally envisioned in the grid, the city looked inward on itself, toward Center Square in the middle, without privileging a few sites over others, much like the way benches in a Quaker meeting house all face each other. New ideas for city planning swirled in the seventeenth century, but many—Versailles comes quickly to mind—attempted to organize space for grand displays of power. Washington, D.C., with its overwide diagonals cutting through its rectilinear grid, has become the city where Americans use space to display power. A product of the baroque period, there is nothing at all baroque about Penn's grid.

More than that, the plan embodied brotherly love through what it did not include: a wall or any other fortifications. City walls were on the wane in Europe as the medieval world passed into the modern one, but they were certainly still regarded as a necessity in the rough frontier of America. Penn believed, however, that his would be a city of peace, and thus Philadelphia was founded to be an open city.

William Penn began his "holy experiment" as a way to answer the question: how can we build a city that is both livable and prosperous and that can be shared peacefully by people with varieties of cultural, religious and ethnic experiences? As we look around the world today—from Rwanda to Zimbabwe, from Northern Ireland to Kosovo—that question seems as urgent as it was in 1683. No one would claim that Philadelphia has answered that question finally or definitively, but I think it is fair to say that Philadelphia has been confronting that question longer than just about any place else. That confrontation, while not unique to Philadelphia, has been more self-conscious here. In this sense, it has been at the heart of the region's identity.

Yet deep within Penn's vision for Philadelphia lay a profound ambivalence about cities altogether. John Winthrop imagined the Massachusetts Bay Colony explicitly as a "city upon a hill," but Penn hoped for a more pastoral sounding "greene countrie towne." While he told the world in *Some Account of the Province of Pennsylvania* that some of the best land in title "shall be set out for towns or cities," he simultaneously confided to his wife Gulielma, "of Citys and towns of concourse beware, . . . a country life and estate I like best for my Children." He advertised Philadelphia to the rest of the world, but for himself he built a country estate—Pennsbury Manor—on the Delaware River well north of the city.

Penn was thus simultaneously the city's founder and its first suburbanite. In this sense, Penn also stands as the first resident of a Greater Philadelphia, the first to negotiate between the city and its surrounding region. Historically, Quakers, Penn among them, desired to be in the world but not of it. They worried about the corruption of "worldly" influences, and more often than not "worldly" was a synonym for cities. Paradoxically, then, the great city of Philadelphia was founded by a man deeply anxious about cities in the first place.

Cities are in their essence public affairs, places where people inhabit and negotiate over public space, where they create a sense of what constitutes the public good. Quakerism, at one level, is inward looking, and certainly in the seventeenth and eighteenth centuries Quakers had a profound suspicion of the public world. Americans have always had a complicated reaction to their cities, attraction and repulsion all at once. Usually we trace that love-hate impulse to Thomas Jefferson, as urbane and cosmopolitan as anyone in the trans-Atlantic world of the eighteenth century, who hoped the United States would always remain a nation of yeoman farmers. In fact, the uneasy relationship Americans have had with their cities began with William Penn and his "holy experiment" in the Delaware Valley. Philadelphia thus stands, to borrow from the historian Sam Bass Warner, however oxymoronically, as a "private city."

In Warner's view, "privatism," personal independence, the accumulation of wealth, and the attention only to one's family rather than the larger community, defined Philadelphia from the very beginning.[4] "Privatism," according to Warner, isn't merely the Philadelphia ethos but the American ethos, and in this sense Philadelphia again serves as a national model. As Americans, we are guaranteed life, liberty, and the pursuit of happiness—a succinct summary of personal rather than collective ideals. That line was written by a Virginian, but he wrote it in a room at Seventh and Market Streets.

This chapter will look at what has happened over three centuries to this two-part utopian vision and will muse a bit on what that vision means for the current residents of Penn's region.

At one level, the experiment proved an enormous success.

During its first one hundred years the city boomed. Penn was right that the port held great commercial potential. Trade drove the economy of the city and connected it to the rest of the Eastern Seaboard, to the West Indies, to Europe, and eventually even to China. Religious freedom attracted all kinds of people to the area, some of whom stayed in the city, others of whom passed through it on their way to settlements in the hinterlands. Germans settled widely and created their own center at Germantown, and Welsh farmers have left their mark on the place names that surround Philadelphia—Bryn Mawr and Bala Cynwyd, for example. Immigrants of many sorts constituted one of the largest imports coming in to the port of Philadelphia. It was neither accidental nor coincidental that by the last quarter of the eighteenth century, Philadelphia played host to the events associated with the American Revolution and the founding of the republic. By that time,

Fig. 6. By the end of the eighteenth century, Philadelphia had the most influential free black population of any American city. That community erected the Bethel African Methodist Episcopal Church at Sixth and Lombard. "Mother Bethel" is still there today. Courtesy of the Library Company of Philadelphia.

Philadelphia had grown to become the largest city in the Western Hemisphere and the most prosperous one to boot.

Because of Penn's "holy experiment," the region looms large in any religious history of the nation. Presbyterians rooted themselves first in Philadelphia, establishing the first presbytery in the country. So did the Baptists, shaped by the Philadelphia Association, founded in 1707. In fact, the American Baptist Convention is still headquartered in Philadelphia. Philadelphia served as the place where the Protestant Episcopal Church was founded in this country, its first bishop residing in an elegant house on Walnut Street. And south of his house, at Sixth and Lombard Streets, members of the city's free black community came together to found the African Methodist Episcopal Church, the first independent black denomination in the country.

The city's religious tolerance was initially conceived of primarily for Protestants. But the colonial city also attracted Catholics, who first congregated at what is now called "Old" St. Joe's church. While the city's welcome to Catholics was tentative—they found themselves living largely on the edge of the city—their treatment here certainly contrasted to what they found in Boston, where they were persecuted. So too Jews came to Philadelphia in the eighteenth century and while they weren't necessarily embraced, neither were they tormented. The city's first Jewish community buried its dead at the Mikveh Israel Cemetery, still located on Spruce Street.

This religious pluralism meant that the region became home to a remarkably diverse population, especially of German speakers. The Pennsylvania Dutch—more properly Pennsylvania Deutsch— who came through Philadelphia are familiar to most people. But those Amish were only one group of German-speaking religious dissenters who left their homes for Philadelphia. Mennonites came too, as did Moravians, who established their community in the 1740s in a town they called Bethlehem north of the city on the Delaware.

The first Schwenkfelders, fleeing persecution by the Catholic Church, arrived in Philadelphia in 1731. The Dunkers arrived at about the same time. In 1720 Conrad Beissel, another renegade Protestant, stepped off a boat on the docks of Philadelphia. He moved west into the wilderness of what is now Lancaster County and by 1732 had founded the cloistered and celibate religious community at Ephrata. Though the community itself did not last long—celibate utopias seldom do—Beissel and his followers left behind beautifully illuminated manuscripts, their own music, and at Ephrata itself some of the most interesting late medieval German vernacular architecture still standing here or in Germany.

The architecture of Ephrata serves as a reminder that while the Delaware Valley was a remote and distant outpost of Europe, Penn's notion of religious tolerance made the area a central part of Europe's religious and political upheavals. As the eighteenth century wore on, of course, Philadelphia's role on the stage of world affairs would only increase.

More so even than its centrality to the nation's religious life, the religious freedom established by William Penn made Philadelphia the first city to negotiate the function of religion in secular public life, the place where the line between church and state was first drawn. Religious plurality meant that no single religion predominated—indeed, Quakers quickly found themselves a statistical minority in the Quaker City. As a consequence, while Philadelphians enjoyed freedom in their private religious affairs, they created a secular public culture. As the historian Sydney Ahlstrom has put it, Philadelphia and its surroundings became the place where a great variety of religious groups first "experienced the difficulties and discovered the possibilities for fruitful coexistence that American democracy was to offer."[5]

Eighteenth-century Philadelphia was the New World center of

Fig. 7. Penn's proclamation of religious tolerance made Philadelphia the port of entry for a wide variety of European religious groups. The Moravians settled north of the city in Bethlehem. Courtesy of the Library Company of Philadelphia.

the Enlightenment. It was no accident either that when the teen-aged Ben Franklin left his home in Boston he came to Philadel-phia. When he got to Philadelphia, Franklin found a remarkable and unique "free market" of religious ideas.[6] That free market meant that religious ideas could be evaluated on their merits by anyone interested in doing so. For Franklin, as he tells us in his *Autobiography*, the religious freedom he found in Philadelphia meant choosing not to affiliate with any denomination at all. God and sect, for Franklin and many others, seemed almost entirely disconnected.

Religion thus became, at least for those who participated in debates, a matter of choice, not of tradition, habit, law, or even the educational apparatus. Transplanted to Philadelphia, Franklin would, of course, become America's greatest contribution to that Enlightenment. Among Franklin's myriad projects was the school that would become the University of Pennsylvania, the first insti-tution of higher learning in the country founded without a denom-inational affiliation.

That "free market" of religion was a central element of the American Enlightenment in Philadelphia. Religion became just one more topic to be debated in the coffee houses, street corners, and parlors of polite Philadelphia. Religious freedom and plurality in Philadelphia meant that the practice of religion remained as part of, and thus helped to define, the private sphere, not as part of the public realm of policy and law. As a witness to the reli-giously inspired violence of the English Civil War, Penn under-stood not so much the importance of keeping the church out of the state, but rather of keeping the state out of the church. It is a lesson we seem to have forgotten in this country three hundred years after he granted his Charter of Privileges.

If imitation is the highest form of flattery, then Philadelphia was flattered indeed in the early years of the republic. City after city planned itself with the grid. New York City, which started its life as a random tangle of streets, imposed the grid early in the nineteenth century, though without Penn's public spaces. From New York to San Francisco, with dozens of places in between, in the nineteenth century the grid became the quintessentially American urban form. After Philadelphia, virtually every American town and city came to look like Philadelphia. (Washington, D.C. stands as the exception. There Jefferson and his engineer Pierre L'Enfant tried to meld Penn's grid with Louis XIV's Versailles, which may explain why the traffic in D.C. is so unworkable.)

For Penn, the grid did not constitute an end unto itself, but rather a means to an end. I mentioned those ends briefly already: the green country town, a place free of fire and disease, a harmonious, orderly place.

Almost immediately, however, Penn's vision for the city became a victim of the city's very success. With migrants a major "import" on the docks of Philadelphia, the city's population grew quickly and strained the wide grid plan. Almost immediately, the original blocks of Penn's city were sold and subdivided. The result was a honeycomb of narrow streets, all lined densely with housing. Those streets and alleys quickly became filthy and disease-ridden, most catastrophically in the summers of the 1790s when yellow fever raged through crowded neighborhoods. After its first one hundred years, Philadelphia had grown to become the most important, prosperous urban center in North America, and it had ceased to resemble Penn's notion of a green country town.

Still, the Philadelphia grid proved remarkably influential. Indeed, the whole of the Northwest Territory was gridded, and its towns were planned around a central square. Small towns and county seats throughout the Midwest and the upper South built around a town square owe a debt to the Philadelphia plan.[7] As the nineteenth century wore on small towns grew up along the railroad lines that radiated out from the center of Philadelphia.

These too used the grid plan, most of them, and several—Narberth, Media, Ardmore come quickly to mind—grew to develop their own identities as satellites of the larger metropolis.

The grid isn't perfect, of course, and many have complained over the years that it lends a certain sameness and a certain blandness to the city's streetscape—no great vistas, no small idiosyncrasies, only the predictable, precise rhythm of geometry. As a consequence of that perception, perhaps, the grid was challenged in the twentieth century. First, in the city itself, planners created a vast diagonal through the rectangles in the 1920s. The Benjamin Franklin Parkway serves to connect the center of the city with its great municipal art museum and park system beyond. A product of the "city beautiful" movement in urban planning, the parkway creates French drama in a city defined by Quaker plainness.[8]

After the Second World War, Philadelphians, like everyone else, forgot about the grid entirely. As the city's suburbs sprawled they did so around kidney-shaped streets, cul-de-sacs, and access roads. In this sense, Philadelphia's suburbs are largely indistinguishable from most postwar suburban development. They have also had identical results: the disappearence of open space and farm land, demoralizing traffic congestion, and a loss of any sense of community.

What makes Philadelphia's ill-planned suburbia so disappointing, though, is that it has grown in the shadow of the most innovative city plan in America. We should have known better, and we surely could have done better. The challenge of the next fifty years will be to relearn Philadelphia's lessons of good urban design and transform the region accordingly.

Recently, smart growth advocates and their allies among the new urbanist architects have tried to get Americans to rethink how we develop our towns. These planners and designers stress towns where streets can be walked on, rather than driven through, public spaces that are sources of civic pride and centers of civic life, and concentrated, mixed-use development rather than unfocused and decentralized sprawl. Among the most eloquent and influential of these advocates is Thomas Hylton, a journalist, activist, and thinker who works in Pottstown, but whose ideas have had an impact all over the nation. He and others are trying to bring back urban planning with people—rather than cars, malls, and interchanges—at the center. William Penn may have the last laugh yet.

Anyone who has looked up at William Penn standing atop City Hall's tower has probably been perplexed. The tower sits at the center of Penn's original grid, and the grid is oriented rigorously north-south, east-west. Penn himself, however, isn't. He faces slightly to the north and east, and his right hand rises a little in what is an obvious if subtle gesture. It isn't exactly clear where Penn is looking or what he is gesturing at.

Alexander Calder, the sculptor, wanted his creation pointed south, down Broad Street, so that its face would always face the sun. Rather than align William Penn with his grid, those who designed and built City Hall in the last quarter of the nineteenth century chose instead to have the statue of the founder face off toward Penn Treaty Park, the place where he signed his famous treaty with the Lenni Lenape Indians. Indirectly then, Penn's is a gesture toward the natives who lived in the Delaware Valley first, and it is a gesture of welcome, tolerance, and peace.

The treaty was made in 1682 under a great spreading elm in a place that is now the city neighborhood of Kensington but which was at the time well outside the boundaries of Philadelphia. Penn had left Europe when religious warfare raged. He landed in the New World shortly after savage wars between settlers and natives—the so-called King Philip's War in New England, and Bacon's War in the Virginia colony—had ended. Through his treaty, he essentially bought out the claims of the Lenape to the land he wanted and paid them quite well, at least by the standards of the time. Penn's city had no fortification, and through this treaty Penn ensured peaceful relations with the Indians. It remains the only treaty negotiated between Europeans and Native Americans never to have been broken. As Penn himself wrote: "Let us then try what love will do for if men did see we love them they could not harm us."

Or so the legend goes.

We know that Penn made some sort of payment to the locals in 1682 and again in 1684. But beyond that we don't really know much about the transaction—who was there, what terms were negotiated, or even where it took place—with any high degree of certainty. Nobody involved seems to have thought it necessary to take notes. No matter. Two hundred years later, when they hoisted the thirty-six-foot-high William Penn to his perch on City Hall's tower, they pointed him at the place everyone now believed Penn had met with the Lenape.

If, however, you can conjure the scene up in your mind, it is probably because you have seen, in one version or another, the painting by Benjamin West, *Penn's Treaty with the Indians*, which he completed in 1771. West, who grew up around Quakers in the hinterland of what is now Swarthmore, was already in London by the time he received the commission to do *Penn's Treaty*. The commission came from Thomas Penn, William's grandson, who was running the colony from the great distance of his country estate in England. By 1771, of course, his rule, along with the rest of the British colonial enterprise in North America, had become difficult and contentious. Thomas Penn seems to have commissioned the painting as a way of reminding Philadelphians of their heritage as a "peaceable kingdom" and of his connection to the founder's dream of peace and harmony. By extension, presumably, he hoped that reminder might get Philadelphians to stop causing so many problems for him. Already, by the end of the eighteenth century, Penn's "peaceable kingdom" had become mythologized—the treaty with the Indians represented a fall from grace and measured the distance the city had traveled in less than a hundred years from a place of brotherly love to a caldron of decidedly unbrotherly conflict.

For Thomas Penn at least, the painting did not have the desired effect, and after 1776 he became a historical footnote. The image, however, went on to have an extraordinary life. Reproduced countless times in every conceivable way, *Penn's Treaty* became a near ubiquitous image in the United States in the nineteenth century, especially in the Delaware Valley. Even Quaker homes, usually devoid of decoration, would often have a lithograph or two of the painting on the wall. By the middle of that century it was perfectly conceivable to see a framed print of the scene while eating from ceramic plates with the image on them, pause in the meal to stare through window curtains embroidered with it, finish the meal with a shot from a *Penn's Treaty* whiskey glass, and tuck oneself into bed under a *Penn's Treaty* quilt. The enthusiasm for the image only increased when Joseph Harrison bought the actual painting itself and brought it to Philadelphia in 1851.

Among those who copied the image and helped spread both it and its message was the painter Edward Hicks, who did several versions of the painting, themselves copied from some sort of reproduction, since Hicks never saw the original (the reproductions and Hicks's versions are all mirror images of the original). Born in 1780, Hicks spent most of his life in the Quaker communities of Bucks County, north of Philadelphia (among his neighbors was the Quaker abolitionist and feminist Lucretia Mott). Hicks is best known today as the "folk" painter of *The Peaceable Kingdom*. Some have read Hicks's scene of lions lying down with lambs as a visualization of the Quaker notion of inner light and as

Fig. 8. The story of Penn's treaty with the Indians had become a central part of the city's and the nation's mythology by the nineteenth century. Here the image painted by Benjamin West has been turned into a child's jigsaw puzzle. Courtesy of the Library Company of Philadelphia.

a vision of peace for humanity. Others have seen in *The Peaceable Kingdom* an allegory of the rift that developed within Quakerism after 1827 and of Hicks's desire to heal it. By the time he died in 1849 he had executed over one hundred variations on the peaceable kingdom theme. Many have a tiny rendition of *Penn's Treaty* off to the side and in the background, underscoring the message of the animals in the foreground.[9]

By the time *Penn's Treaty* came to Philadelphia, though, the meaning of the image had shifted. By the mid-nineteenth century the United States was embarked fully and irrevocably on a path to destroy Native America as the only way to manifest our destiny. People found in West's painting a sense of lost possibilities. Penn, after all, proved that relations between white and Native America could be different. When subscribers to the *Philadelphia Ledger* received a complimentary engraving of *Penn's Treaty* in 1857 it came with this piece of Hallmarkian schlock:

How beautiful the scene portrayed above

A treaty, framed in Justice, Truth and Love,

Our City's Founder and the peaceful "Friends"

Stoop to no subterfuge, to gain their ends;

While with unswerving confidence around

Their Indian brethren occupy the ground,

This incident, a maxim may afford,

And prove *our* PENN was "mightier than the sword."

Penn imagined his utopia in the age of religious wars; that imagining, as translated by Benjamin West, spoke to the nation during the age of Indian wars. By the late nineteenth century, at least for some Americans, Penn and his treaty underscored a fundamental failure to live up to utopia, measuring the distance from Philadelphia to Wounded Knee, from the peaceable kingdom to the reservation system, from brotherly love to genocide. It is the distance measured by that small gesture from a very large statue.

That Penn should occupy pride of place on City Hall's tower also underscored that just as no other American city is so associated with its founder, no other city is still associated with a single religion as Philadelphia is with Quakerism. Boston might have been founded as a haven for Puritans, but practicing Calvinists are hard to find these days. In contrast, Philadelphia can still be called the Quaker City without causing too many perplexed looks, and this despite the fact that very few in the region actually attend Sunday meeting.

Indeed, Quakerism provides us with another way to draw boundaries around the region. The Friends Center, home of the Philadelphia Yearly Meeting, is located in the very center of the city, two blocks from City Hall. The center serves as the headquarters for a network of meetings and schools that are scattered widely. Some of these meetings are quite old, and they once functioned as the heart of Quaker communities in the wilderness in the seventeenth and eighteenth centuries. Quakers started schools, which have become some of the finest educational institutions of this or any region. And in the nineteenth century Quakers created two superb colleges for their children to attend, one in Swarthmore and the other in Haverford. Most of the students who attend these schools today do not enter as practicing Quakers. In the 1970s a joke circulated locally asking: How can you identify a Jewish family these days? The answer: They send their kids to Quaker school. Through those schools, and the thousands of students they have educated, Quakerism still exerts a cultural influence in the region.

Yet by the time the statue was affixed on its tower, Quakers probably constituted less than 1 percent of the region's population, and their characteristic plain style was in fact disappearing so that they no longer stood out. At roughly this moment, however, Quakerism was being reinvented by a Quaker from a small town in Maine.

Ironically, war framed Rufus Jones's life. Born during the Civil War (1863), he died in 1948 as the convulsions of the Second World War were still fresh. He took a B.A. from Haverford College in 1885 and then taught at several different Quaker schools in New York and Rhode Island. In 1901 he received an M.A. in philosophy from Harvard and that year he returned to Haverford as a professor of philosophy. He stands, alongside Albert Schweitzer, with whom he was compared, as one of the most interesting and influential Christian activists of his age, and he stands as the most significant Quaker theologian since George Fox, the founder of the Society of Friends.

Fox was one of those remarkable, charismatic evangelicals that the seventeenth century produced in such abundance. He committed the entire Bible to memory and could outquote any opponent in a religious debate. Buried within his writings is this exhortation: "Be patterns, be examples in all countries, places, islands, nations, wherever you come; that your carriage and life may preach among all sorts of people, and to them. Then you will come to walk cheerfully over the world, answering that of God in everyone." This universalist understanding that the "inner light" resides in all of us has always been a part of Quaker belief. As early as 1688, it prompted members of the Germantown Meeting—now a part of the city, but then an outpost several miles from Philadelphia proper—to issue the Germantown Protest against slavery. (The first school for the city's black children, founded in the late eighteenth century, was the Friends' Negro Schoolhouse.) It is what drove the Quaker abolitionists and feminists in the mid-nineteenth century. It made Quakers more energetic advocates for Native American rights than members of other religious groups after the Civil War was over. Rufus Jones, however, in his writings and in his other work, pulled the last part of the quote— "that of God in everyone"—and moved it to the center of what Quakerism means.

Jones surely responded to debates and developments that were internal to Quakerism in the late nineteenth century—the resolution of the Hicksite/Orthodox schism among other things. But his ideas grew out of several external influences as well. As a student at Harvard, Jones studied with William James, the philosopher most associated with Pragmatism. More broadly, Jones matured during the era of Progressive reform and during the era of the Social Gospel Movement. The latter was an attempt by many Protestant ministers to reinvigorate what they saw as a stagnating Christianity and to give it a relevance it seemed to be losing in the wake of industrial dislocation and the challenges to religious belief posed by Darwin and other scientific developments. Social Gospelers attempted to create a Protestantism that stressed service, engagement, and social justice, a muscular, energetic Christianity that would, in the words of the Reverend Walter Rauschenbusch, reassert the "social aims of Jesus." Industrial capitalism, coming into full maturity, was, after all, in Rauschenbusch's view only "semi-Christian."

In this context, Jones reinvigorated Quakerism by confronting the tension inherent in the desire to be in the world but not of it. Jones, and other Quaker thinkers, helped turn the notion of "inner light" into a social imperative. In Jones's vision of it, Quakerism could be an activist faith, driven both by one's own inner light and the duty to respect and protect "that of God in everyone" as well. In a sense, Quakerism was reinvented to stress those aspects of the religion most people already associated with it. And certainly this is how most of us think of the religion today, much to the frustration of many Quakers who worry that the emphasis on peace and social justice activism risks overwhelming other important aspects of Quaker spirituality.

The reinvention brought about by Jones and his colleagues reached a culmination of sorts with the creation of the American Friends Service Committee (AFSC) in 1917. The initial impulse behind the AFSC was to provide conscientious objectors, those young men whose religious principles would not permit them to participate in the combat of World War I, with alternative forms of service. In 1917 the federal government restricted the draft category of conscientious objector to members of just a few religious groups—Amish, Mennonites, and, of course Quakers. (Greater Philadelphia thus stood as the center of the moral opposition to war in the twentieth century, another item to put on the list of "firsts.") Over the course of the twentieth century the definition of conscientious objection grew to include members of other faiths and eventually to those whose objection to war grew out of ethical or moral imperatives even if those imperatives were not specifically religious.

After World War I, the AFSC found itself even busier. Members provided all sorts of vital post-war relief service in Europe and in Russia. They were busy during the 1930s helping those fleeing Nazi Germany and Fascist Spain. In the 1940s, the AFSC went to India to help deal with the refugee crisis created by the partition of India and Pakistan, and to the Middle East, where it helped provide relief to Palestinians in Gaza after the creation of the state of Israel. In 1966, the AFSC began a program to aid Vietnamese civilian victims of the American war there. Today, the AFSC continues to work all over the world dealing with issues that might broadly be described as pertaining to development and social justice. The AFSC stands as the most internationally visible face of Philadelphia Quakerism, of the attempt to create some sense of peaceable kingdom in a world desperately in need of it.

In 1947, thirty years after its founding and shortly before Jones's death, the AFSC's work around the world earned it the Nobel Peace Prize. The recognition was surely deserved, even if it probably embarrassed some of the more deferential Quakers in the organization. In the citation accompanying the prize, the Nobel committee captured nicely the way the AFSC combines its public activism with the more inward-looking nature of Quakerism: "It is through silent assistance from the nameless to the nameless that they have worked to promote the fraternity between nations. . . ." Silent and nameless, like a Sunday meeting.

The twentieth century also saw a parallel reinvention of Quaker schools. Quakers, as I mentioned earlier, founded schools almost immediately upon their arrival in the Delaware Valley, but their purpose initially was to provide a Quaker education to Quaker children. This "guarded education," as it was sometimes called, would protect young Quakers from "worldly" influences. By the twentieth century Quaker schools had begun to lose some their insularity and to accept non-Quakers in greater and greater numbers. (I should mention here that the Mennonites too responded to the changes brought by the twentieth century. In 1954, and in response to the Second World War, Philadelphia-area Mennonites opened the Christopher Dock Mennonite High School. One of the impulses behind founding the school was a concern that too many Mennonite men had enlisted in the army, violating the church's pacifist doctrine. The Dock School is a much more explicitly religious and denominational school than any of the region's Quaker schools are.)

The struggle for Quaker schools, then, has been to retain their own sense of mission and purpose while accommodating students, very few of whom now are practicing Quakers. Just what a Quaker education means is a bit elusive. "Like veteran artisans," Samuel Caldwell, the former general secretary of the Philadelphia Yearly Meeting, has written, "we seem to know just how to perform our craft, but we can no longer explain how or why we do it." Tom Hoopes, himself a product of Quaker schools and a member of a family whose Quaker roots stretch back to the seventeenth century, now works for the Philadelphia Yearly Meeting as its liaison with the Quaker schools in the region. He puts the issue more pithily: "We pluck the fruits of Quakerism and make them palatable to high school students."[10]

What Quaker schools offer, Hoopes continues, is "a coherent culture," one that stands in opposition to what he calls the "toxic culture" of mainstream America. By "toxic" Hoopes means several things, but perhaps the most comprehensive synonym for it would be "violent." Quakers see most social ills as varying forms of violence—done to individuals, communities, races, the environment, and so on—and nonviolence as the only solution to those ills. A banner hanging over the entrance to the Friends Center quotes A. J. Muste: "There is no way to peace. Peace is the way." Quaker schools thus provide places to analyze, critique, and reflect upon that culture of violence, and further, they provide the model of nonviolence as its alternative. Schools as peaceable kingdoms.

In this, Quaker schools still wrestle with that tension fundamental to Quaker life since the seventeenth century—how to live in the world but not be quite of it. As Hoopes explains, he believes that "the meta-agenda" of Quaker schools is to produce "world citizens." And yet these schools, in their very oppositional stance, can stand as islands in the midst of hostile waters. Quaker schools try to negotiate this divide, a tension nicely summarized by Kathy Paulmier, a Quaker and graduate of Germantown Friends School, in an interview with the writer Nathaniel Popkin: "When I get up in the morning I don't know whether to enjoy the world or to save it."[11]

Each Quaker school has its own mission statement, and while they vary a bit in the details, they all have important things in common. Teaching at the Abington Friends School, for example, "is rooted in Quaker beliefs, combining reflection with action and balancing the needs of individuals with those of the community." Achieving that balance is also a part of the philosophy of Friends Select School. Meeting for Worship "based on silence where each may speak when moved to speak . . . remains central" to the life at Germantown Friends School. Wherever it is offered, a Quaker education is an experience that is both academically rigorous and spiritually deep. To develop a sense of spirituality that is not explicitly religious, and certainly not specifically denominational, is for Caldwell what distinguishes Quaker schools. He borrows a phrase from Rufus Jones and writes that Quaker schools should produce people with "eyes for invisibles." In statements of philosophy at every Quaker school is a commitment to George Fox's idea that there is "that of God in everyone" and the pledge to develop students who can see that.

It would be hard to claim that the thousands of students who have graduated with a Quaker education have made Greater Philadelphia a less violent place than any other. Hoopes is right that ours is a culture steeped in violence, where guns are more readily available than health insurance and where my own small children regularly ask me to explain why people are being killed in Iraq. Still, in my own travels I have always found it remarkable to discover just how many of the people who have devoted their lives, in big ways and small, to the quest for social justice are products of Quaker schools.

Quakers are in theory supposed to commit to five core values: peace, simplicity, community, quality, and integrity. In that same interview, Kathy Paulmier notes, "It's hard to be a Quaker! Nearly impossible." To which her husband responds, "It's impossible not to be a Quaker."[12] But there is also a specifically Quaker way of doing business, at least the business of the meeting. Eschewing centralized authority as a foundational principle, Quakers give each meeting tremendous authority to make decisions. In so doing, members of the meeting gather to arrive at a "sense of the meeting." It is a process in which all members can participate and through which members hope to figure out God's will in the context of the meeting's business.

Secularized and removed from the benches of the meeting house, that process has become known as consensus decision making. The business of politics in Greater Philadelphia is carried on much the same way as it is anywhere else—parties fight, candidates run, voters rally, money and favors are traded, and winners defeat losers. If, however, you choose to participate in the extraordinarily rich grassroots civic life of the Delaware Valley, then you may find yourself sitting in a meeting—facilitated, not chaired, and run by consensus.

Decisions aren't finally made by voting in a consensus-based meeting. The process of consensus allows everyone in an organization an equal voice. It avoids the tyranny of the majority, and it empowers any individual with the authority to hold up the organization's business by blocking the consensus. At its base, consensus works only when participants are willing both to speak and to listen, to be honest about those things that are of primary importance and those that are of only secondary importance. It is predicated on compromise and negotiation and on the personal integrity of the participants.

The process can be maddening, and I speak from hours upon hours of personal experience. Oscar Wilde once quipped that he could never be a socialist because it required too many meetings. He didn't know the half of it. Consensus meetings can go on and on, often without any apparent movement. They can founder without a skillful facilitator. They can be hijacked quite easily by those who either don't understand or don't respect the process.

But when the process works, as it usually does when it is handled well, it creates a sense of unity and strength and enthusiasm among participants that simply can't be matched by groups operating in conventional ways where some people get to go home as winners and others as losers. This I also know from personal experience.

Consensus-driven organizations are no longer unique to Greater Philadelphia, of course. The process has been adopted widely, especially by organizations working on the left of the political spectrum. For these groups, consensus is a way of ensuring a close relationship between means and ends, and of guaranteeing that the goals of democracy and equality have been arrived at by a process that puts democracy and equality at its center. ACT UP New York, an AIDS activist group, for example, has a very thorough explanation of how consensus works on its web site. Most of its members, I suspect, like most of those in similar organizations around the country, probably don't realize that their process is rooted in Quakerism. But then the Quaker influence has always been quiet and subtle.

Etymologically speaking, pacifism, perhaps the belief for which Quakers are best known, does not derive from the word "passive" despite the similarity of the sound, and it certainly does not mean the same thing. Rather, pacifism comes from the Latin word *pace*—peace. In the twentieth century, few Americans thought more about the relationship between peace and pacifism than Bayard Rustin.

Born in 1912, Rustin grew up in West Chester, Pennsylvania in the small, tight, black community that had lived there since before the Civil War. He was not born a Quaker, but he grew up among and around them and by the time he attended nearby Cheyney State Teachers College, a school for black students founded by Quakers—and after he heard a lecture by Rufus Jones—he had become one.

His movement in Quakerism accompanied a more general radicalization that Rustin underwent in the crucible of the 1930s. By 1941, with America's involvement in World War II looming, Rustin joined the Fellowship of Reconciliation as one of its youth secretaries. The FOR had been founded by A. J. Muste in 1915, its creation having been driven by many of the same impulses behind the founding of the American Friends Service Committee. As early as the 1920s, Muste had become interested in the movement Gandhi was then leading in India, and in particular the kind of nonviolent resistance Gandhi was using against the British. Muste was eager to meld Gandhian nonviolence with traditions of Christian pacifism to achieve social change in the United States. Rustin became Muste's most influential student.

The nation would feel that influence most during the civil rights movement. Rustin first met Martin Luther King Jr. in Montgomery, Alabama in 1955 during the epochal bus boycott there. For the next thirteen years, until King's assassination in Memphis, Rustin was a central advisor to King, the movement's philosopher of nonviolent strategy. We remember King now as the apostle of nonviolence. In fact, in 1955 King knew almost nothing about Gandhi or pacifism. As Rustin himself remembered, "The fact of the matter is, when I got to Montgomery, Dr. King had very limited notions about how nonviolent protest should be carried out." Indeed, when Rustin arrived at King's house and base in Montgomery the place was full of guns. King did become the most important—and successful—practitioner of nonviolent action in American history, and he did so because Rustin, a black West Chester Quaker, was whispering in his ear.[13]

Nearly three hundred years after Germantown Quakers had condemned slavery, Quakerism shaped the very core of the civil rights movement. It is almost unimaginable what the freedom struggle of the 1950s and 1960s would have been like without it.

In the world but not of it.

There is another, perhaps more frustrating legacy of Quakerism, explored most fully by the social theorist and Philadelphia scion E. Digby Baltzell. In 1979, Baltzell, who is probably best known for having coined the acronym WASP, wrote a comparative study of Philadelphia and Boston that remains wonderfully readable and insightful. Baltzell wrote his study as the dust of the 1960s and early 1970s settled. Not surprisingly, given the issues raised in that decade, he was primarily interested in questions of authority and leadership, and he focused on how the two cities' upper classes wielded authority. As a self-described member of the Proper Philadelphian class—he lived his life from birth to death in Philadelphia's WASPy Chestnut Hill neighborhood—Baltzell wondered why Boston's elite had produced a long tradition of leaders while Philadelphia's had not. His book attempted to answer that question.

Baltzell defined and measured leadership in a way that strikes us now as old-fashioned and shamelessly elitist—political leaders, business leaders, intellectual figures. Still, his points of comparison are, for Philadelphians at least, chastening. He begins the book by staring at the portraits of Nathaniel Hawthorne, Henry Wadsworth Longfellow, and Franklin Pierce, novelist, poet, president, in the Bowdoin College library. The three were classmates at the tiny Maine college, and yet as Baltzell writes: "No three individuals of comparable stature . . . had ever graduated from . . . my own university [Penn] or from any other college in the state of Pennsylvania."[14] Boston and New England produced the Adams and Kennedy families in politics (were he writing now, he might also have included the Bush dynasty) whereas Greater Philadelphia has produced no comparable political leadership. Indeed, Pennsylvania has sent exactly one man to the White House, in 1856, and James Buchanan's claim to fame is primarily that he was ousted by Abraham Lincoln in 1860. Baltzell collated the entries in the *Dictionary of American Biography* geographically and discovered that far more of those included there came from New England than from the mid-Atlantic. On and on it goes.

For Baltzell, the key to understanding the differences between the two places lay in what he called their different Protestant "ethics," and he summarized that difference in the book's very title: *Puritan Boston and Quaker Philadelphia*. Puritanism bequeathed two things to Boston that interested Baltzell. First, it was an intensely intellectual religion. It demanded the close reading of texts and produced lengthy exegeses of those texts. Thus, New England developed early on a culture of intellectualism—high literacy rates and the founding of colleges—that served as the soil out of which leadership grew. Second, the practice of Puritanism centered around the figure of the minister. When New

Englanders went to church on Sundays they went to hear, sometimes for several hours, what those ministers had to say. Puritan divines constituted, especially in the seventeenth century and the early eighteenth, a primary source of intellectual activity in the New World. Indeed, in the early days of New England, ministers served as community leaders as well as religious ones. That those ministers were often products of, and then leaders of, the educational institutions only reinforced this connection between intellectual life and community leadership.

Quakerism, by contrast, was an altogether different form of religious practice. The most radical gesture Quakers made was to do away with a professional clergy. Quakers believe in the possibility that all members of a meeting might feel the call to ministry. But since every member might take on a ministerial role then there is surely no need for a professional clergy. Quakers sitting in their meetings sat silently—and still do—unless the spirit moved any member of the meeting to speak. (There were once Quaker "preachers" but they had no real ministerial authority in the sense that other denominations have it.) Further, because of its inward-looking focus, Quakerism has stressed the emotional and interior over the cerebral and intellectual. With the exception of its founders, Quakers produced no great theologians to match the Mathers and Jonathan Edwardses of New England. Their schools provided a basic instruction, but most Quakers seem to have been suspicious of higher learning, and in the nineteenth century Quakerism was accused of being decidedly anti-intellectual.

Having designed a religious practice that deliberately did not create its own leadership, Quakers had a deeply ambivalent view of leadership outside the confines of their meeting houses as well. In the eighteenth century, Philadelphia became home to the leading figures of the American Enlightenment, but almost none of them were Quakers, nor did Quakers play a particularly important role in the events surrounding independence and the creation of the new nation. (Though neither came from Greater Philadelphia, there have been two Quaker presidents, Herbert Hoover and Richard Nixon, from which we might conclude that Quakers have generally been right to avoid political leadership.) As Baltzell saw it, these two traditions have created two different ethics, which he paired this way: Puritan Boston is a place with a low level of social tolerance and a correspondingly well-developed sense of civic responsibility on the part of its elite. Quaker Philadelphia, in contrast, is a place with a high level of social tolerance and a very low sense of civic responsibility among those who, in Baltzell's view, ought to be its leaders.

At one level, Baltzell simply elaborated and theorized the observation made by the muckracker journalist Lincoln Steffens in 1903 when he called Philadelphia "corrupt and contented."[15] While the phrase is still invoked often in the region, I suspect many people have forgotten what Steffens meant to say about Philadelphia. Philadelphia, Steffens contended, was no more corrupt than any other big American city at the turn of the twentieth century. What set the place apart was that no one seemed to care about the rampant corruption. While reformers in other cities struggled to clean up their municipal messes, no important figures stepped forward to lead a crusade for reform. Philadelphians thus remained content.

Writing at almost exactly the same moment, Henry James put the problem just a bit differently. James had exiled himself from the United States in 1883. He returned twenty years later to make a tour of the country he knew had changed dramatically, and in his estimation almost entirely for the worse. What he found in Philadelphia was a perfect bifurcation between what he called "Society" and the "City." The former was "the most genial and delightful one could think of"; the latter existed "parallel to this, and not within it, nor quite altogether above it, but beside it and beneath it, behind it and before it," and it existed "all for plunder and rapine, the gross satisfaction of official appetite, organized for eternal iniquity and impunity."[16] And it is easy to argue that little has changed. Almost one hundred years to the day after Steffens's essay appeared, Philadelphia's mayor, John Street, surged to a landslide reelection, *because* of, many observers felt, not despite, revelations of a widespread federal investigation of his administration. Indictments started raining down on City Hall in the summer of 2004. Embarrassed by the investigation, the City Council grudgingly began to debate an ethics bill, only to have influential members of the council defend the widespread practice of nepotism.

There is much that can be debated about Baltzell's analysis, as there is with any grand attempt at social theorizing, starting with his very notion of leadership in the first place. And yet his dichotomy strikes me as having captured something quite important. It isn't simply that Metropolitan Philadelphia has and does still suffer from mediocre, disappointing political leadership. It certainly does, but most places in the United States do too. More than that, its institutional and private sector leaders do not exert as much civic leadership as they do in other regions. In New York, Chicago, even in Minneapolis/St. Paul the sense of civic responsibility is more highly developed. Over the years, more often than not, Philadelphia's CEOs, its high-priced lawyers, its institution presidents, while none of them Quakers themselves, have adopted that Quaker ethos of privatism. (One result of this can be seen at some of the region's cultural institutions. They are among the finest of their kind in the country and are often run by well-connected but parsimonious boards.)[17]

Further, those Philadelphians who do emerge as leaders of one sort or another often find themselves slighted, ignored, or ridiculed for their efforts. Greater Philadelphia is second to none in its enthusiasm for professional sports, but those fans make a regular habit of heaping scorn on the city's star athletes. Mike Schmidt, the Hall of Fame third baseman for the Philadelphia Phillies, once quipped that Philadelphia was the only place where you could experience the thrill of victory and the agony of reading about it the next day in the paper. In the last one hundred years, Philadelphia has produced three of the most innovative, independent, and influential architects in the world—Frank Furness, Louis Kahn, and Robert Venturi. Kahn received only one major commission in the city, and that early in his career, and Venturi is coming to the end of his career without have received even one. Greater Philadelphia was once dotted with wild, wonderful Furness buildings, but most were systematically torn down after his death, leaving only a few to remind us of his genius. Philadelphians seem not only reluctant to assume leadership, but to resent it in their fellow citizens as well.

At the level of elected government, there is also a history of parochialism, mistrust, and an inability to communicate, which keeps cooperation across political borders from happening. At a basic level, city politicians refuse to see a connection between their own inefficiency, ineptitude, and outright corruption and the unwillingness of state legislators to contribute more thoroughly to the health of the city. At the same time, suburbanites refuse to acknowledge—much less pay for—all the ways in which their lives depend on a healthy city. Nor do they care much that Philadelphia virtually alone must bear the high costs of the region's poverty. Many simply want the city to provide them with recreational and cultural opportunities while resolutely closing their eyes to any sense of shared responsibility or common destiny. The high-flying, Cherry Hill–based Commerce Bank may have a better understanding that the fate of the region is bound to the health of the city. Commerce Bank, the fastest-growing retail bank in the nation, is at the center of the federal influence-peddling investigation.[18]

These are the common divides between urban and suburban America, between haves and have nots, between black and white. These tensions are no different, nor any worse in Greater Philadelphia than they are in Greater New York or in Chicagoland. They are the tensions that have defined metropolitan regions everywhere in the wake of the postwar suburban expansion.

The consequences and costs of these divides may, however, be more acute, not just for the city but for the whole region. Consider the comparison with Chicago: there, business leaders—largely suburban and Republican—have come to an effective working relationship with city politicians, most of whom are Democrats. The results of this famous "combine" are that business gets a friendly environment in which to operate within the city, and in exchange those business interests beat on their suburban legislators to get more for the city out of state government. Thus, Chicago receives 16 percent of its annual revenue from the reallocation of state tax dollars while Philadelphia only gets 10 percent.[19] Plenty of people in the region know all this, but it remains to be seen whether a critical mass of leaders in the Delaware Valley will emerge to do something about it.

It is no surprise either that the inability of regional leaders to work together has largely resulted in bad news for the city, weakened politically by its smaller size. In recent years, the state has taken away the city's control over its own Parking Authority and Convention Center, among other things. Again, the comparison with Chicago is instructive: when state legislators in Springfield decided that Chicago's failing school system needed a drastic overhaul, they gave that control almost entirely to the mayor. In Philadelphia, whose schools are no worse, the state stepped in and took a large measure of control away from city leaders.

Writing with the 1960s fresh in mind, Baltzell called the Quaker ethos "left-wing" and "anti-authoritarian," and he worried about its consequences. But at the same time, Philadelphia is replete with leadership at the community and neighborhood level. Thanks to that leadership, often mobilized against the exercise of the elite power Baltzell seemed to yearn for, Philadelphia was spared some of the worst excesses of urban "renewal" in the 1950s and 1960s. After all, the combine that runs Chicago so effectively also created the Robert Taylor Homes and Cabrini-Green, perhaps the most infamous housing projects in the nation, and it tore out much of the downtown loop to make room for corporate office towers.

The track record of elite leadership in urban America, especially during the postwar period, is decidedly mixed, replete with big projects that strike us now, looking back on them, as big mistakes. Perhaps we should thank the Philadelphia ethos that the city was spared some of the worst abuses of the "urban renewal" era, and for the fact that the downtown was not simply given away to large business interests, as has been the case in cities such as Los Angeles, Columbus, and Houston, all cities with the sort of leadership Baltzell might admire. As the urban historian and Philadelphia son Wendell Pritchett put it to me: "I agree that we have less elite leaderships, but I also think we have more democracy. Democracy is not a pretty system, but I'd chose our politics over [Chicago's]."[20]

Here too may be a Quaker legacy. Quakerism represents a deeply egalitarian impulse. It is perhaps the most democratic of the religious experiments to emerge from the seventeenth century, something that strikes us now as a fundamentally American characteristic. For over one hundred years critics, especially European ones, have accused the United States of living in the gloomy shadow of Puritanism. That may or may not be right in terms of our social mores and prudery. But it is more accurate to say that in our egalitarianism and our suspicion of a self-conscious and self-identified elite authority and leadership, the United States may be more Quaker than Puritan.

* * *

The utopian impulse that shaped so much of American life in the eighteenth and nineteenth centuries subsided to a large extent in the first half of the twentieth. It emerged again in the late 1960s and early 1970s as young people—and some not so young—tried to reimagine how life might be lived in the wake of the tumults of that era.

As was the case in previous centuries, this new effloresence of utopianism was largely a rural phenomenon. Small groups of people established alternative communities on old farmsteads in New England, especially in Massachusetts and Vermont, in California, and in a host of places in between. In those communes, they experimented with back-to-the-land communitarianism and with self-sufficient, organic agriculture, and they explored the relationship between the natural and the spiritual in ways that reached back at least as far as Henry David Thoreau.

Except for the experiment that called itself the Movement for a New Society.

Beginning in 1970 a group of roughly twenty-five to thirty Quakers, peace activists, and civil rights veterans including Richard K. Taylor and Bill Moyer, both of whom had worked with Martin Luther King Jr., began meeting in Philadelphia to discuss what might come next both for the movement and for themselves. The Movement for a New Society was the result of those meetings and it was launched in 1971.

As George Lakey, one of the founders of the MNS, explains it, the movement grew out of a sense that despite a rhetoric of progressive social change, most of the activity associated with the 1960s was still mired in "old thinking," especially when it came to the dynamics of gender, class, and race. Likewise, the energy of the 1960s consumed people at a great rate, burning them out and often leaving them damaged in the process. A primary goal for the MNS, then, was to create a community that would organize itself and live collectively, and that would provide a context in which participants could be sustained and nurtured in their political work. As George put it, with an equal mix of pride and exasperation: "Steve, it was hard, it was hard."

And the people who came together to begin the MNS made a self-conscious and deliberate choice that their experiment would be urban. As George acknowledges, those who went "back to the land" in the late 1960s and early 1970s were in some sense retreating. Most of the really difficult social issues facing the nation, from race relations to economic inequality to declining public education, are urban problems. Many of the New Left utopians, however, had made the City their enemy, along with the Establishment and the System. In this, they were little different from the hundreds of thousands of white city dwellers around the nation who left the city for their own version of bucolic paradise in the suburbs, except that they did so for slightly different reasons and went ever farther away. Indeed, as the decade of the 1960s came to a close, roughly two hundred thousand white Philadelphians had moved out to the surrounding suburbs to escape crime and violence, falling real estate values, and new black neighbors they could not abide. Almost three hundred years after William Penn began his revolutionary urban utopia, those who committed to the MNS committed to stay in the city.

The Philadelphia neighborhood where they chose to plant their roots had become, by the early 1970s, no one's idea of a peaceable kingdom. Located west of Penn's campus and along Baltimore Avenue—the old colonial road—it had grown up in the late nineteenth century as a classic example of a "street car suburb." Its large, elegant, late Victorian houses were home to prosperous Anglo-Protestants and Irish Catholics. The Catholics, in a show of their own ethno-religious pride, built the Church of St. Francis de Sales, a remarkable, vaguely Byzantine structure, whose bells still ring throughout the neighborhood and whose dome can be seen from points all over the city. Not to be outdone, the Methodists built the magnificent Calvary Church at 48th and Baltimore and topped their sanctuary with a breath-taking Tiffany glass dome. Residents of the neighborhood took their leisure at Clark Park, once the site of a Union hospital during the Civil War and now a leafy strolling park. And to underscore the bourgeois domesticity of it all, the neighbors erected a statue of Charles Dickens—the only one of him in the United States—with Little Nell at his feet in one corner of the park.

In the postwar years, that prosperity diminished somewhat. Many of the houses were subdivided into rental units and the population became more decidedly middle and working class. By the late 1960s, black residents began to move in from other surrounding neighborhoods. By 1971 the neighborhood seemed poised for the kind of collapse that had become so common in cities around the country. Crime became such a scourge that few people ventured out after dark, and many put bars up on their windows. Real estate agents went door to door goading white home owners to sell immediately—black people, after all, were moving in, and home values were only going to drop.

While the people who joined the MNS came with concerns about the big issues, the neighborhood itself became the first test case for their ideas. They began by addressing the problem of safety—organizing a system of block captains, neighborhood patrols, and neighborhood alerts. They helped calm the fears of at least some of those older residents who were poised to flee and persuaded many of them to stay. And they made sure that in all their efforts black and white residents worked together. The neighborhood stabilized. At a time when neighborhoods from the South Bronx to South Central Los Angeles descended into chaos largely because of racial tensions, the MNS created a model of how neighborhood transition did not have to mean neighborhood implosion.

The MNS was busy with other things as well, campaigns against the B-1 bomber and against nuclear power to name just two. But whatever the issue, as George explains, the eighteen houses that collectively constituted the MNS Life Center served as the laboratory to try out new ideas about strategy, organizing, decision making, and so forth. "We were our own guinea pigs," George remembers, and all these experiments were driven by the group's maxim: "Most of what we need to know to be effective we have yet to learn." The result was a profusion of creative ideas, some of which flopped, many of which were hugely successful. The 1970s and 1980s were, as George points out, disappointing times for Americans on the left. The promise of the 1960s proved if not illusory then at least a long way off. To sustain themselves, MNS members "set proximate goals for ourselves," George explains, "so there was always some victory to celebrate."

The MNS hit the peak of its influence in the late 1970s, when roughly three hundred people identified with it in cities such as Atlanta, Baltimore, Seattle, Toronto and even in the tiny village of Yellow Springs, Ohio. Back in West Philadelphia, the MNS established New Society Publishers and a food co-op, which is still selling food on Baltimore Avenue.

The MNS was officially laid to rest in 1989, its remaining membership deciding that this particular experiment had run its course.[21] There are still several group houses owned by the Life Center and they continue to provide a home and a haven for young people involved in community and political activism. George Lakey too still lives in the neighborhood and since 1992 he has run Training for Change. He travels around the world helping to build the capacity of activist groups to work for democratic change. He helped establish a network of activists in Russia in the tumultuous period after the Soviet Union collapsed and has been smuggled into Burma to train pro-democracy student groups there. The last time we spoke, George had just returned from Zimbabwe. When I pointed out to him that he was merely exporting the utopian idealism of his West Philadelphia neighborhood around the world, he laughed and agreed.

In 1982, a German television crew came to Philadelphia to mark the three hundredth anniversary of the founding of Philadelphia. German speakers, of course, constituted a major stream of migrants to Penn's city; they came seeking religious freedom, and the television crew wanted to know what had become of the "holy experiment." After talking with people at the Friends Center, they were sent to West Philadelphia. There, they were told, Penn's dream was best being kept alive.

I should confess: this has been my neighborhood too, on and off for the last fifteen years. It is a remarkably diverse, remarkably harmonious place. It still has a vibrant—indeed, sometimes exhausting—civic life, filled with community projects, political engagement, and festivals in Clark Park. It is where I have learned much of what I know about community and coexistence, about both the difficulties and the exhilarating possibilities of urban life. One of my neighbors (and my electrician, as it happens) has a bumper sticker that reads: "Heaven is a mixed neighborhood." It may not be heaven, and it certainly is not immune to some of the city's grinding problems, but it is still the closest thing I have known to a peaceable kingdom.

Religious pluralism, born in Philadelphia, has remained a central part of the nation since its founding, so much so that we don't pause over it much. Even so, in Metropolitan Philadelphia there are still particular reminders of those who were drawn to Penn's holy experiment in the eighteenth century. The Amish are still around, of course, and many in the region buy their food from them. But so too are the Dunkers and the Schwenkfelders. In fact, the Schwenkfelder Library and Heritage Center is located—how fitting—in Pennsbury, Pennsylvania, and it has recently received a grant to conserve examples of fraktur, the beautiful tradition of illuminated manuscript that Schwenkfelders, along with other German Protestants, produced in the eighteenth century. More remarkable, one of the remaining Schwenkfelder congregations is located in a tough North Philadelphia neighborhood that no one would mistake for a green country town. The Mennonites are still here too, and they have embraced some of the newer arrivals to the city. Penn's city now boasts a Chinese Mennonite Fellowship, a Vietnamese Mennonite Church, and the Iglesia Menonita Comunidad do Amor among others. Mennonites own and run my favorite coffee shop, just a few blocks from where I write this in West Philadelphia, and this afternoon I bought eggs at the farmer's market in my marvelously mixed neighborhood from an Amish family who live—where else?—in Quakertown.

On a recent visit to the Philadelphia Zoo I saw two groups of picnickers seated next to each other. One group was Muslim, the women fully veiled; the other Amish. There was a certain incongruity to this sight, but frankly it is no longer as improbable as it once might have been. Still, it reminded me that when John Sedgwick decided to write a book chronicling a year in the life of the Philadelphia Zoo—a wonderful, charming book, by the way—the title must have been as irresistible to him as it was obvious: *Peaceable Kingdom.*[22]

City of Brotherly Love. These days, the city's name is usually invoked in a cynical way. Sportscasters love to toss it out for a giggle just after Philadelphia fans have behaved boorishly. The legendary football coach Bill Parcells once warned his team when it visited Philadelphia: "They call it the City of Brotherly Love, but really it's a banana republic." Or it is used as an expression of despair or disgust after some act of tragic violence. It isn't a city of brotherly love, of course. No place is. When Thomas More coined the word "utopia" in 1516 he used it to describe an imaginary island where there existed a perfect social, political, and legal system. But Philadelphians, I think, are reminded more pointedly than people in other regions of the distance between reality and that imaginary island. Those who honor Penn's vision are those who make the attempt to get there.

CHAPTER TWO

The Ghosts That Haunt Us

The moviemaker M. Night Shyamalan has provided another kind of imaginative geography, a decidedly spooky one, for Greater Philadelphia. Shyamalan himself lives on Philadelphia's Main Line and he has set—and filmed—all his movies in the region. Through Shyamalan's lens, Bucks County has become a place of weird crop circles, and nineteenth-century Chester County the home to a plagued village.

Shyamalan broke into the national movie scene in 1999 with his wildly successful film *The Sixth Sense*. The plot revolves around Cole Sear (Haley Joel Osment), an eight-year-old boy who is haunted by ghosts, and Dr. Malcolm Crow (Bruce Willis), a child therapist who tries to help him through his difficulties, and if you are one of the tiny handful who hasn't seen the picture, I won't tell you how it resolves, except to say it will take you utterly by surprise.

The Sixth Sense is set in the city of Philadelphia and it makes marvelous use of the city to achieve its moody, scary tone. Everywhere the camera takes us, it seems, ghosts seem to pop out to terrify poor Cole. In a particularly taut scene, Cole tells Dr. Crowe his dreadful secret: "I see dead people."

I have a theory about *The Sixth Sense*. For most people who saw the movie around the country, it was simply a wonderfully crafted, slightly creepy, psychological thriller. For audiences in the Delaware Valley, however, the film also captured brilliantly a central fact of life in the region: the whole place is haunted by its own ghosts.

All real cities can be read as rich historical textbooks. Indeed, one of the best descriptions of a city I have ever come across defines them as layers of human history visible to the eye. In this sense, Philadelphia is no different than Chicago or Seattle, except perhaps in having more historical accumulation. Nor did Philadelphians develop what we might call a historical consciousness faster than anyone else. The first published history of the city appeared in the nineteenth century, roughly a century and a half after the city was founded. This was just at the moment when the nation itself was developing a modern sense of its own history.[1]

Still, there is some sense in which the Philadelphia region steeps more in its own past than any other place in the nation. When Henry James returned to the United States he was thoroughly alienated by most of what he found. When he came to stay in Philadelphia he felt at home and largely because of the way the city lived with a sense of its own history. "The place 'went back,'" he wrote in *The American Scene*, "or, in other words, the social equilibrium . . . had begun early, had had plenty of time on its side, and thus had its history behind it—the past looms through it, not at all luridly, but [ ] squarely and substantially. . . . The backward extension, in short, is the very making of Philadelphia. . . . To walk her streets is to note with all promptness that William Penn *must* have laid them out."[2] The company that insures my house was founded in 1752 and its 250-year-old logo is still on the top of all its policies. History is indeed behind it, and it looms.

To bolster their sense of their own history, Philadelphians did found a collection of institutions, unmatched perhaps anywhere else in the country, charged, at least in part, with preserving a sense of the city's past: The Library Company and the American Philosophical Society date to the eighteenth century; the Athenaeum and the Historical Society of Pennsylvania were founded early in the nineteenth century. All are still thriving research centers today.[3] The HSP was matched as well by county historical societies of uncommon holdings and energy, especially the Bucks County Historical Society in Doylestown and the Chester County Historical Society in West Chester early in the twentieth century. In 1897, members of the city's black intellegentsia came together to found the Afro-American Historical Society of Philadelphia, making it probably the first African American historical organization in the nation.[4]

Yet these institutions are not solely the reason for the particular historical sensibility in the Philadelphia region. More so, it is the city and region's role in the founding of the nation—from Washington's crossing of the Delaware, to the winter at Valley Forge, to the political debates and documents produced in Independence Hall—that have created a dialogue between local and national history, and between past and present, unique in the country. This connection between the regional and the national is one of the reasons the distinguished historian Gary Nash titled his book on the way Philadelphians have remembered and preserved the past *First City*.

The Philadelphia region serves as an extraordinary repository of the nation's collective memory—collective memories, more accurately, contested and contradictory as some of them are. When W. E. B. Du Bois wanted to study the problems of America's black urbanites at the end of the nineteenth century, he did so in Philadelphia.[5] Just a few years later, Lincoln Steffens even saw garden-variety municipal corruption in Philadelphia through the lens of national significance: "But I say that if Philadelphia is a disgrace, it is a disgrace not to itself alone, nor to Pennsylvania, but to the United States and to American character." In this,

Henry James, the aristocratic, aloof man of letters, could agree with the muckraking journalist. Philadelphia "was an American *case*, and presumably one of the best . . . for some study of the wondrous problem . . . : the way in which sane Society and pestilent City, in the United States, successfully cohabit, each keeping it up with so little of fear or flutter from the other."[6] In this chapter, I want to look at the way an awareness of history, the constant presence of the past, shapes Greater Philadelphia, for better and worse.

It used to be the case that school children in metropolitan Philadelphia would learn local history with a lesson on "Philadelphia Firsts." (I don't know if this is still a part of the area's curriculum—perhaps I've just dated myself.) The list is familiar, but it is still worth reviewing, or dredging from my memory, in no particular order:

—first lending library,
—first volunteer fire company,
—first hospital in the New World,
—first insurance company,
—first skyscraper done in the international modern style,
—first municipal water system,
—first penitentiary,
—first medical school in the Western Hemisphere.

The list could go on for some time.

And, of course, Philadelphia was home to the first American: Benjamin Franklin. William Penn might preside over the city from the distant vantage of City Hall's tower, but Franklin is still our ubiquitous man about town. There he is, toga clad, over the door to his American Philosophical Society on Fifth Street. There he is, three different times no less, on the campus of the University of

Pennsylvania. His head serves as the cornerstones of the arches in the gates of City Hall. And there he goes, walking down Chestnut or Third, portrayed by an actor. When the bust of Franklin created in 1779 by the French sculptor Jean-Antoine Houdon came up for sale in 1996, the Philadelphia Museum of Art, which has not had the money or inclination to be a major player in the art market, felt a special compulsion to buy it, and for a large sum. We all know Franklin's story, at least in broad outline, but it is worth revisiting it briefly. He left his native Boston as a teenager and came to Philadelphia in 1723. Boston was in a period of stagnation early in the eighteenth century and Franklin calculated, absolutely correctly as it turned out, that a lad of ambition and talent could better make his fortune in Philadelphia. He went into the printing business, did well for himself, and retired to pursue the life of a gentleman by the time he was forty. As a gentleman, Franklin played the roles of diplomat, scientist, political philosopher, and writer. He became the most celebrated American of the eighteenth century, the preeminent American contribution to the Enlightenment.[7]

We know Franklin's story because Franklin told it to us in his most famous publication, the *Autobiography*. In it, Franklin tells us, with his characteristic common sense, how his life of hard work, steady habits, moderation, and purpose not only led to his success but could be easily emulated, though Franklin's own public modesty would never have permitted him to say that explicitly. It is a rags-to-riches story, the story of a poor boy made good, a parable of what is possible in America, where success is not predetermined by birth but made through hard work and sober habits. We know Franklin's story because it is the archetypical American story, and every subsequent American autobiography, from Frederick Douglass's and Booker T. Washington's to Sam Walton's, has responded to Franklin's.

To see Franklin's life only as an affirmation of an up-by-the-bootstraps individuality, however, misses an important part of its significance. Franklin was a great founder of institutions, the aforementioned Library Company and American Philosophical Society two among them. Through these institutions Franklin answered a basic question about life in the New World: Where does the authority come from to solve our civic problems and work for the collective good in the absence of religious hegemony and when the king lives three thousand miles away? The answer Franklin came up with over and over again was the voluntary association. A group, Franklin reasoned, could better act in a disinterested way for the public good than any single individual. Through the voluntary association Franklin helped define a secular, public sphere in a city where many religions flourished privately and none dominated. (Franklin, famously, was a man of desultory religious faith, who had disdain for organized religion. He muses in his *Autobiography* about inventing one of his own but concedes that he never got around to it.) Franklin, it needs remembering, had such an expansive view of what constituted the public sphere that most present day conservatives who claim his mantle would cringe if they acknowledged it. In Franklin's view, all property beyond basic necessities belonged "to the public, who by their laws have created it." Franklin stands as the first American then in his ability to balance the pursuit of individual success with a sense of civic duty, and his story was only possible in the essentially secular space created in William Penn's religious utopia during the eighteenth century.

Being the City of Firsts, being America's First City, having produced the First American—all of these are points of civic pride to be sure. But being first becomes a slightly hollow distinction if the initial impulse to innovation cannot be maintained over the years. Take, for example, the case of the Philadelphia Zoo. America's First Zoo, as it still calls itself, was opened to the public shortly before the grand centennial celebrations of 1876. For those who strolled the grounds of the Zoological Garden, the first modern zoo in the United States, they were novel and remarkable. With some imagination you can still conjure the original zoo—its boundaries have remained fixed, and you still enter the same gates as visitors did in 1876.

At just over forty acres, however, the Philadelphia Zoo is now among the smallest of the nation's major zoos, and it isn't at all clear where or how the Zoo can grow. The zoo, shaped roughly like a half moon, is hemmed in on its curved side by busy railroad tracks and on its straight edge by four lanes of equally busy traffic. In what can only be described as a short-sighted design decision during the era of big road projects, the zoo was cut off from the Schuylkill River by yet more lanes of high speed traffic. Philadelphia's Noah's Ark, sitting amid an angry sea of cars and trains.

As a consequence, the zoo struggles to keep up with changing standards for animal exhibits, which demand more space for animals. There is no small irony in this, since the Philadelphia Zoo once set the scientific standard on how to keep animals in captivity. While the zoo remains perhaps the most popular destination for regional visitors, it does not draw visitors from around the country the way the Bronx, San Diego, or National Zoos do.

Likewise, perhaps the last, that is to say most recent, item on most people's list of Philadelphia Firsts is the Electronic Numerical Integrator and Computer, ENIAC. The world's first digital computer, ENIAC began crunching numbers at high speed toward the end of the Second World War. It had its formal dedication on February 15, 1946. ENIAC was produced by the demands of the war when the Army needed a faster way to calculate firing and bombing tables for ordnance. The Army granted a contract to develop such a machine to the Moore School of Engineering at the University of Pennsylvania. By the time ENIAC was finished it had grown enormous: 30 separate units, 19,000 vacuum tubes, 1,500 relays. Its 30 tons consumed 200 kilowatts of electricity to run.

ENIAC's builders applied for a patent in 1947 and in their application they described the need for greater speed in making the calculations necessary for modern scientific problems and they promised that "the present invention is intended to reduce to seconds such lengthy calculations." They were right. Despite it size, it really did represent a quantum improvement over other mechanical calculating devices. At the time, a skilled person using a desk calculator took roughly twenty hours to calculate a sixty-second trajectory; an analog differential analyzer made the calculation in fifteen minutes. It took ENIAC all of thirty seconds.[8]

The digital age began at the corner of Thirty-third and Walnut Streets on Penn's campus, but it grew up elsewhere. In 1947 as well, all thirty tons of ENIAC were packed up and moved down to the Army's Aberdeen Proving Ground in Maryland, the major site for ordnance testing. Having produced the first digital computer, Philadelphia and the region would largely be a bystander to the digital revolution. The Delaware Valley did not become Silicon Valley.

Just a year after ENIAC moved to Maryland, in what strikes me now as heavy if unintentional symbolism, President Harry Truman signed the legislation authorizing the establishment of Independence National Historical Park. Work began on the park in 1949 in the heart of Philadelphia's original city. With the founding of the park, Philadelphia, at least in the minds of many, became an eighteenth-century city again, and much of the region's future became staked to its past.

Independence National Historical Park is what most people outside the region think of when they think of Philadelphia. More specifically, they think of the park's twin icons: Independence Hall and the Liberty Bell. For those who live in the region, the park is the place your out-of-town relatives want to see when they come to visit. The city keeps its official annual count of tourists at the Liberty Bell.

More formally, Independence National Historical Park preserves a number of buildings associated with Philadelphia's role in the events of American independence and maintains them amid lovely gardens and green spaces. It is, for my money at least, one of the most pleasant parks anywhere in urban America, with its collection of elegant architecture, museums, and open spaces. It is this nation's shrine to liberty and its most interesting, moving commemoration of the founding of the nation.

It is also a fiction of sorts, a fantasy of what the park's planners wanted eighteenth-century Philadelphia to look like. In this sense, Independence National Historical Park mirrors the 1950s as much as it preserves the 1770s.

That Congress felt it necessary to create the park in the first place surely reflects the growing tensions of the Cold War. As an iron curtain descended across Europe, and the United States mobilized for a titanic struggle against the Soviet Union, Independence National Historical Park served a symbolic purpose, reminding Americans and the world of values central to the nation, values antithetical to those of state socialism. Since it was built in the middle of a dense but by then deteriorating urban neighborhood, the park was also shaped by the ideas about urban renewal circulating in the 1950s. Though the grand plan for the park went through several iterations during the decade, it was clear from the beginning that restoring Philadelphia's eighteenth century meant demolishing much of what had accumulated on the site after Franklin died, including a magnificent bank designed by Frank Furness.[9]

The result, however lovely, erased much of what remained from Philadelphia's eighteenth-century working class and the poor, thus turning revolutionary Philadelphia into a city populated almost entirely by prosperous patriots. Not Disney so much as Williamsburg, which, especially in the 1950s and 1960s, was a colonial history theme park organized around archaeologically reconstructed buildings where never was heard a discouraging word about slavery or social inequality.[10] It was the eighteenth century as we wish it had been—all graciousness and gentility.[11]

We can see INHP as the final culmination of a "colonial revival" that swept the country beginning in the early years of the twentieth century. Among its local products are dozens of "colonial" style homes around Philadelphia's suburbs, most built in the 1920s, and the Colonial Dames, a women's club reserved for those who can trace their ancestry back to the eighteenth century. Founded in 1890, the Colonial Dames predate the more (in)famous Daughters of the American Revolution and they still have an active clubhouse—in a 1920s-era colonial-style building—just off Rittenhouse Square.

In 1926 the colonial revival, and all that it implied about America's eighteenth-century past, was brought to the public in grand fashion at the Sesquicentennial Exposition. Philadelphia, of course, had played host to the first of the big world's fair events in 1876 to celebrate the centennial. Fifty years later, the city tried to recapture the magic and excitement.

It didn't work. Everything that the Centennial Exposition was, the Sesqui was not. It opened late and even then wasn't entirely complete, its construction mired in epic levels of municipal corruption.[12] The anticipated crowds never came. The weather didn't even cooperate: of the 184 days the Sesqui was opened to public, it rained on 107 of them.

The fair sat at the very bottom of Broad Street, in what was then an undeveloped area of marsh and open space, and it has largely vanished from the public imagination (though I think it may have provided fodder for W. C. Fields, a son of Philadelphia, to make jokes about the city). On one half of the site now sits the complex of sports venues and their parking lots. On the west side of Broad, the Sesqui bequeathed Franklin Delano Roosevelt Park, and the American Swedish Historical Museum, built for the fair as a way for Swedish Americans to claim their connection to the nation's First City. Both, frankly, stand a little forlorn these days.

But the Sesqui did produce one smash hit. Amid the curvilinear paths running through the grounds, "High Street" ran on a straight axis, and was far and away the most popular exhibit at the event. It consisted of twenty "houses" recreating Philadelphia's High Street (now called Market Street) circa 1776.

It was the creation of the Sesqui's Women's Committee, and each of the buildings along the faux street was built and maintained by a different women's patriotic association: the DAR presided over "Washington's House," while the War Mothers maintained the "Little Wooden House." Women from the Pennsylvania Horticultural Society planted and tended the gardens along the street. It was such a huge hit that many in the city clamored that it be reinstalled in the Philadelphia Museum of Art.

High Street presented eighteenth-century Philadelphia as a thoroughly domestic affair. While the fair itself ostensibly celebrated the political act of independence, High Street immersed visitors in the cozy, liveried interior life of the founders—at least as society ladies of the 1920s assumed they had lived it. The hostess at the recreated Stephen Girard house (Girard made a fortune in Philadelphia and may have been the richest man in the nation when he died) explained the didactic purpose of High Street: "It needs an actual street like this, reconstructed before our eyes, to reveal the fine heritage of beauty and dignity in ordinary everyday life which our ancestors have passed on to us. It proves that our beginnings were not chaotic, lawless, cheap, or tawdry, but essentially noble, dignified."[13] How this entirely ersatz street "proved" anything the hostess did not explain.

This genteel, quasi-aristocratic version of eighteenth-century

America reached a kind of apotheosis at Winterthur. Located just outside Wilmington, Delaware, Winterthur was built over a number of years by Henry Francis DuPont (1880–1969) as a sprawling pleasure garden, a collection of decorative arts, and a center for research about American material culture. The gardens cover nearly one thousand acres. The collection, comprised of over eighty-five thousand objects now displayed in a house-museum DuPont built for the purpose, has grown to be, quite simply, incomparable in its scope and quality. It covers all sorts of American decorative arts made between 1640 and 1860, but its focus, primarily, has been on the finest and the best. In conjunction with the University of Delaware, it offers a master's degree in art history. Through this research arm, Winterthur has trained connoisseurs, who have gone on to work for Sotheby's and Christie's and as museum curators around the nation.

Winterthur was founded to be unapologetically aristocratic— the very name of the place in its advertising even carries the subtitle: "An American Country Estate." The brochure reveals the kind of Anglophilia that lay behind much of the colonial revival, even influencing this descendant of French immigrants: "[DuPont] created an extraordinary country estate on par with English examples that had evolved over centuries."

In this way, Winterthur gave a museum and an academic home to the sense of the American eighteenth century as having been essentially as refined as European aristocracy of the same period. Touring Winterthur, even today, it is easy to come away with the impression that the domestic lives of eighteenth-century Americans were lived surrounded by Chippendale and Hepplewhite, their elegance and sophistication reflected by highly polished and exquisitely crafted silver. Without any sense of qualification or irony, Winterthur describes its museum as "the ideal place to rediscover America's heritage," begging the question of exactly whose heritage is to be rediscovered.[14] And for those who want to bring this heritage home, Winterthur offers handmade "museum quality" reproductions of its furniture for staggering prices.

Were Benjamin Franklin to stroll the grounds of Winterthur, or had he descended onto the grounds of the Sesqui, he would not have recognized the eighteenth century on display: missing are any of eighteenth-century Philadelphia's metaphorical or literal messes. By 1926, the real High Street the DAR and its sisters imagined had vanished under the accumulation of real city life. High Street, the exhibit, vanished too after the fair closed. But in a sense its influence was felt a generation later, when the builders of Independence National Historical Park scrubbed Ben Franklin's old neighborhood clean.

Having determined which buildings would be saved and restored between Second and Sixth Streets, and having cleared away the buildings that had grown up around those, the wrecking crews turned north from Independence Hall and mercilessly cleared three entire city blocks to create, this being the 1950s, Independence Mall.

Whatever version of the eighteenth century is presented in the rest of INHP, the mall was pure mid-century modernism. As I mentioned in the previous chapter, Penn planned his grid without any grand axes. It is a spatial representation of a kind of egalitarianism. The mall repudiates that gesture, oblivious to the irony. The mall's purpose, as I understand it, was to have a great plaza in front of Independence Hall, thus creating an unimpeded view of the building and a grand approach to it—something on the order of the Mall in front of the U.S. Capitol.

And it has been, since the very day it opened, an urban planning disappointment. The plaza spaces themselves, planned again with a 1950s sensibility, have been lifeless and sterile. They did not fall into disuse, because they were never used at all in the first place. (It did not help that in subsequent years, the federal

Fig. 9a

Figs. 9a & b. Independence Hall before (Fig. 9a, ca. 1936) and after (Fig. 9b, ca. 1962) the creation of Independence National Historical Park. In this case, preserving the eighteenth-century past meant erasing most of what had come later. Courtesy of Independence National Historical Park.

government walled in the perimeter of the mall with a series of equally brutal, lifeless buildings—the federal courthouse, the Federal Reserve Bank, and the windowless, heavily fortified U.S. Mint.) Yet despite being devoid of human activity, they crumbled. As the front yard for Independence Hall, the mall was no better. The building itself is simply too modest to hold the yawning space it was now asked to command. Rather than help us appreciate this fine piece of mid-eighteenth century architecture, the mall simply made Independence Hall seem small and inadequate. The mall was a vast, featureless table, as Penn professor Tony Garvan once quipped, and Independence Hall became an overwhelmed table-weight at its southern end.[15]

In the 1990s the mall underwent a major—though many would argue not major enough—transformation. The table was shortened, its northern most leaf filled in with the National Constitution Center; and the western boundary was edged with the new Independence Visitors Center in one block and a new building for the Liberty Bell in another. The National Constitution Center is a work of genuine architectural distinction, designed by the modernist Henry Cobb. Its use of glass and light stone creates a wonderful juxtaposition to the heavier red brick that predominates in the area. Inside, the exhibits and programming are both fun and important. Taken together, these three additions have injected much more vitality into INHP than has been there before.

These new buildings, however, were supposed to be accompanied by a major change in the overall landscape design. That

Fig. 9b

plan, developed by the Olin Partnership, the nation's leading landscape architecture firm, located just a block from the mall, would have connected the plaza more effectively to the original street grid, which the mall had obliterated. The buildings went up, but the landscape plan became yet one more victim of the September 11 attacks. Openness and access have been replaced by security fences and metal detectors.

The National Park Service, whose orders came from Secretary of the Interior Gale Norton, has clashed repeatedly with groups of residents and businesses around INHP, with designers, planners, and architects, and with many people from around the country who simply see the security response as overblown, ill-conceived, and perhaps even a bit paranoid. The park simply cannot be made secure from car bombs, rocket attacks, or from some lunatic tossing a grenade, so planners at the park service have decided to defend the site against individuals carrying explosives in backpacks. With this spurious logic, the park has now mostly been made a hassle for tourists. For a while after September 11, visitors had to endure two separate security screenings, one to get in to see the Liberty Bell, the other to see Independence Hall. Most onerously, if you found yourself in need of a bathroom at Independence Hall, you were forced outside the secured area and back through a screening point to relieve yourself.

In the summer of 2004, INHP began to develop a new, alas more permanent, security design that includes erecting a six-foot-high metal fence around the southern side of Independence Hall and building a permanent security building next to it. It is a grisly plan. As John Gallery, head of Philadelphia's Preservation Alliance, points out: "The space, to me, is as significant as the building. It was the place where the Declaration was first read. It was the place . . . that Jefferson walked around when he contemplated what to write." Charlene Mires, who teaches history at nearby Villanova University, believes that as a result of this plan visitors will not confront the historical questions about American liberty. Instead, visitors will be confronted with a different experience: "What does it mean when you are standing in a place called Independence Square and the fundamental activity is security?"[16] This plan is still under development as I write. For the moment, America's shrine to liberty now resembles nothing so much as a cheap minimum security prison.[17] It has also thus become an irony-free zone.

If Cold War posturing helped create INHP originally, then the war for tourists drove these new developments. Having watched too many tourists zip past the Philadelphia area on their way to and from New York and Washington, leaders in the region decided to market the city much more aggressively as a tourist destination. The improvements on Independence Mall—roughly 200 million dollars worth—were a major part of those plans. In a post-industrial age when cities no longer manufacture much beyond tourist and conventions, the region's leaders decided that Philadelphia's most marketable tourist commodity was its history. Back to the future, as it were.

Building a tourist economy around Philadelphia's historic resources faces several dilemmas. Not the least of these, as Kyle Farley points out, is that "most Americans have historical amnesia." Farley, a graduate student in history at the University of Pennsylvania, is a cofounder of Poor Richard's Walking Tours. He and other Penn grad students give well-researched historical tours of the city. From a historical point of view, they are simply the best tours in the city. "People come here," he continues, "and they know they're supposed to see the Liberty Bell and Independence Hall, but they don't remember why." Furthermore, his clients want some history, but "not too much history."[18]

Philadelphia, of course, can be used to illustrate almost every major episode of American history, but the historical commodity being marketed is a specific thirty year period: 1770–1800. Not a bad thirty years, given everything that took place in the city during that stretch, but that marketing therefore neglects Philadelphia's fascinating industrial past and its multiplicitous ethnic past, and it even risks downplaying the city's rich contemporary cultural life. Further, as Farley reports, the city's marketing people want to stress a Whiggish, hagiographic version of those thirty years. "Discussing all the tensions that existed in revolutionary Philadelphia makes the marketing people nervous," he says. But, he quickly adds, discussing those tensions, making links between the contentious past and the fractious present, is precisely what the people who take his tours find most interesting.

Quite apart from the marketing questions that confront the region's tourism boosters, there is a difficult tension inherent in building the Delaware Valley's tourist economy on the foundation of its eighteenth-century history. Emphasizing the theme of the city as the birthplace of the nation may well mean that the tourists who do come are not actually interested in seeing the city but rather come for a set of isolated historical sites. As Farley puts it, many people don't see Philadelphia as a living city but as a museum holding a handful of historical artifacts that belong not so much to the city but to the whole nation. Tourists to New York or Chicago go to experience the places they associate with those cities. When they come to Philadelphia they come to see the birthplace of the nation, which happens to be located in Philadelphia. They may or may not be interested in exploring much beyond the national parks and eighteenth-century historic sites. After seeing the Liberty Bell and Independence Hall many tourists, at least in Farley's experience, don't have any sense of what else there might be to do.

The good news, according to Farley, is that when he is finished walking groups of visitors around the city they invariably say: "I had no idea there was so much more here!" The bad news is, as he puts it, "the city only gets people's lunch money." What he means is that Philadelphia's identity as a tourist destination is still primarily for day-trippers coming to see the Bell. By and large, they don't come for extended stays, spending serious cash. Farley's experience notwithstanding, the situation does seem to be changing. The region's tourist marketers have become much smarter and much more aggressive in recent years. They are also marketing the entire region, not merely the few square blocks around the Liberty Bell. For those who want history, there is plenty of that from one end of the Delaware Valley to the other; for those who want the arts there are an abundance of these; for those who want flowers and trees there is no finer constellation of gardens and arboreta, starting, of course, with Bartram's Gardens, the very first such place in the New World, which dates back to the mid-eighteenth century. And these efforts do seem to be paying off—hotel stays are up, even after September 11 when tourist travel was down almost everywhere else. In recent years, the region has also seen a dramatic increase in the number of foreign visitors. Tourism is now the world's largest "industry," and Greater Philadelphia is getting a larger and growing share of it.

Indeed, according to one recent study, Philadelphia now ranks second in the nation in the volume of "heritage tourism," surpassing Boston and trailing only Washington, D.C. There are a whopping 450 historical sites within a fifty-mile radius of William Penn's statue—museums, societies, battlefields, and so forth. Over 100 of these are related to the eighteenth century. Ghosts from one end of the region to the other.[19]

Nowhere, however, do they whisper in your ear quite like they do at Eastern State Penitentiary. Eastern State is another Philadelphia "first," the first correctional facility design to rehabilitate, rather than simply to punish. In this sense, our penal system today descends directly from Eastern State. It stands also as another monument to Quaker humanitarianism. The Quakers who

Fig. 10. The geography of historical tourism. Recently, marketers
have made a concerted effort to
promote the history of the whole
region as a tourist commodity.
Data from the maps *Bucks
County and Surrounding Area,
Chester County & the Brandywine Valley,* and *Montgomery
County and Surrounding Area* ©
2002 PCVB and C.C. Salvatico,
rev. 9/02, and *Philadelphia and
Its Countryside* © 2001–2 PCVB
and C.C. Salvatico, rev. 9/02.

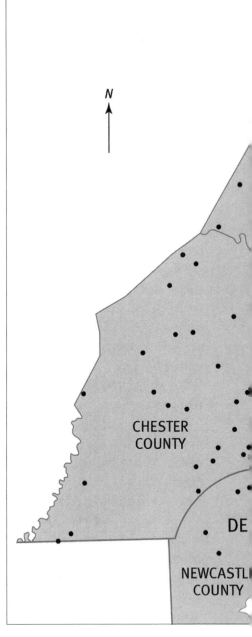

N
↑

CHESTER
COUNTY

DE

NEWCASTL
COUNTY

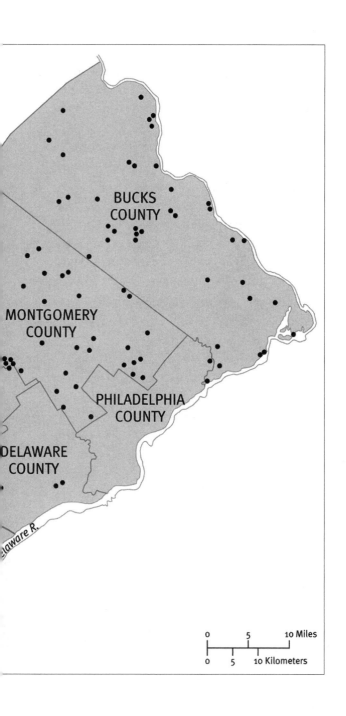

BUCKS
COUNTY

MONTGOMERY
COUNTY

PHILADELPHIA
COUNTY

DELAWARE
COUNTY

elaware R.

0   5   10 Miles

0   5   10 Kilometers

founded the place believed that that any criminal could, with enough penitence—hence "penitentiary"—return to life outside the walls and live as a productive citizen. The way that transformation would be achieved was through solitary and silent confinement, days filled with labor.

It was a celebrated and radical experiment and it was visited by people from all over the world. Alexis de Tocqueville came to see it on his American tour in 1831, and Eastern State's system and design became enormously influential. When the first prison was built in the penal colony at Sydney, Australia, it was modeled on Eastern State. When Eastern State opened in 1829, inmates generally received short sentences. The goal of this grand experiment, after all, was to return convicts to civilian life, not to keep them confined. Instead, many went mad. Charles Dickens, another famous tourist to the site, recognized as much and denounced the prison in his 1842 book *American Notes*.

Built well out in the country in 1829, Eastern State became surrounded as the city grew up around it in the late nineteenth century. A huge, hulking, intimidating gothic castle, it is now bordered incongruously by three-storey row houses.

Crowded and deteriorating, Eastern State was closed in 1971. And there it sat, empty, forbidding, and falling apart still further, until in 1988, with this remarkable site threatened, the city turned the prison over to the Pennsylvania Prison Society. The group endeavored to open the prison as a museum and started giving tours in 1994.

Since then, Eastern State has been run by a collection of energetic, creative staff and volunteers. In addition to giving tours through the prison, which themselves are haunting, disturbing, and utterly fascinating, they have also run art exhibits, theater performances, and events such as the annual Halloween tour and the July 14 storming of the Bastille ("Let them eat Tastykake"), to name just a few of the activities that have turned this historic site into one of the most dynamic cultural institutions in the region. Still, the tourist economy has Independence National Historical Park at its center. Whether the mandate of the National Park Service to run and interpret INHP can be made to mesh more cooperatively with the region's desire to attract more tourist revenue remains to be seen. In fact, over the years, the park service has been alternately hostile or indifferent to the city's economic development concerns. One gets the sense sometimes that the park service sees INHP as an island floating completely independently from the rest of the city. This tension is embodied at the tourist information desk at the new visitor's center on Independence Mall. One half of the desk is staffed by national park rangers, who will answer questions about anything administered by the park service. If you want to know about anything else in the area, they direct you to the other half of the desk, staffed by volunteers who provide you with tourist information for the rest of the region.

Finally, there is, I think, a deep ambivalence on the part of many Philadelphians about the whole notion of becoming a tourist attraction in the first place. Philadelphians think of their city as a "real" city, and whatever that phrase means it is surely the antonym of a theme park. This ambivalence was captured perfectly for me in the summer of 2000 when the city "welcomed" thousands of Republicans for the Republican National Convention. I passed a woman on Market Street wearing a t-shirt that read: "Welcome to Philadelphia! Now go home." Such are the growing pains the region is feeling as it develops a new, postindustrial tourist economy.

Independence National Historical Park sits at the center of a regional complex of sites associated with the Revolutionary War and with the colonial period more generally. North along the Delaware is the little town of Washington's Crossing, located—yes—at the point where Washington made his famous crossing of the Delaware in the dead of night. That event is reenacted regularly, though usually during the day and, in one measure of our warming climate, the reenactors almost never have to contend with ice. Washington's Crossing is also the home of the David Library of the American Revolution, a small research facility specializing in material from the revolutionary period. The library was founded in 1959 by Sol Feinstone, a Lithuanian immigrant who came to this country in 1902. When it opened to the public in 1974, it became his gift to his adopted home, and it joined the other area institutions charged with preserving and disseminating American history.

To the south, almost at the Delaware state border, is the Brandywine Battlefield site. It is small, and perhaps a bit overlooked, sitting as it does just off of Route 1 and surrounded increasingly by the traffic and development of suburban and exurban sprawl. It doesn't help Brandywine's visibility that the battle did not go well for the patriots. They lost the fight, in the fall of 1777, and as a result the British kept marching north, where they captured Philadelphia. Still, the Battle of Brandywine is reenacted every so often, and the site itself is an interesting, peaceful remnant of the eighteenth-century Chester County landscape.

The British kept chasing General Washington and engaged his troops again, this time at the Battle of Germantown. This battle went a bit better for the Americans, though they still lost in the end. Germantown retains at least some of its historic town center, with several extraordinary eighteenth-century buildings extant, and this battle too is reenacted, though patriots and red coats must do so amid the bustle of a busy, if somewhat down-at-the-heels, urban neighborhood.

The defeat at Germantown sent Washington packing north and

west, where he made camp at Valley Forge, spending his famous winter there from December of 1777 through the following spring. These defeats, and the Valley Forge encampment, were the immediate events that prompted Thomas Paine to write "These are the times that try men's souls." The Delaware Valley, put simply, was the heart of the Revolutionary War. It is still dotted with sites associated with that moment, and filled with the ghosts of eighteenth-century patriots, redcoats, and others.

Selling history as a tourist commodity presents certain challenges, however. In Kyle Farley's experience, very few people who come to see the Liberty Bell know why they are coming to see it. "It's something to check off their list," he says a bit wearily, "but they don't know what its significance is. I've even listened to park rangers explain how the bell was cast, what kind of metal used, and not explain what it all means."

So quickly, let's review:

To begin with, the Liberty Bell has little to do with 1776 or the Revolutionary War, though it and the city's other bells were evacuated to Allentown when the British captured Philadelphia. That it rang out on July 4, 1776 is a fiction created in the nineteenth century by the writer George Lippard. It was cast to commemorate the fiftieth anniversary of William Penn's epochal 1701 Charter of Privileges. The bell arrived in Philadelphia a year late in 1752 and cracked upon its first ringing. It was recast again and then hung in the State House in 1753.

The bell did ring on certain ceremonial occasions in the eighteenth century and early nineteenth—for the ascension of George III to the throne in 1761, to gather people to discuss the Sugar and Stamp Acts in 1764 and 1765. The bell tolled its last to mark George Washington's birthday in 1846, at which point the crack had widened so much that the bell became unringable.

Even before that, however, the bell had already begun its journey from functional to symbolic. When the bell was commissioned

"By Order of the Assembly of the Province of Pensylvania [sic] for the State House in Philada," it was cast with a quote from Leviticus, 25:10: "Proclaim Liberty throughout all the land unto all the inhabitants thereof." Seizing on this quote, and on the bell's location in Philadelphia, abolitionists turned the cracked bell into an icon of liberty. The bell appeared as the frontispiece to an 1837 edition of *Liberty*, a New York publication of the Anti-Slavery Society. In 1839, in his Boston-based paper *The Liberator*, William Lloyd Garrison reprinted a poem about the bell entitled "The Liberty Bell." With that poem, the State House bell began its transformation into the Liberty Bell, a process largely completed by the time of the World's Columbian Exposition in 1893. There visitors could see a thirteen thousand pound replica called the Columbian Liberty Bell, and one made entirely out of California oranges. The Liberty Bell itself was well traveled at the turn of the twentieth century, visiting big world's fairs in Atlanta, New Orleans, and St. Louis, where it was venerated by pilgrims as a sacred relic.

Garrison stands as the best known of the white abolitionists. He made his famous denunciation of slavery and the Constitution in Boston's Park Street Church in 1829. A year later he launched the *Liberator*. But when he and others attempted to build a national coalition for abolition in 1833, the delegates gathered in Philadelphia. The sixty-three participants, many of them clergy from different denominations, were chaired by Beriah Green, who opened the proceedings in Quaker fashion with a moment of silent reflection.[20]

At this meeting Garrison drafted a "declaration" for the antislavery movement in which he declared: "We plant ourselves upon the truths of Divine Revelation and the Declaration of our Independence as upon the EVERLASTING ROCK . . . to deliver our land from its deadliest curse."[21] Sixty-three delegates signed the declaration and Garrison joked that that was seven more signatures than on the Declaration of Independence.

The connection between abolition and the Liberty Bell represents probably the first major example of how Philadelphia's history has been used by various groups to establish a link between their particular concerns and the founding of the nation. It is a peculiar aspect of most American opposition movements that they seek a link with the national past rather than a break from it. Abolition, women's suffrage, civil rights—all have called upon the nation to fulfill the promises made in Philadelphia about life and liberty and freedom. Philadelphia's history and its collection of historic icons have thus served since the 1830s as the stage set upon which different groups have tried to establish their historical legitimacy and to demonstrate their connections to the founding ideals.

Throughout the nineteenth century Philadelphia certainly had no monopoly on dissent. All kinds of people in big cities and small towns marched, demonstrated, protested, and organized for a whole host of causes. But whatever the tenor and cast of those efforts in other places, in Philadelphia they often self-consciously drew from the well of the city's association with 1776. So when in 1835 laborers participated in the nation's first general strike, they marched to Independence Hall. The largest demonstration to take place on Independence Square during the antebellum period may have been the multiethnic gathering of immigrants who assembled on the square in 1848 in support of the revolutions taking place in Europe. Later, in 1912, suffragists stood on the site to read Susan B. Anthony's Declaration of Women's Rights, which she had delivered to the vice president during the centennial celebrations in 1876. Before Washington, D.C. served as the backdrop by which citizens of varying beliefs linked their causes to the national agenda, people came to Independence Hall.[22]

Even after Washington replaced Philadelphia in this role, the symbolism of Philadelphia remained important. At the Lincoln

Memorial Martin Luther King Jr. exhorted the nation to live up to its creed that all men are created equal and challenged us to imagine a day when freedom would truly ring. He spoke those words in Washington D.C., but he was remembering the document signed in Independence Hall and the bell that would become synonymous with liberty.

As a creation of the Cold War, Independence Mall and the national park played host to many events designed to bolster an anti-communist, patriotic agenda by organizations such as the Veterans of Foreign Wars and the Young Americans for Freedom. This use of Independence Hall reached a climax of sorts when President John Kennedy gave a July Fourth address to thousands on the mall in 1962. Referring to the building behind him, Kennedy urged the crowd to resist communist aggression.

By the 1960s, however, the hall and the bell were being reappropriated by a new generation of activists, who were interested in the expansion of civil rights and opposed to the war in Vietnam, and who believed that in taking these positions they best honored the founders. By 1968, a college guide book to Philadelphia could write: "In the last few years, the spirit of political controversy enshrined here in 1776 has been revived by picketers and protesters. Police grumble and tourists look on amazed, but nothing could be more appropriate at the place where the hot-headed Founding Fathers declared their independence."[23]

And so it was in this shifting context, less than two years after King made his famous speech, that visitors to Independence Hall on July 4, 1965 found themselves in the middle of a quiet demonstration by members of ECHO—the East Coast Homophile Organizations.

A small group of gay men and lesbians, ECHO had come to Independence Hall to demonstrate for the right to be included as part of American society. Its members were entirely, almost painfully, respectable, the men dressed in suits and ties, the

Fig. 11. The birthplace of gay rights. Before Stonewall, Philadelphia's gays and lesbians used Independence Hall as the backdrop for their pickets. Temple University, Paley Library, Urban Archives, with thanks to Marc Stein.

women in dresses and heels. They carried signs with such slogans as "All men are created equal. Homosexuals ask for their equality." Four years before the Stonewall riots in New York, this march was among the very first public demonstrations for gay rights in the nation.

Political organizing among Delaware Valley gays and lesbians had taken an important first step in the Main Line town of Radnor in 1960 when nearly one hundred people gathered to discuss the formation of a "homophile" political group. (The meeting was raided by the local police, who arrested eighty-four of the participants on vague charges of indecency.)

ECHO included activists from New York and Washington, D.C.

as well as Philadelphia, and their march of July 4, 1965, in the shadow of Independence Hall, marked an important coming out—pardon—for the gay rights movement. They marched in annual reminders until 1969, when their version of respectable picketing in front of the nation's great symbols was eclipsed by the more boisterous gay liberation movement born of the Stonewall riots. These symbolic uses of Independence Hall were not necessarily the biggest, nor the most attention grabbing, but they were often the first attempts on the part of marginalized Americans to forge their predicament to the nation's founding ideals.

Despite the fact that the United States owes its very existence to the Revolutionary War and to the documents written by Jefferson, Paine, and others, most Americans have only the vaguest historical sense of the event. As wars go, it probably ranks a distant third in our popular interest behind the Civil War and World War II. We celebrate July 4 every year, but I suspect fewer than two out of every ten Americans know what actually happened on that day (the Declaration of Independence was signed, though not read publicly until July 8). This should not come as any surprise, given that so many Americans have so little knowledge of or interest in our own history. But this historical lacuna about the Revolutionary War has been particularly galling to some, and they have big plans to fix it at Valley Forge.

The park itself constitutes thirty-five hundred preserved acres and is the only other revolutionary site in the region to have been turned into a national park. That happened officially on July 4, 1976 as part of the nation's bicentennial. Before that, it had been a state park—indeed, the first state park in Pennsylvania—created out of the patriotic fervor that flowed from the 1876 Centennial. Between 1878 and 1893, a private group raised money and lobbied politicians to preserve Valley Forge from the threat of industrial uses. And by the end of the nineteenth century their efforts paid off.

At the end of the twentieth century, the private nonprofit National Center for the American Revolution entered into a partnership with the National Park Service and the Commonwealth of Pennsylvania to build a large museum devoted to the Revolutionary War to be located at Valley Forge. Currently tagged at roughly one hundred million dollars, the project has at its center a three-storey, one hundred thousand square foot museum designed by the marquee architect Robert Stern.

The project has created an interesting coalition. Its intellectual content will be shaped in part by a distinguished board of scholars. But more to the point, Pennsylvania has already committed $20 million to it, largely on the hopes contained in an economic development report that concluded that the new museum would draw seven hundred thousand new visitors to the region annually, who would generate $48 million in new spending each year. The Oneida Indian Nation has also been poised to donate money to the project, one assumes as a way of making sure Native Americans receive their due consideration in the museum. High-profile conservatives have also praised the idea, including the ideologue Lynn Cheney, largely because they feel that Americans need to be taught to appreciate the American Revolution more than they currently do.[24]

It is this last group of advocates that may help explain why such a project would be located in Valley Forge in the first place—as opposed to Philadelphia, or Boston, or even on the Mall in Washington. If in the theater of national politics Independence Hall and the Liberty Bell have been placed stage left by groups such as abolitionists and gays who believe that the historic mission of the United States is to expand notions of individual freedom and liberty, then Valley Forge has been increasingly placed stage right by those who stress a slightly different set of ideas as forming the core of the nation.²⁵ Philadelphia and Independence Hall stand for a set of principles associated with Enlightenment rationality. Valley Forge stands for more martial values.

In the heart of a region steeped in the religious traditions of pacifism resides what is advertised as the nation's premier preparatory school whose pedagogical philosophy is based on the military model. Valley Forge Military Academy sits in the middle of Philadelphia's Main Line suburbs, just four miles from the park itself. It is an all-male affair, originally designed for boys in grades 7 through 12, adding more recently a two-year junior college program as well.

The Forge, as its students, staff, and faculty all call it, stresses five "cornerstones": academic excellence, character development, personal motivation, physical development, and leadership. Built upon these cornerstones, the goal of the Forge is, according to its mission statement: "To foster love of God and country, gentlemanly qualities, and high moral standards; characteristics that will make [students] a credit to themselves, their families, their alma mater, their country, and their God." It is a striking contrast to the mission of the region's Quaker schools.

While military men are common in the faculty, most graduates of the Forge do not pursue careers in the military, though the institution is clearly proud of those who do, such as General Norman Schwarzkopf, the affably rotund commander of American forces during the First Gulf War. The Forge also graduated the writer J. D. Salinger, though one hesitates to speculate on the relationship between Salinger's time at the Forge and his life as a bizarre recluse.

The Forge was founded in 1928, in the wake of the First World War. Twenty years later, immediately after the Second World War, a group of influential businessmen founded the Freedoms Foundation, and they located it even closer to Valley Forge. It was "established to honor patriotism and good citizenship," and President Dwight Eisenhower served as chairman of its board from 1949 to 1969.

The Freedoms Foundation is a nonprofit educational operation that works primarily with schoolchildren and their teachers. It is "dedicated to teaching young people the principles upon which our nation was founded," according to some of its promotional material. Just what those principles are, of course, and what constitutes the definition of patriotism and good citizenship is not quite specified. In keeping with so much of the conservative discourse in American political life, the truths of what constitute these things are self-evident, singular, and certainly not debatable.

Like Independence National Historical Park itself, the Freedoms Foundation grew in the context of the Cold War. Not surprisingly, then, it began perhaps its most far-reaching initiative in 1985, when the last of the great Cold Warriors, President Ronald Reagan, was riding highest. Convinced that at the root of many of the nation's problems was the untrammeled exercise of individual liberty, those at the Freedoms Foundation countered the Bill of Rights with their own Bill of Responsibilities. Modeled on the Bill of Rights, complete with a preamble, the Bill of Responsibilities outlines ten precepts. The first few of these might well have come out of a Boy Scouts manual: 1) "To be fully responsible for our own actions and for the consequences of those actions"; 2) "To respect the rights and beliefs of others"; 3) "To give sympathy, understanding and help to others." Several of the others seem to me more toward the libertarian: 5) "To respect and obey the laws"; 6) "To respect the property of others": 9) "To help freedom survive by assuming personal responsibility for its defense." There is something almost innocent about this litany, reading as it does like a civics textbook from a pre–civil rights, pre-Vietnam era. Written, as it was, in 1985, however, there is something almost insidious about it.

Behind the bill is the Freedoms Foundation's belief that "with Rights come Responsibilities," which seems fair enough. But in case you missed the overarching political tenor of these responsibilities, the marble tablet upon which they are inscribed on the foundation's Valley Forge campus reminds you. At the bottom of all this—and in this case, literally at the bottom of the monument—is the phrase "FUNDAMENTAL BELIEF IN GOD" carved in stone. The foundation reports that three million copies of the Bill of Responsibilities have been circulated internationally.

It is within the context of this particular meaning of Valley Forge that the new museum project is taking shape. The values the National Center for the American Revolution hopes to promulgate are encapsulated in a line President Gerald Ford spoke in 1976 at the bicentennial celebration, a line that the center uses to define itself: "Though prosperity is a good thing, a nation survives only so long as the spirit of sacrifice and self-discipline is strong within its people." Putting aside for a moment that the Center may be the only organization in the nation to draw its inspiration from Gerald Ford, the quote downplays prosperity in favor of "sacrifice and self-discipline." These are the values, the Center believes, represented by Valley Forge: "Of all the places associated with the American War for Independence, perhaps none has come to symbolize perserverance and sacrifice more than Valley Forge." (Notice too that here the American Revolution has been replaced by the American War for Independence. This subtle shift also has a political implication dating back at least to the Nixon administration. As Nixon and the nation prepared for the bicentennial, Nixon turned the American Revolution Bicentennial Commission into an instrument of shameless partisan promotion. Part of this involved sponsoring projects that equated

Fig. 12. The Freedoms Foundation wants its Bill of Responsibilities to balance the Bill of Rights. Conservative groups have linked their agendas to the region's history at Valley Forge, while liberal groups do so at Independence Hall.

patriotism solely with militarism. Another part was to strip the American Revolution of its revolutionariness. As the California State Bicentennial Commission resolved formally and officially: "The American Revolution was not a 'revolution.'")[26]

As I write, this project is still in the planning, approval, and fund-raising stage. Assuming, however, that it will eventually be built, it will join the new Independence Visitors Center, Liberty Bell pavilion, the National Constitution Center, and Independence

National Historical Park as a major center of gravity for the region's tourist economy built around its late eighteenth-century past. It will also embody some of the most difficult tensions in American life: liberty, freedom, and the pursuit of happiness at Sixth and Chestnut Streets; perserverance, sacrifice, and self-discipline at Valley Forge.

I don't know whether or not the Freedoms Foundation saw the irony of it or not.

In 2002 the National Parks Conservation Association (NPCA), a nonprofit advocacy group for the national parks, listed Valley Forge National Park as one of "America's 10 Most Endangered National Parks." The threat that prompted this listing came from Toll Brothers, a developer that had announced plans to build over sixty McMansions on eighty acres of privately held land on the northern edge of the park. The sanctity of private property, number 6 in the Bill of Responsibilities—and the sacred right of developers to do whatever they want with their land—came crashing up against the public good and the sanctity of Valley Forge.

Toll Brothers, based in Huntingdon Valley, Montgomery County, ranks as the largest builder of "luxury" housing in the country. It follows the formula set out over fifty years ago by Levitt and Sons in Levittown: purchase large tracts, usually of agricultural land (in this case, the eighty acres in question had been the Schwoebel family's tree nursery), grade away the landscape features to a certain uniformity, assemble housing units all based on two or three variations of the same plan, and finally, market the units aggressively to a largely affluent demographic.

Toll Brothers knew exactly what it had when it acquired the Schwoebel site. It planned to market the subdivision as "Valley Forge Overlook," a name that not only trades on the cachet of the park but accurately describes the site itself. The McMansions would have overlooked much of the park from highlands along the Schuylkill River and in turn might have been one of the most prominent features of the park for visitors. If only George Washington and his troops had had housing from Toll Brothers during the winter of 1777–78, life at Valley Forge would not have been so rough.

The development had been in the works for a few years before it generated any public reaction, but once it did, the reaction was furious. Historians, preservationists, environmentalists, school children all protested the idea. That in turn brought local politicians into the dispute. For its part, Toll Brothers seemed miffed at the outcry. They were doing nothing wrong, after all. Crass, perhaps, but not illegal. As the Toll Brothers CEO Robert Toll put it in a written statement, the tract "is already in a residential area next to existing homes" and is already zoned residential.

The Battle of Valley Forge Overlook ended in the summer of 2004 when the federal government purchased the land from the Toll Brothers and set it aside for inclusion in the park. The exact figure has not been disclosed as I write this, but estimates are that it might be in excess of $7 million. Toll Brothers purchased the property for $3.15 million.[27]

History (and cash) triumphed over Toll Brothers at Valley Forge. At virtually the same time, historic preservation lost at Philadelphia's Naval Home site, where Toll Brothers has been permitted to have its wicked way with an extraordinary historic resource.

The Naval Home was founded in 1799 and built between 1826 and 1829 on the banks of the Schuylkill River by the architect William Strickland, one of the early republic's leading architects. In addition to providing a rest home for the nation's sailors, the site and complex of buildings also served as the Naval Academy's first home until it moved to Annapolis in 1846. It is a remarkable and important collection of buildings, rich with both military and architectural history. The navy closed it finally in 1976, sold it to Toll Brothers in 1988, and the site sat derelict for fifteen years.

Acquiring the Naval Home site is part of a larger strategy for Toll Brothers. Recognizing that big tracts of cheap land in the suburbs have become scarce (and since such developers often face more opposition from anti-sprawl activists), Toll Brothers and some other sprawlers as well have turned their gaze toward urban tracts, hoping to bring high-end suburban sprawl right into the city. The only obstacle to such plans is that the sites often have existing structures, though rarely as significant as the Naval Home. Since historic preservation usually does not fit the cookie-cutter design schemes used by Toll Brothers, and since it could never get a demolition permit to tear down the Naval Home buildings, Toll Brothers opted for the time-honored strategy of "demolition by neglect."

After fifteen years, during which the site sat empty, unprotected, unsecured—Toll Brothers neglected even to mow the weeds, much less maintain the buildings—the strategy seemed to pay off. Early on the morning of February 3, 2003 an arson fire broke out in Biddle Hall, which had been designated a national historic landmark. In an official press release Toll Brothers said the fire "marks the loss of a great landmark." On February 10, 2003, Toll Brothers CEO Robert Toll received a 46 percent raise, making his annual compensation nearly $10 million.

Toll Brothers spoke too soon, however. The fire damaged but did not destroy Biddle Hall and after the smoke cleared it became apparent that the building could be saved. Apparently Strickland's buildings are made of stronger stuff than a Toll Brothers McMansion.

With its feet held, however briefly, to the fire by a Philadelphia judge, Toll Brothers came back with a new design for the site. The historic buildings will stay, but the rest of the twenty acres will be filled with ticky-tacky, fake Georgetown-style townhouses—a "candyland of kitsch" as described by Harris Steinberg, an architect and a member of the Historic Commission. And it will have a big surface parking lot. This plan, as banal and unimaginative as it is, received all the necessary city approvals by the Historic

Commission (Steinberg dissented) and the Zoning Board, which is known for its acquiescence to the wishes of big and well-connected developers.

The actions of Toll Brothers seem to demonstrate that the easy equation the Freedoms Foundation makes between patriotism and the veneration of private property may not really be quite so simple. Developers don't like the restrictions that come with historic preservation; preservationists recognize that once a building, site, or landscape is developed our connection to the past is severed irrevocably. Balancing those two sets of concerns in a region as thick with history as the Delaware Valley is no easy task.

Trivia question: Which of the thirteen colonies saw more fighting during the Revolutionary War than any other? Answer: New Jersey. And in New Jersey redevelopment and sprawl are having more luck than the redcoats and Hessians did defeating the armies of George Washington. Trenton's eighteenth-century remains, for example, have not been treated with much respect. As the historian Sally Lane puts it: "If you did a true eighteenth century walking tour of Trenton, you would have to say 'Under this parking lot' . . . a great deal." Down the road, the Institute for Advanced Study at Princeton recently announced plans to put fifteen houses on part of a battlefield site it owns. Since much of the fighting in New Jersey took place in rural locations, much of that landscape has disappeared without too much notice or outcry. As Lane quips, New Jersey "is where more fighting took place . . . and we have paved over it."[28]

The struggle to preserve and nurture what remains of the eighteenth century constitutes another division between the city and the rest of the region. We expect Philadelphia to preserve its eighteenth-century history—our eighteenth-century history, after all—and every threat to that history brings a big fight. And yet at the same time, as Philadelphia has worked to preserve and promote itself as a repository of the eighteenth century, that same history is largely disappearing from the surrounding area. Farmsteads, country estates, and the agricultural landscapes that constituted the Delaware Valley during the Revolutionary moment are increasingly difficult to find. They disappear without much fuss. So, for example, when the National Trust for Historic Preservation issued its annual list of the nation's most threatened sites for 2005, many were surprised to see a sixty-acre tract in Springettsbury Township. On that site, the American government built Camp Security and between 1781 and 1783 kept fifteen hundred British troops imprisoned there. There has only been one archaeological excavation done on the site, and that one in 1979 was small and quick. And now the tract has been sold to a developer who plans yet more sprawl. Few knew about this episode in the American Revolution, and fewer seemed to care about the fate of the land.

Many metropolitan areas, of course, are struggling to figure out how to preserve their historic buildings and landscapes. That struggle pits two large, growing forces in American life against each other. On the one hand, metropolitan regions, facilitated by corporations like Toll Brothers, continue to sprawl in reckless, unplanned, unsustainable ways. On the other, more and more Americans want to see connections with the past preserved and maintained. The difference in the Delaware Valley is that these local fights often quickly assume a national significance.

According to market research, Philadelphia ranks first in the nation as an urban tourist destination for African American tourists. There are all kinds of reasons why this might be true, but the Greater Philadelphia Tourism and Marketing Council has highlighted Philadelphia's African American history as it sells the city to this demographic.

In particular, the GPTMC points to Mother Bethel church, the first AME church in the nation, and to the eighteenth-century careers of Richard Allen and Absolom Jones, who founded the nation's first black self-help organization, the Free African Society. (Du Bois recounted the history at the beginning of *The Philadelphia Negro*, writing of the Free African Society: "How great a step this was, we of to-day scarcely realize; we must remind ourselves that it was the first wavering step of a people toward organized social life.")[29] There are also important nineteenth-century sites associated with the underground railroad and with the struggle against slavery. More recently, Philadelphia was home to some of the key African American religious and artistic figures, including the Reverends Paul Washington and Leon Sullivan, John Coltrane, Marian Anderson, and Paul Robeson. The houses of those latter three are open to the public.

It does not overstate it to say that until the beginning of the twentieth century, Philadelphia's was the largest, most influential, most accomplished black community of any of the nation's cities. Indeed, in 1830, African Americans made up nearly 10 percent of the city's entire population.[30] Still, despite the centrality of Philadelphia to the development of black America, the connection between the African American experience and the "birthplace of freedom" is complicated to say the least. The national shrines of the nation's birth stand also as reminders that not all people were believed to be created equal in eighteenth-century America and that the promises made in those documents remain in many ways unfulfilled. For many people, the largely celebratory story told at these shrines glared with omission.

That changed in January of 2002.

In the January 2002 issue of the Historical Society of Pennsylvania's scholarly journal *Pennsylvania Magazine of History and Biography*, the local historian Edward Lawler published an article on George Washington's Executive Mansion—the first White

House. The building itself was razed in 1832, leaving only the most inexact sense of its location and plan. Lawler, in a historian-as-sleuth role, demonstrated definitively where it had been and, even more dramatically, where President Washington housed the slaves he brought with him from Virginia.

All of this would have made Lawler something of a hero in the small, dusty world of professional historians. But what thrust Lawler into the bright lights of a larger public was his final conclusion: part of the mansion lay underneath the new Liberty Bell building, then under construction, and visitors to it would walk directly over the slave quarters to enter the building devoted to the Liberty Bell. History proves, once again, to be far more ironic than any fiction.

Lawler's article, appearing as it did while the site itself was in such flux, prompted a group of historians (who somewhat unimaginatively called themselves the Ad Hoc Historians) to lobby the park service to include slavery in some meaningful way as part of the new bell building. As Randall Miller, one of the Ad Hoc Historians, told the New York Times, "This was an opportunity to get people interested in the contested nature of freedom."[31]

But whereas historians and others were genuinely excited about the pedagogical possibilities, the National Park Service was less enthusiastic. It waffled, it avoided, it hoped the issue would go away. Officials met with the historians in May of 2002 and promised to consider changes to the exhibit plans. A year later, INHP Superintendent Mary Bomar had retreated to a position that questioned whether we really knew that the slave quarters extension to the building had been built. By late 2003 the park service seemed to favor some sort of tracing to mark the outline of the Executive Mansion without anything to outline the slave quarters, a position Ed Lawler called "deceptive and intellectually dishonest."[32]

Meanwhile, a group somewhat more imaginatively named the

Fig. 13. Trying to avenge the ancestors. Washington quartered his slaves at the first White House, at a site now at the entrance to the Liberty Bell pavilion. The National Park Service has been reluctant to acknowledge this. Photo courtesy of Joseph Becton.

Avenging the Ancestors Coalition began to pressure the park service to incorporate the slave quarters into a reconfigured site and to use some space nearby for a national memorial to slaves and slavery. They gathered signatures on petitions and held street demonstrations while the Ad Hoc Historians were banging away inside meeting rooms.

We know that Washington brought at least eight and perhaps more slaves to Philadelphia. We also know that Washington worried a great deal about doing so, believing that once in the city they might run away. It turns out that his anxieties were well founded. Among those who lived with the Washingtons was Oney Judge. The city, and her friends among Philadelphia's free black community, filled her with what she later called a "thirst for compleat freedom," and she escaped to Portsmouth, New Hampshire in 1796. The Washingtons were furious and sent agents to pursue and recapture her. They failed. Still fuming about this insolent young woman, who fled, as Washington believed, "without the least provocation," the Washingtons were preparing to return to Mount Vernon when their cook Hercules ran away too. In 1791 Washington had written to Tobias Lear that "the idea of freedom might be too great a temptation to resist." It was and is.

Washington's slaves escaped while living at Sixth and Market Streets in Philadelphia, but their personal act of liberation and defiance, like so much of the region's history, rings with national significance. The nation comes to Philadelphia to visit the monuments associated with freedom and liberty, and it is hard to imagine a more effective and dramatic way to talk about those precious things than to tell the story of Washington and his slaves. Nor can I imagine a better backdrop to talk about the relationship between past and present. If this can happen in an honest way at Independence National Historical Park, then African Americans too will take their proper place on the stage set of our national intentions.

Slavery may well be the ghost that haunts this nation more than any other. Perhaps at Independence Mall in Philadelphia we will be able to confront it.

CHAPTER THREE

The Delaware Valley Makes the Middle Class

I play a game with my students: Raise your hand if you are middle class. All hands invariably go up.

And there it is. We are all middle class in America. I have heard doctors and lawyers, whose annual incomes top half a million dollars, insist that they too are middle class. It is more central to our sense of ourselves than apple pie, baseball, or moms.

The purpose of my game, of course, is precisely to get my students to examine just a bit more closely what we mean by middle class and just what constitutes membership in it. After all, if everyone thinks of themselves as middle class, then don't we risk another version of Garrison Keillor's Lake Wobegone, where all the children are above average?

The definitional problem is tricky. We get our understanding of class categories from Karl Marx, more or less, and Marx himself didn't think much of the middle class. He theorized only two classes: those who owned the means of production, and the proletariat, the rest of us, who labored for the former. Insofar as there were some people occupying a class in between, Marx believed, they wouldn't last long. Eventually a very few of them might become owners; the vast bulk would become prols.

In strictly economic terms, it seems as if this is yet another thing Marx got wrong. History may yet prove the middle class to be ephemeral in the grand economic scheme of things, but they—we—certainly seem to be the bulk of the income earners in the economy today, even if the precise terms of what constitutes a middle-class income keep shifting.

But income is really only one of the things we mean when we use the label "middle class." Perhaps a better way to think of the middle class, then, is as a culture—a set of values, behaviors, sensibilities, and so on that define what we mean when we identify ourselves as middle class. And in this cultural sense—whatever may turn out in the great dialectic of history—the middle class is triumphant. The label appeals to our cultural sense of ourselves, in a nation where to admit to being poor—much less to be poor—is the worst evidence of personal failure and where, at least until recently, being unashamedly, unapologetically, flauntingly rich carried certain stigmas. We are all middle class in America, and we have been for some time. Writing in 1858, the poet and newspaperman Walt Whitman told his readers: "The most valuable class in any community is the middle class. . . ."[1]

More than anything else, the promise of the middle class is the promise of fluidity. What makes the middle class such an attractive identity for Americans is the sense inherent in it that we can aspire to rise even higher. Never mind whether that aspiration can realistically be fulfilled. Never mind that statistically speaking there is a class structure that traps a large number of us and always has. Americans don't live their lives in aggregate statistics or longitudinal studies. They live them in their aspirational dreams, and the middle class has proved the best place from which to dream those dreams.

In this chapter I want to look at the Delaware Valley's contribution to the creation of the middle class, of what we mean culturally when we talk in those terms. Perhaps more than any other place in the United States, Metropolitan Philadelphia invented the American notion of what it means to be middle class. I am not suggesting so much that Philadelphia has been a typical middle-class region as I am arguing that it has been archetypical. Just as the Delaware Valley served as the cradle of the nation in the eighteenth century, it gave birth to that now ubiquitous thing we call the middle class.

Before Philadelphia and its environs became the Workshop of the World—its nickname by the early twentieth century when its industrial economy had reached full maturity—it was known as "the best poor man's country in the world." This phrase appeared to describe Philadelphia as early as 1724 and was used regularly throughout the eighteenth century to denote the vast hinterland around the city, stretching from the Delaware River all the way to the Susquehanna. The whole Philadelphia region constituted "the best poor man's country in the world."[2]

As it happens, William Penn established his holy experiment in the middle of what would prove to be some of the best agricultural land in the Western world, stretching fifty miles in every direction from the city. The area was sparsely populated by Native Americans when Europeans began arriving in significant numbers, and thus there was no Pennsylvania equivalent to New England's King Phillip's War or Virginia's Bacon's Rebellion. The terrain is rolling and gentle and well watered. Its climate is generally even, without extremes of heat or cold; rarely is the region hit with big weather "events." Horticulturally speaking, Greater Philadelphia sits at the edge of two growing zones, making it possible to grow almost anything.

This set Greater Philadelphia quite apart from its two east coast siblings, New York and Boston. In the eighteenth century, New York was a busy, if small, seaport, its life clustered at the very tip of Manhattan; Boston especially in the first half of the

Fig. 14. "The best poor man's country in the world." Farmsteads like this were home to a very prosperous agricultural class. Courtesy of the Library Company of Philadelphia.

eighteenth century presided over a struggling region. New England, as anyone who has tried knows, is a terrible place to farm—the weather is hard and unreliable and the soil produces rocks more abundantly than anything else. Those Yankees who fled New England in the early republic to settle the flat, open spaces of the midwest must have thought they had died and gone to heaven. By contrast, because of Greater Philadelphia's natural advantages, the region experienced no "starving time" at its founding, as was the case in virtually every other European colony in the New World.

By the middle third of the eighteenth century, subsistence farming in the Philadelphia region was evolving into market farming. The Welsh, Scotch-Irish, and German-speaking farmers who came to the area through the port of Philadelphia and then moved into its hinterlands began producing in such abundance that they could export back through the port and around the trans-Atlantic world. Farmers in Greater Philadelphia might find their products shipped to other east coast ports, the West Indies, Great Britain and Ireland, France and the Iberian peninsula. By the 1740s, farmers of the "middling" sort were selling anywhere from one-third to one-half of their production for export.[3]

And all this without much by way of what we might call technological advances. The European immigrants who came into Philadelphia brought with them traditional methods of farming and
continued to use them throughout the eighteenth century. It
didn't matter. The natural resources of the region were so generous and productive that yields continued to go up, as did the
prosperity of the region's farmers. By 1800, the population of the
city had grown to somewhere between sixty and seventy thousand while the population of the region stood at roughly three
hundred thousand, most of them farmers.

By that time, the centrality of Philadelphia's port to the region's agricultural trade had been challenged by the remarkable
growth of Baltimore. Farmers at the western edge of Greater Philadelphia found they could get their products to market more effi-
ciently by shipping them down the Susquehanna rather than
overland to Philadelphia. Either way, however, by the beginning
of the nineteenth century, according to the historical geographer
James T. Lemon, the farmers of the Philadelphia region enjoyed a
greater prosperity and higher standard of living than perhaps any
other comparable number of agriculturalists anywhere in the
Western world.[4] Over the first century of its European life, Greater
Philadelphia did indeed seem to be "the best poor man's country
in the world."

Here, then, is the first example of how city and region were
inextricably bound. Without Philadelphia, its port, its merchants,
and its financial resources, little of that vast agricultural production would have had much value. Certainly those farmers produced
far more wheat and pigs, apples and oats than the local population
could consume. Without a wider national and international export
market, those farmers might have enjoyed a comfortable subsistence life but not the more expansive prosperity they wanted.
Philadelphia was the key to those markets and that prosperity.

In turn, without its abundant agricultural hinterland, one wonders whether the city would have developed as remarkably as it did during the eighteenth century, becoming the most important urban center in the Western Hemisphere. In fact, while Philadelphia's port was commodious, at least by eighteenth-century standards, it was two hundred additional miles from London than New York, the Delaware River itself was tricky to navigate up from the mouth of the bay, and, being a fresh water port, it did freeze regularly during the winter months. In some sense, the port's major advantage was its easy access to all that agricultural export.

Put briefly then, in the eighteenth century, the city made the region, even while the region made the city. And the region made other cities, or towns, as well. Especially during the middle years of the eighteenth century, many followed William Penn's lead and established new towns as intermediate centers of this agricultural trade. This wave of new urbanization within Greater Philadelphia included the founding of places such as Chester, West Chester, Reading, and Easton. Faced with competition from Baltimore, Philadelphians built the first paved turnpike in America to connect Philadelphia with Lancaster, another of these eighteenth-century satellite cities founded as part of the commercial network of Greater Philadelphia. By 1800, there were three hundred such places scattered across the region.[5]

Historians generally see the creation of "classes" as a product of the nineteenth-century industrial transformation. To use the term "class" to describe groups in the eighteenth century is to use the term anachronistically. What eighteenth-century observers did recognize were people in the "middling ranks," "people of the middle condition," and "middling sorts." In an urban context, these descriptions referred to artisans and craftsman who, while certainly not merchants or professionals, had become successful enough to achieve some measure of status and independence.

Perhaps then the final significance of the best poor man's

country was that it was a place where even farmers in the eighteenth century, not too far removed from European peasantry, could aspire to the middle ranks.

The region's farms, small scale, tidy, well ordered, continued to prosper throughout the nineteenth century. However, by the second quarter of that century, Greater Philadelphia ceded its role as the bread basket of the nation and the trans-Atlantic world to the even richer, even flatter prairie lands of the Midwest and Great Plains, and Chicago became the hub of that activity. If Chicago, as the historian Bill Cronon has demonstrated, stands as the preeminent example of a metropolis shaped by—and in turn shaping—a vast hinterland of natural abundance, then Philadelphia was probably the first great city in America to exist because of such relationships.[6]

By the time Chicago surpassed Philadelphia in this respect, however, Greater Philadelphia's economy had shifted from farm to factory, and its new middle class would be a creation of that economy.

Most historians agree that the middle class, as a creation of the urban, industrial economy, did not really begin to emerge as an identifiable group until the middle years of the nineteenth century and was not fully formed until the period after the Civil War. Certainly it was visible enough by 1858 for Whitman to sing its praises.

One consequence of the new industrialism was to move the locus of the region's economy from country to city. The port remained central to economic life, but now because it was moving industrial production in and out of the area rather than crops. Philadelphia's hinterland still grew a great abundance of crops, but its anthracite coal was even more valuable. Nationally, by 1890, according to the federal census, the value of manufactured goods exceeded the value of agricultural goods for the first time.

That switch probably took place in the Philadelphia area much sooner. In this sense, then, as we consider the formation of the middle class our attention moves from the country to the city.

The historian Stuart Blumin has come up with what I think is the best historical analysis of what he calls the middle-class "way of life" as it emerged in the nineteenth century. Without ignoring the economic basis of the term "class," Blumin instead develops a definition of the middle class based around a set of new workplaces, living spaces, social associations—in short, a cultural, rather than strictly economic definition of what it meant to be middle class.[7]

Blumin's experiential definition of the nineteenth-century middle class stresses how those in the middle class became segregated—at work, at home, at church, and elsewhere—from the working class. Insofar as they had contact with those different from themselves it was with their employers, whose manners they emulated and whose social position they aspired to achieve, rather than with those below them on the economic and social ladder.

Work, as Blumin sees it, constitutes the most significant of the experiences that defined the new middle class. More specifically, the growth of the industrial economy in Philadelphia generated a new world of nonmanual labor. The middle class consisted of those who went to work wearing a white collar, rather than a blue one, who worked with their heads rather than with their hands.

That differentiation, in turn, led to a differentiation in the kinds of spaces where Philadelphia's workers worked. As the production of goods and the selling of those goods increasingly took place in separate spaces, retail spaces, where many of these new nonmanual laborers worked, grew to be considerably more attractive places—brighter, cleaner, often grander, certainly more genteel than the factory shops where goods were made, which continued to be dirty, dusty, and otherwise unpleasant.

Different working environments accompanied different living

environments as well. As the nineteenth century wore on, the "walking city" of the eighteenth century, a city where all of the city's peoples and functions coexisted heterogeneously on top of one another, stretched into a much larger, less dense city where functions and people became increasingly segregated. Put another way, after the Civil War, Philadelphia's middle class moved into its own new neighborhoods.

Many members of the middle class followed new train and streetcar lines, which radiated out from Center City to "streetcar suburbs" in West Philadelphia and Spring Garden and to close-in railroad suburbs such as Mount Airy.[8] There, they lived among people like themselves, in leafy enclaves quite unlike the more crowded, older parts of the city. With work and residence now taking place in different places, home became a purely domestic place with a proliferation of bedrooms, parlors, and libraries. We call those houses, sometimes twins, sometimes freestanding, "Victorian," a label that denotes both certain architectural styles and the sense of bourgeois domesticity that those houses were intended to foster.

In their new "streetcar suburbs," members of this new middle class spent their nonworking hours in a host of new civic, social, and cultural enterprises largely of their own making. Members of what we might call the "moral" middle class centered their lives around churches. In 1855, seventy-four out of eighty-four male members of the Philadelphia's First Presbyterian Church, for example, were nonmanual workers.[9] Those churches often led their congregants to involvement in the temperance movement, and for a few to the abolitionist cause. Beyond church groups, Philadelphia's middle class formed book clubs, musical and choral groups, participated in the new sports of baseball and rowing, and gathered in any number of fraternal and voluntary organizations. Along with their work and their homes, these social networks defined what it meant to be middle class.

As a result, by the end of the nineteenth century Philadelphians had created a city more thoroughly "middle class" than perhaps any other major city in America. If our image of New York in those years is of a place teeming with immigrants crowded into tenements of the sort Jacob Riis chronicled in his book *How the Other Half Lives*, and if, likewise, our image of Chicago comes to us from Upton Sinclair's *The Jungle*, that scarifying story of stockyards and the immigrants who worked there, then our image of Philadelphia remains one of tidy streets and single family houses, fostering a certain staid bourgeois domesticity. Not so much a city of neighborhoods—another of Philadelphia's nicknames—but a city of middle-class neighborhoods.

The growth of those neighborhoods paralleled the growth of the city itself. In a foreshadowing of demographic trends to come in the late twentieth century, by the 1840s the center of the region's population was no longer inside the city's boundaries, still technically the two square miles laid out by William Penn, but north of it. By 1850 or so, over 200,000 people lived in the areas north of Vine Street, while 188,000 lived in the city proper. More than this even, the rates of population growth in sections such as Spring Garden and Kensington out-paced the more modest growth of the city's population.

This represented a problem for many city leaders, and the solution to that problem seemed obvious: consolidation. And so it came to pass that early in 1854 the state legislature approved a massive redrawing of the city's boundaries. The city of Philadelphia grew from a tiny 2 square miles to nearly 130, swallowing up many of its first- and second-generation suburbs: Northern Liberties, Southwark, Spring Garden, Germantown, Kensington, Frankford, and West Philadelphia.

Apart from the burgeoning concentrations of people, much of the land within the newly consolidated Philadelphia was still rural, pockets of which would remain until after the Second World

War. Indeed, as of 1854, fifteen hundred farmers made their living and ten thousand head of cattle grazed on farms now inside the second largest city in America.[10]

In its 1854 consolidation Philadelphia proved once again to be archetypical. It was the first of the big, older American cities to redraw its own map to accommodate the dramatic changes brought about by industrialization. Over the rest of the nineteenth century many other cities followed suit, most spectacularly in 1898 when Manhattan gobbled up four other boroughs to create New York City.

With a prescience he could not have known, Anthony Trollope quipped that if all American cities followed Philadelphia's example, "there would soon be no rural population left at all."[11] In the era of consolidation, metropolitan expansion allowed a middle class uneasy about being in the city—at least that crowded, heterogeneous, "promiscuous" city—to remain of the city.

The transformation of space and experience brought about by the rise of Philadelphia's middle class within the city had an analogue in the suburbs as well. And if streetcars and trolleys facilitated the growth of "streetcar suburbs" such as West Philadelphia, then railroad service allowed commuter towns to grow up along many of the same middle-class lines. Places such as Lansdowne, Yeadon, Ardmore, Cynwyd, Drexel Hill, and a dozen other towns emerged, and each in its own way recapitulated the middle-class way of life that had developed first inside the city.

In an era when public transportation systems are underfunded and underutilized—and when Metropolitan Philadelphia's own SEPTA is the butt of so many jokes—it may be hard to remember just how much of the region as we know it today was shaped by the railroads. Their lines alternately traversed the region, making possible the physical expansion of the area, and stitched it together in a semicoherent, dependable network of stations, schedules, and terminals. The little town of Cynwyd makes a perfect case study in the role of the railroad in the growth of middle-class Philadelphia.

Cynwyd, though located near Center City, had only a few hundred residents at the end of the nineteenth century largely because the closest train station, Merion, was over a mile away. When the Pennsylvania Railroad's Schuylkill Division built a line from Center City out to Norristown and Reading with a stop at Cynwyd, the sleepy place found itself connected to the vast regional network. Real estate speculators flocked to the area, carving up farm fields and estates into building lots. In the space of just over a decade the population of Cynwyd nearly tripled and by 1916 the Pennsylvania Railroad could claim that Cynwyd had become "one of the most rapidly growing and most popular suburbs of Philadelphia."[12] Those flocking to Cynwyd were middle-class people—not the wealthy or those who worked on the shop floor—underscoring the fundamental equation: the middle class was a product of the railroad age.

More than anything else, I suspect, homeownership lies at the center of what people mean when they talk about the American middle class. Homeownership remains the barometer by which we measure the aspiration of middle-class Americans to social status and financial security. All the attributes we associate with bourgeois domesticity are products of—and sheltered in—the single family home, and home buying remains most people's single largest financial investment. There may be more that constitutes the "American dream" than owning a home, but there is surely nothing larger.

Here too, Philadelphia invented the middle class as we understand it today. It was in Philadelphia that craftsmen, artisans, and others of the "middling sort" could rise to social respectability by living in, and in many cases owning, their own homes. It was no mere booster's invention to call Philadelphia the "City of Homes."

Fig. 15. The row house became the distinctive Philadelphia housing style, and it became the place where the American dream of single-family homeownership was born. These are of 1920s vintage. Courtesy of the Library Company of Philadelphia.

The equation between housing and the middle class was formulated in the first half of the nineteenth century. As the historian Donna Rilling has amply demonstrated, house building itself was a major part of Philadelphia's economy during those years. By her calculations, roughly 25 percent of Philadelphia's male workers were a part of or depended upon the building economy. And between 1790 and 1850 those builders added fifty-two thousand new residences to the existing stock of city houses.[13]

Part of that growth can be attributed to the growth of the city's population, which rose from less than fifty-thousand to nearly four hundred thousand souls during that sixty-year stretch. But New York and Boston grew dramatically too during those same years and neither of those places housed their residents in the single-family row houses that came to typify the streetscape of Philadelphia.

To understand why the single-family home came to predominate in Philadelphia, in turn defining the city as a "city of homes," we need to understand a bit about the city's particular craft tradi-

tions and building culture. Put a different way, we need to understand the extraordinary impact of something called a "ground
rent."

As Rilling explains it, many of Philadelphia's largest landown-
ers, some of whom traced their holdings well back into the eighteenth century, would commonly divide their land and sell the
subdivided lots to a purchaser in exchange for an annual rent that
was, typically, to be paid as long as the purchaser held title to
the lot. The purchaser, with title in hand and paying this annual
rent on the ground itself, was free to do with that land whatever
he chose.

More often than not, the purchaser was a building mechanic,
carpenter, or other craftsman, and more often than not he chose
to build a two- or three-storey house on the lot. The builder, in
turn, sold or rented the building and enjoyed the profits to be
made in so doing.[14]

The ground rent system had several related consequences
through the first half of the nineteenth century. It enabled builders and craftsmen to get into the real estate development business because it reduced their capital requirements. They only had
to pay for the price of "improving" the lot, rather than that sum
plus the price of the land itself. This meant that numbers of these
independent builders could themselves raise their economic
status through real estate development, even if they did not actually own land, or have quite enough capital to do so. Development
on this small, more entrepreneurial scale led, in turn, to the small
scale of the row-house unit, rather than the larger sorts of tene-
ment and apartment blocks that emerged in other cities—more
than 80 percent of the new construction during the 1840s was of
the three-storey variety.[15] This meant that the prices for that
housing were lower than comparable units in other cities (real
estate in the Philadelphia area is still cheaper than comparable
real estate in the Northeast Corridor). The ground rent system

both served to house the middle class in single family homes and permitted manual laborers such as carpenters and builders to themselves become middle class.

The ground rent system was a fundamentally conservative way to develop the city, a European holdover, a nearly medieval system of land tenure adapted by Philadelphians to the exigencies of nineteenth-century city building. And it was unique, or nearly so, to Philadelphia. No other large American city grew this way, and as a consequence, no other American city developed both the physical stock and culture of the single family home. In his 1857 study of Philadelphia's manufactures, Edwin Freedley noted that the ground rent system "gives to the man of small means facilities he cannot ordinarily obtain in other cities. . . . By this means, it is quite common for mechanics, small tradesmen, and even laborers, to become owners of homesteads." Likewise, in 1881, Addison Burk concluded "Philadelphia was a city of homes, made primarily so by the ground-rent system."[16]

As was the case with farmers in the eighteenth century, Greater Philadelphia didn't simply invent the middle class. Philadelphia, as the "city of homes," was the place where people with working-class jobs and incomes could successfully aspire to a middle-class world.

The ground rent system came to an abrupt end in 1854, the same year that Philadelphia's boundaries were redrawn to incorporate its first ring of suburban and other settlements. The state legislature put an end to any form of "perpetual" contracts, ground rent contracts among them. In the second half of the nineteenth century, other financial mechanisms of home building in Philadelphia would replace the ground rent system. But if in the antebellum period the single family home was a by-product of the way the building economy was structured, then after the Civil War single family homes were the goal of building in the first place. By 1867, a scant two years after the war was over, Philadelphia grew by an average of forty-five hundred new row houses each year.[17]

Between the Civil War and the First World War Philadelphia would add roughly one million people to its population. Many of those lived their lives in the second generation of row houses. These surrounded factory buildings in industrial neighborhoods in North Philadelphia and near the Northeast, and they lined the streets of the Italian and Jewish enclaves of South Philadelphia. Again, in its explosive growth in the late nineteenth century Philadelphia did not stand alone. New York, Chicago, St. Louis, Detroit—all the great American cities grew spectacularly during the industrial age. But whereas new New Yorkers found themselves living in multi-storey tenements, new Bostonians in "triple deckers," and new Chicagoans in any manner of ramshackle accommodation, new Philadelphians lived, by and large, in row houses.

We should not romanticize. Life in late nineteenth-century Philadelphia could be nasty and brutish, especially for those at the bottom end of the economic totem pole, or on the wrong side of the color line. Still, according to one estimate, in 1880 an average of 8.25 people occupied a single dwelling in Boston, a whopping 16.36 people in New York, and only 5.7 people in Philadelphia. A single family in a single home. The home ownership rate stood at about 25 percent, and a family earning twenty-five dollars per week (more than most laborers earned themselves but not outside the reach of working-class families with more than one income earner) was considered a potential homeowner.[18]

If Philadelphia presented an exterior facade of single-family row houses to the world—thousands upon thousands of them, block after block, neighborhood after neighborhood—Philadelphia also helped shape the middle-class domestic life that took place behind those facades and inside tens of thousands of middle-class homes around the country.

After coming home from work, early in the twentieth century, dad might sit down to read the *Saturday Evening Post*. The *Post* was part of the Curtis publishing empire, which by the early twentieth century operated from an imposing headquarters just opposite Independence Hall on Sixth Street. Taken over by the editor Edward Bok in 1889, the *Post* featured lots of colorful illustrations and advertising to go along with its thoroughly middle-brow features aimed largely at a male audience. By the First World War, roughly five hundred thousand men read the *Post*.

In fact, Philadelphia publishing companies had been shaping the tastes and worldview of the emerging middle class since 1830, when *Godey's Ladies Book* first appeared. Each issue included a piece of music, needlework patterns, and general reading material "always moral and instructive." By the 1840s it boasted the largest monthly circulation of any magazine in the nation. *Godey's* successor by the late nineteenth century was surely another of Curtis's publications: *Ladies Home Journal*, which began its run in 1883 with Mrs. Curtis at the editorial helm. The *Journal* offered recipes, advice on home decoration, and lessons on manners and morals, and it was immensely popular.

Not content to cater to those who already lived in their own home, the *Journal* began marketing its own house plans for the sum of one dollar in the 1920s. By then, the Curtis Publishing Company was printing 16 million magazines every month. Such was the connection between the Curtis Publishing Company and the growth of middle-class domesticity that the architect Stanford White, of the renowned firm McKim, Meade and White, said, "I firmly believe that Edward Bok has more completely influenced domestic architecture for the better than any man in his generation."[19]

Middle-class life in the first quarter of the twentieth century bore Philadelphia's stamp in other ways too. While dad might be enjoying the *Post*, mom might well be preparing a dinner that included a canned product from Campbell's, manufactured at the company's huge plant in Camden. After dinner, the family might sit down perhaps to listen to RCA recordings on the Victrola, both made in Camden as well. When commercially broadcast radio arrived in the United States in the 1920s, that same family might have gathered 'round the Philco to listen. The Philco was a product of the Atwater Kent company, by the 1920s the largest producer of radios in the nation. And on a special Sunday in 1929, that family could hear Leopold Stokowski lead the Philadelphia Orchestra in the first radio broadcast concert by an American symphony, which was carried on fifty stations coast to coast.

For these reasons, and for a dozen others, the actor and playwright John Cecil Holm, himself the son of a successful electrician, looked back on early twentieth-century Philadelphia as "one great big stretch of middle class."²⁰ And in these ways, Philadelphia was central to making the rest of the nation one great big stretch of middle class as well.

In the mid-1960s the sociologist Herbert Gans moved into a small house on the Jersey side of the Philadelphia suburbs and produced the classic study *Levittowners*.²¹ That Gans chose the Philadelphia suburbs for his study probably had more to do with the fact that he was then teaching at the University of Pennsylvania than anything else. But *Levittowners* underscores, if inadvertently, that metropolitan Philadelphia was at the vanguard of the great postwar demographic and cultural shift of the middle class from the city to the suburbs. Once again, not so much typical as archetypical.

The story of the middle-class migration to the crabgrass frontier of the new suburbs usually begins with the first Levittown on Long Island, which opened shortly after the war came to an end. What the Levitt brothers understood was that the demand for housing, pent up to bursting after nearly fifteen years of depression and war, would provide a tremendous opportunity for any builder ready to capitalize on it.

Their breathtaking engineering innovation was to figure out a way to mass produce single-family detached housing, achieving both unprecedented speed in construction and economies of scale. In essence the Levitt brothers turned home building, once the realm of craftsmen and contractors, into another factory product like a GM car or a McDonald's hamburger. Only in this case, the assembly line moved from unit to unit, rather than the other way round.

The Levitts and their Levittowns created the blueprint for postwar suburban development that developers still follow, with slight variations, today. Find a large parcel of green space in a metropolitan area—agricultural land is preferable because it has already been cleared. Wipe the natural features of the landscape clean; lay out a set of curvilinear roads (gridded streets smack too much of the city); and then erect some number of virtually identical housing units, lot size and square footage dependent on how much the developer hopes to charge. In this sense, everywhere in postwar America is Levittown.

The postwar suburbs represent perhaps—I mean not to exaggerate—the most profound social revolution since human beings first began to congregate in cities six thousand to eight thousand years ago. In the new American suburb for the first time large numbers of people live not in a densely concentrated urban environment, enmeshed in complex economic, ethnic, religious, and other kinds of networks. Nor do they live in smaller settlements—towns or villages—more directly tied to food production and connected to the rhythms of rural life. The social configuration of the postwar suburb is something altogether different and new—neither city nor country, disconnected from communities larger than the nuclear family, and dependent on a level of resource consumption—land, water, fossil fuels, time—that would have humbled the Romanovs.

The Levitts initiated this revolution outside New York, but it is surely no coincidence that they built their other two large projects in suburban Philadelphia, the first, north of the city in Bucks County, and the other in New Jersey where Herbert Gans moved. (It's no coincidence, either, that Toll Brothers that we met in the last chapter, the Levitts' most successful descendants, are head-quartered in the Philadelphia suburbs.)

The demand for housing in the postwar period was real. The census of 1950 records the peak of Philadelphia's population: 2,071,605 souls. But those two million people lived in crowded quarters, the result of the fact that virtually no new housing had been built since 1929. Sixty-five thousand Philadelphia families lived "doubled up"—two families sharing a space intended for one—and vacancy rates for rentals and properties for sale barely registered at 0.5–1 percent.

Like most large metropolitan areas, Philadelphia went on a building spree. Between 1946 and 1953 roughly 140,000 new homes sprouted around the region. Some were built in under-developed land within the city, in deepest South Philadelphia and in the section of the city called the Northeast, for example. But much of it got built in surrounding counties thus transforming country into suburb.

When the U.S. Steel Corporation announced plans to open its huge new Fairless Works in lower Bucks county, William Levitt decided to bring his house-building operation to the Delaware Valley. On December 8, 1951 houses in Levittown, Pennsylvania went on sale. By 1953 fifty-five thousand Levittowners lived in roughly sixteen thousand Levitt houses.

Levitt imagined that his houses would be occupied by steel workers from the Fairless plant. That physical proximity between plant and suburb underscores the phenomenon I discussed previously. Philadelphia was the place where the working class—the blue collar, lunch pail guy—could achieve a middle-class status through the mechanism of the single family home. At the turn of the twentieth century that meant a row house; by the 1950s that meant a modest house in Levittown or some similar place.

Levittown set a pattern for suburban development in another way too. On December 8, 1951 a white prospective buyer told the sales clerk that he had a friend who was also interested in buying. The friend, as it happened, was black. The sales clerk simply responded that Levittown was to be "a white community." So it was, and so too were the vast, vast bulk of new suburban houses.

By 1957 not a single one of Levittown's fifty-five thousand residents was black. On August 13 of that year, Bill and Daisy Myers tried to break the color line in Levittown. By midnight, a crowd of over two hundred stone-throwing Levittowners had driven the Myerses back to their old house. The Myerses continued to be subjected to a variety of racial harassments through the fall, until arrests and indictments finally cooled things down.

Those Levittowners willing to discuss what happened to the Myerses voiced their opinion with an almost refreshing honesty. A Mrs. Robert Gross, who commuted from suburban Levittown to a waitressing job in suburban New Jersey, told a reporter that she didn't want "Negroes living in my neighborhood, and I don't want my children going to school with Negroes." Steel worker George Bessam averred that he was no racist: "I don't have any objections to colored people, but I don't think they ought to live in white neighborhoods." He reminded the reporter that "a lot of people moved into Levittown from Philadelphia and other places for just one reason, to get away from colored people."[22]

Variations of what happened to the Myerses happened to untold numbers of black Americans who moved into white neighborhoods after the Second World War. It happened in Chicago, Detroit, St. Louis, and Cleveland. In the postwar North, the struggle over race took place on the terrain of real estate. As William Levitt himself famously said, "We can solve a housing problem, or we can try to solve a racial problem. But we cannot combine the two." In early 1953 a delegation of activists, led by the Nobel Prize winner Pearl Buck, met with William Levitt to discuss housing discrimination. He fell back on the impersonal, and thus ungovernable, forces of the market to defend the racial exclusivity in Levittown, and by extension in all of suburbia: "People are terribly prejudiced in Pennsylvania, just like anywhere else. They are not ready for Negro neighbors," he told Buck and the others, but continued generously: "When the whites get ready for Negro neighbors, I'll be among the first to open up my sales policy."

William Levitt might claim that housing and race were two entirely separate issues in postwar America, but George Bessam and his friends recognized the inextricable connection between the two. Black migrants from the American south continued to move to Philadelphia during the 1930s and 1940s. Indeed, in that latter decade the city's black population grew dramatically, while the white population increased barely at all. When Philadelphians caught their breath after the twin traumas of the Great Depression and World War II, they found their city much blacker than it had ever been. Many Philadelphians felt the need for new housing acutely; they felt the desire for racially exclusive housing just as strongly.

It is hard to know what to conclude from the Myerses' experience as Levittown's black pioneers. They themselves left in 1961, though Daisy Myers insisted that homesickness for their original town, not racist pressure, prompted the move. They were followed to Levittown in 1958 by the Mosbys, whose arrival did not generate the same public anger and resistance. Perhaps the Myerses bore the brunt of white racist rage which burned out as quickly as it flared. At the same time, Levittown has remained stubbornly white in the fifty years since it opened. By the turn of the millennium, less than 5 percent of Levittowners were black.

The Myerses did not stumble accidentally or innocently into Levittown. Like many civil rights actions in the 1950s, this one was well planned. Bill and Daisy had been part of the Human Relations Council, an organization with links to the NAACP and the Urban League. And, this being the Delaware Valley, with links to the American Friends Service Committee.

Quakers were central to the civil rights movement generally—we have already met Bayard Rustin, a Quaker from West Chester—and they were no less active locally. The AFSC sponsored an important study of housing discrimination patterns in two Levittowns in 1957, at the same moment that the Myers moved in. And Quakers were deeply involved in perhaps the most ambitious experiments at integrated suburban housing to take place in the 1950s.

If the story of Levittown is generally familiar, the story of Concord Park is not, which is ironic since the two places sit about five miles apart. Concord Park was the brainchild of the trade unionist and real estate developer Morris Milgram and the Bucks County Quaker businessman George Otto. Otto had served as chair of the Friends Social Order Committee and as treasurer of the Friends General Conference; Milgram, who stumbled into the real estate business by inheriting it from his father, had been on the boards of the Philadelphia branch of Americans for Democratic Action and the NAACP.

By 1952, upset by the discrimination already evident in the new housing business, Milgram had vowed to himself that he would build no more houses unless they could be sold regardless of race. He committed himself to building a new development that would be intentionally integrated to demonstrate that integration was indeed possible and to tap into the unmet demand of black buyers for suburban housing.

That decision of conscience had very practical consequences. Milgram was repeatedly turned down by lenders when he tried to secure financing for Concord Park. By 1954, after two years spent searching for money, units at Concord Park finally went on sale.

Concord Park's developers realized that simply opening up their houses to an interracial market would not ensure the integration they wanted, so they settled on a carefully crafted formula: 55 percent of the houses would be marketed to whites; 45 percent to blacks. After all the houses were sold, which happened in 1957, then Concord Park residents could sell to whomever they chose. Ironically, maintaining this racial balance meant turning away numbers of black buyers who could afford the move to the suburbs but had precious few choices in an otherwise racially restrictive housing market.

Concord Park was an experiment in social engineering, and by all accounts it seems to have been a grand success, a rebuke to those who insisted (as some still do) that residential integration inevitably leads to social conflict and declining property values. Because it was such an unusual project, it was quickly studied. A team from the University of Pennsylvania came out in 1957 to interview residents and discovered that 75 percent of white residents felt an "unqualified approval" of their black neighbors, while another 11 percent expressed a "general approval."

Residents understood that they were living a grand experiment, and many clearly thrilled in the experience. In a 2000 interview, Joyce Hadley, one of the original black residents of Concord Park, looked back at the place with genuine fondness and recalled a particular friendship with a German immigrant neighbor. "That was the point of Concord Park," she told the reporter. "You absorbed each person individually." Similarly, Warren Swartzbeck, the last of the original white residents to move (he and his wife left in 2000), recalled moving into Concord Park as "our little effort to heal the nation."[23] A split-level peaceable kingdom, with a garage and a driveway.

Utopia didn't last. By 2000 the makeup of Concord Park had

become almost entirely black, mirroring precisely the all-white demographics down the road in Levittown. Concord Park used the same kind of restrictive deeds to maintain its racial quota that other developments used to keep blacks out. Both were ultimately outlawed and in the end Concord Park couldn't preserve its racial balance under the demand of black buyers.

The "white flight" to the suburbs in the postwar era was part of the larger process of deindustrialization that left Philadelphia and other big cities poorer and blacker. U.S. Steel, after all, chose to build its new plant not in the city, but outside it. Today, it too is closed. The tectonic shift in the economy we call deindustrialization, with its attendant suburbanization, might well have been inevitable. The example of Concord Park, however, stands as a reminder that it need not have happened the way it did. Who can know what the nation would be now if suburbia looked more like Concord Park?

Down the shore.

It is, let us be frank, an ungrammatical, ugly phrase. And yet, for millions of Philadelphians those three words have defined the very essence of summer.

The shore in question, of course, is a shorthand for the beaches of South Jersey, which Philadelphians have claimed as their own from roughly Long Beach Island in the north all the way to the tip of Cape May Point. And Philadelphians have been going down the shore to escape the summer heat of the city since the early nineteenth century.

Until those vacationers started arriving, humans had made light use of the Jersey Shore. From what we can deduce archaeologically, Native Americans—bands of Lenapi—like later Europeans, made seasonal trips there, primarily for fish and oysters. Nor did the Jersey Shore develop a maritime economy and culture of the sort the grew up in eighteenth- and nineteenth-century New

England. There are no great fishing towns along the Jersey Shore, not like Gloucester, Massachusetts, nor any mighty whaling ports like Nantucket or New Bedford. Few people ever sang sea shanties or carved scrimshaw in New Jersey.[24]

Perhaps one reason that Native Americans did not establish a network of more permanent settlements lies in the extraordinary ecosystem that covers much of South Jersey: the Pine Barrens. A vast area, roughly a thousand square miles stretching originally from Cape May Point to Asbury Park, the Barrens consist of flat, sandy soil cut through with small, lazy rivers, interspersed with bogs and swamps and otherwise covered in pine forest.

The early European settlers called the place a Barrens because the soil is poor. The trees themselves could tell you that. Much of the Barrens is covered in scrub forest, with trees that in other places might reach forty feet scarcely topping out at ten. It is not what we might call a resource-rich environment, at least not for seminomads and early agriculturalists and not compared to the environments farther north and west, which may explain why Native Americans went down the shore for only short periods of time.

But in other ways the Pine Barrens are marvelous. Ecologically speaking, there is simply no other place quite like them anywhere in the mid-Atlantic region. Their closest cousins might be some of the pine forests in the coastal Carolinas, though that observation only begs the question of what a Carolina pine forest is doing several hundred miles too far north. That the Barrens still exist at all is a testament to their strange inhospitableness. They occupy a space roughly the size of Yosemite National Park in what is otherwise the most densely populated state in the nation. As the writer John McPhee pointed out when he came to visit the Pine Barrens in the mid-1960s, if you draw an as-the-crow-flies line on a map from Boston to Richmond—the area of heaviest urbanization in the United States—the Pine Barrens sit exactly in the middle.[25]

In a state that made suburban sprawl its ethos, in which life is organized, at least according to the jokes, around strip malls and exit ramps, there they sit, mysterious, other-worldly, even a bit spooky. The human environment that has now grown around the Pine Barrens looks exactly the same—the same as itself and the same as everywhere else in America—but there really is no place like the Pine Barrens, whose rivers are the color of coffee, stained by the tannic acid of cedar trees.

To get to the beaches, therefore, means traversing the Barrens. And while Philadelphians and others had begun to do so in the antebellum period, the history of going down the shore really began with the building of railroad lines. The first to run from Camden (thus really from Philadelphia) to the shore opened in 1854. The following year a bridge was built to connect Absecon to the adjacent barrier island and Atlantic City was born. By the late nineteenth century most of the shore could be reached by train; by 1880 three different companies made the run from Philadelphia to Atlantic City, while by 1894 Cape May had service from two. Before the railroad, the trip down the shore took two days from Philadelphia; after, it took only a few hours. As Walt Whitman observed while taking a trip from Camden to Atlantic City in 1878, "The whole route . . . has literally been made and opened up by the railroad."[26]

Most of the summer resort towns along the Jersey Shore were founded during the railroad age, from Atlantic City to Cape May, with Ocean City (1879), Sea Isle City (1880), Avalon (1887), and Wildwood (1890) in between. Most of these resort towns grew as places of hotels, some grand, some more modest. Initially, going down the shore meant taking rooms in a hotel. But the great number of trains running to the shore made even day-tripping possible. In 1884, the *Woodbury Constitution* could write: "There never has been a time when the resorts on the New Jersey coast were so easy of access. . . . From Philadelphia 9 express trains leave every week, 2 additional on Saturday and 4 on Sunday. . . . Such facilities place a trip to the seaside within the reach of every class of persons."[27]

That last line might have been an enthusiastic exaggeration. It isn't clear whether Philadelphia's poor, its recently arrived immigrants, and others took trips to the shore in 1884. But what the *Constitution* did understand was that the Jersey Shore was a middle-class resort area. Quite unlike the New England coast, with its exclusive playgrounds like Newport and aristocratic enclaves like Kennebunkport, and unlike what would develop a bit later for New York's wealthy at the Hamptons, the Jersey Shore was surely part of that "one great big stretch of middle class" that defined Greater Philadelphia.

In the late nineteenth century when they went, that middle class brought with them many of the bourgeois anxieties that plagued them back in the city. People came to the ocean during the summer to cool down. That obvious fact in turn generated a problem of Victorian decorum. How to bathe in the ocean and remain, more or less, entirely covered up? An 1878 ordinance in Atlantic City made it illegal for anyone "to bathe in the surf . . . except such person be so clothed as to prevent the indecent exposure of the body." For most people, the law was probably a redundancy. In the late nineteenth century, most middle-class bathers I suspect would have dressed "appropriately" regardless—in loose-fitting wool trousers and flannel coats that covered from neck to ankle. Bathing suits, of course, changed along with changing middle-class notions of public decency, and the outfits worn by Philadelphians down the shore are as a good a barometer of any of how those standards changed. Still, as late as 1935 twenty-five men could still be fined in Atlantic

City for "semi-nude" swimming when their suits did not include tops.[28]

If H. L. Mencken once defined a puritan as a person with the morbid fear that someone, somewhere, might be having fun, then Philadelphia Methodists helped make sure that vacationers didn't have too much, at least in their parts of the Jersey Shore. Ocean City began its life as a Methodist temperance camp, founded by three Methodist ministers. It grew quickly in the 1880s, complete with small cottages and a large auditorium for people to gather for camp meetings. Cape May Point separated from Cape May proper when the department store magnate John Wanamaker founded another Methodist retreat there. At these places, the Sabbath was kept so strictly that swimming in the ocean was forbidden on Sundays. So too were card playing, drinking, dancing, and other suspect entertainments.

Yet even the guardians of virtue and morality at the shore recognized the tensions that strained their summer resorts. Philadelphians, even good Methodists, came to the shore precisely to escape from the city, to behave in ways that would be unacceptable back home. The Methodists farther up the shore at Ocean Grove passed an ordinance reminding vacationers, "All respectable people . . . [should] discountenance the practice of the sexes in assuming attitudes on the sand that would be immoral at their city homes or elsewhere."[29] Yet that such an ordinance was necessary at all attests to the seductive powers of the shore.

The religious camp resorts stood in contrast to—indeed, defined themselves against—the decidedly secular attractions of places like Cape May and most especially Atlantic City. The latter more than any other developed into a mini-urban center by the sea, complete with all the urban vices and vulgarities that so troubled Victorian moralists and reformers. They stood horrified by the proliferation of bars and saloons, and even more by the prostitution and the general sexual promiscuity.

Fig. 16. For the earliest vacationers who went down the shore, Cape May looked like this. Courtesy of the Library Company of Philadelphia.

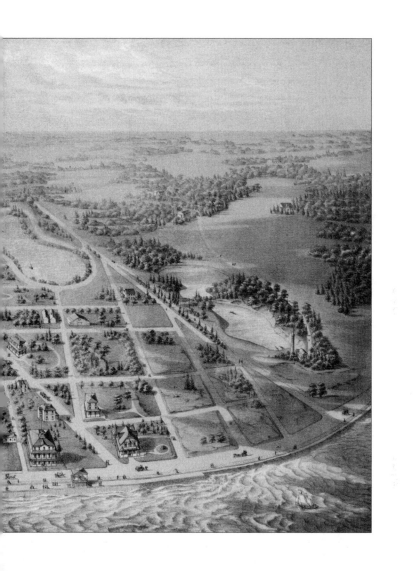

In fact, Atlantic City first and foremost, but other shore towns as well, evolved into epicenters of the kind of urban recreation and entertainment represented by places like Coney Island. Every day of the week was the weekend along Atlantic City's boardwalk, the first and best along the shore. Amusement park rides, theater and movie shows, arcade games—all these were staples of city life by the first quarter of the twentieth century. Not only were they common to American cities, but as David Nasaw has argued, they were places where the working class and the middle class mixed and shared cultural experiences.[30] Philadelphians thus found in Atlantic City versions of the things they already enjoyed back home, only more so. All that and the ocean too.

Surely because Atlantic City stood in the American imagination as the preeminent example of the middle-class resort town by the early twentieth century, it was chosen to play host to the annual event to define the paragon of American womanhood: the Miss America Pageant. The Miss America Pageant, at least in its heyday, combined, however hypocritically, the salaciousness of the beach experience itself—beautiful women in revealing bathing suits—with all the middle-class virtues of female submissiveness and domesticity. In this way, Atlantic City became the showplace for an American middle-class ideal, and the Miss America Pageant became yet another way in which metropolitan Philadelphia shaped the culture of middle-class expectations.

The arrival of the automobile age reshaped the Jersey Shore in a number of ways. Most importantly it enabled vacationers to come in much larger numbers. Between Memorial Day and Labor Day, the worst traffic in the entire Greater Philadelphia region is that between the city and the shore. And it brought to an end the railroad service from Philadelphia. Only Atlantic City remains connected with Philadelphia via train. It brought to an end as well the era of the grand resort hotels which were replaced in part by a new generation of cheaper motels, a few classic examples of

Fig. 17. Metropolitan Philadelphia's middle class re-created much of its life at spots down the shore. And in Wildwood they stayed in fantastic motels like the Bel Air, which was done in the "doo-wop" style. Photo courtesy of Kirk Hastings, Wildwood Crest Historical Society.

which remain up and down the coast. The best, at least according the connoisseurs, are to be found in Wildwood.

If Atlantic City represents a mini-urban center, built for vacationers coming by train, then Wildwood is probably the preeminent example of an automobile-age resort, designed for people driving down the shore. Along with its broad beaches, boardwalk, and amusement park attractions, Wildwood also developed a strip and a culture of cruising along its length. In its dance clubs and drive-throughs, Wildwood became a major epicenter of the youth culture that exploded in the 1950s and 1960s. And at the end of the evening, people stayed at any one of a number of motels, many festooned each season with plastic palm trees and each trying to out-do the others in sparkly glamour.

By the 1970s, however, when Philadelphians began driving down the shore, increasing numbers of them now started their trip in the suburbs. When they got to the shore they expected to stay in single family dwellings not unlike the ones they lived in back home. Many of these are rental properties, available weekly or monthly. But a growing number of Philadelphians have invested in their own houses (or condos) down the shore. No surprise either that the number of year-round shore residents has boomed too. The story of the shore in the recent past, then, has been the story of single family real estate development.

To satisfy the demand for residential real estate, much of the older shore has been demolished, and what remains of it is often threatened. Even in Wildwood condos are replacing the incomparable collection of motels. This being Greater Philadelphia, of course, the demolition of Wildwood's motels has in turn generated a historic preservation movement—they call it "doo-wop" architecture down the shore—with the aim of saving what remains of the 1950s and 1960s.

Put more bluntly: in the age of the automobile, the Jersey Shore, like the rest of metropolitan Philadelphia, has sprawled. The difference, of course, is that while generic suburban sprawl moves anywhere there is enough land and road access, sprawl at the shore is constrained by the availability of land near the beaches. Most of what we think of as the Jersey Shore is actually a string of barrier islands separated from the mainland by inlets, coves, and marshes. Ironically, whereas once Philadelphians went down the shore as a relief from the crowded, sticky Philadelphia summer, now many vacation in places occupied at much greater density than the places they leave behind.

Barrier islands are among the most fragile ecosystems on the planet. Those at the Jersey Shore have surely been overbuilt. While Philadelphia's shore is bordered at each end by gorgeous state parks—Cape May Point and Island Beach—much of the rest in between has become crowded. Because of the middle-class ethos, especially that of homeownership, that has shaped the Jersey Shore, environmentalism has come later to the area than it has in other places. Cape Cod has its national seashore, Cape May does not.

The rise of a "suburban" shore has mirrored the decline of what was once the shore's most glittering attraction and its only real urban center: Atlantic City. By the 1970s, even while other shore towns prospered, Atlantic City had become synonymous with the word seedy. Even the hotels stood empty along the boardwalk once visitors stopped coming. The arrival of casino gambling promised to cure what ailed Atlantic City, but only the most chirpy casino shill would argue that the city has benefited much. The boardwalk twinkles now with the garish bright lights of casinos, but even just a few blocks from the beach, the city remains hard up. Many people do come into Atlantic City now to gamble, but they tend to stay inside the airless, windowless gaming parlors, breathing only as much sea air as their bodies biologically require.

But at the same time, shore towns now resemble old Philadelphia neighborhoods in some ways. Families stay in the same places year after year. They look forward to seeing the same people year in and year out. Kids grow up together on the beaches. Down the shore, people still eat hoagies, complain about the Phillies, and read the *Daily News*. Down the shore, middle-class Philadelphians go on vacation every summer and they have re-created the world they left, for better and worse, to a remarkable degree.

At roughly the same time that health and recreational pioneers began to venture to the Jersey Shore, some went north to the mountainous region known now as the Poconos to look for restorative air and outdoor fun. To call them mountains, of course, overstates the case. Big hills, most of them, more gentle than rugged, more picturesque than dramatic. There is little to find spectacular about the Poconos, though a great deal to find charming and pleasant.

Geologically, the Poconos constitute the top end of the Appalachians, and are made up of two chains of mountains: the Blue (Kittatinny) and the Poconos proper. This hilly plateau covers much of Monroe County and pieces of Pike, Lackawanna, Wayne, Carbon, and Luzerne Counties besides. Generally speaking, therefore, the Poconos can be found south of Scranton, north of Allentown, and west of the Delaware River. They are old mountains, formed during the Cambrian era, and some of the oldest geological formations in the United States. Their rounded contours are the result of tens of millions of years of weathering and erosion.

There has been human activity in the Poconos for almost as long as there have been humans on the continent. The name itself derives from a Native American word. European settlers began arriving, though in small numbers, in the eighteenth century. These were people of the frontier, by and large, trappers, hunters, lumberjacks, and subsistence farmers who tried to scratch out a living in the thin, stony soil. While the farming frontier pushed westward through Pennsylvania and into Ohio and Indiana, those who went north into the Poconos in the eighteenth and early nineteenth centuries found themselves in an economic backwater.

But by 1820, the area's remoteness, thick woods, and trout streams began to attract vacationers from Philadelphia—Quakers who boarded with fellow Quakers who lived around the Delaware Water Gap. Within twenty years several hotels and lodges had opened to cater to summer travelers. These antebellum adventurers had to be hardy. Even to reach the Poconos in that era required a two-day carriage ride over uneven roads.

Nature is an abstraction. The notion that there exists pristine wilderness, unspoiled by any human interference, is a fiction created out of our yearning for such a place. As the historian William Cronon has observed, wilderness "is quite profoundly a human creation—indeed, the creation of very particular human cultures at very particular moments in human history. . . . As we gaze into the mirror it holds up for us, we too easily imagine that what we behold is nature when in fact we see the reflection of our own longings and desires."[31]

Figs. 18 a & b. Some of the earliest Philadelphians to go to the Poconos did so on photographic expeditions to the Delaware Water Gap. Courtesy of the Library Company of Philadelphia.

That particular moment in the Poconos came after the Civil War when railroads made it possible for vast numbers of urbanites—Philadelphians and New Yorkers—to escape the various travails of the city to the antidotal nature that the Poconos came to represent. The Poconos, then, must be understood as part of the urban system emerging in the second half of the nineteenth century. Urban technology made the area accessible in the first place—two-day stagecoach rides were replaced by relatively comfortable train excursions of only a few hours. Urban money built the hotels and lodges and supported the burgeoning tourist economy. And urban people filled up those lodges, bringing with them their par-

ticular prejudices, predispositions, and their hopes that a vacation in the Poconos would prove the cure for ills of urban civilization.

They came to a region that already knew the industrial economy and existed on its fringes. Timber companies cleared the area of its virgin forests. In mid-century, the Poconos supported a tanning industry, which relied on the tannic acid produced from the bark of hemlocks. The tanning business lasted exactly as long as the trees did, which, as it turned out, was only until the 1890s. So too went the small shoepeg and clothespin factories. By the late nineteenth century, when Philadelphians came looking for nature, many of the hills had been entirely denuded of trees, and the region suffered from serious erosion damage.

Likewise, slate and flagstone came out of Poconos quarries to be shipped to urban centers for paving and other uses, but only as long as they lasted, which wasn't all that long. In this sense, the economy of the Poconos resembled many nineteenth-century frontier economies, whether in the north woods of Michigan and Wisconsin or in the mining regions of the West. It relied almost entirely on extractive industries, it experienced periods of boom and bust, and when the booms were over, the wealth they had generated left the area, leaving poverty and deprivation behind.

Unlike the Jersey Shore, then, which really was largely devoid of human activity when vacationers started to arrive, the natural beauty that Philadelphians found in the Poconos in the late nineteenth century masked a local population of poor people. Their descendants aren't hard to find today. Sometimes the encounters between the tourists and the year-rounders have generated friction and resentment; mostly, poverty is a part of the environment that most visitors choose to ignore.

The Pennsylvania Railroad was the major source of Philadelphia tourists to the Poconos, and the Erie-Lackawanna brought in New Yorkers. In fact, the Lakawanna started to promote Poconos vacations as a way of filling up its otherwise empty trains moving westbound to the anthracite fields of Pennsylvania. Yet while the region drew from both cities, the Poconos have generally been regarded as Philadelphia's—Philadelphia radio stations give forecasts for the Poconos while New York stations do not. And the region grew up with a more Philadelphian culture, something more staid, reserved, perhaps stiffer and duller than the more boisterous Catskills, which belong entirely to New York.

The understated natural attractions of the Poconos seemed a perfect fit for Philadelphians with a preference for understatement in the first place. The region did attract the famous, especially in the late nineteenth century and early twentieth, when Presidents Harrison, Cleveland, Roosevelt, and Coolidge came for the fishing. But by and large, according to Lawrence Squeri, the Poconos remained shy of publicity and preferred, like the city itself, to be an insider's sort of place.[32]

Perhaps this represents more of the Quaker influence. Quakers were among the first vacationers to the area after all, and they even recapitulated their own nineteenth-century schism by founding one resort for Hicksites and another for Orthodox Friends. The Hicksites opened the Inn at Buck Hill Falls in 1901, and, in Squeri's words, it "exuded Quaker modesty," at least initially.[33] When it opened, there were no private baths, no electricity, and some of the staff slept on cots. By World War I, however, it was among the most popular of the Pocono resorts. The Inn itself, which now had electricity, long-distance phone service, and steam heat in the winter, was surrounded by 125 private cottages. Not to be outdone or upstaged, the Orthodox opened Pocono Manor in 1902. It too boomed. A half century before the Hicksites and the Orthodox officially ended their split in 1955, theology was being fought out in tennis, bowling and golf tournaments between Buck Hill Falls and Pocono Manor. These Quaker olympiads attracted so many spectators in the 1920s that box lunches were served.[34]

Quaker or not, many Poconos resorts, during their heyday before the Great Depression, advertised themselves as family places, in that most conservative, bourgeois sense of the term. Many of the resorts stayed dry, even if their proprietors never successfully managed to impose prohibition on Poconos counties. Newspapers drew the obvious contrast between the innocent virtues offered in the Poconos and the vulgar vices being peddled in Atlantic City.[35]

It is ironic then that when the Poconos vacation industry had to reinvent itself in the automobile age, it did so as the honeymoon capital of the country. Many of the grand resorts, built around railroad stations, did not survive the 1930s, and the ones

Fig. 19. Later visitors came for the champagne. Image from Caesar's Resort brochure.

that came to replace them tried to capitalize on the postwar marriage boom. By 1959 the *New York Times* could report that the Poconos now rivaled Niagara Falls as the destination for newlyweds. It is in this incarnation that Americans know the Poconos—as the home of places like Honeymoon Haven, tacky more than tawdry, where couples lounge in heart-shaped sunken tubs.

Where once Philadelphians brought their families to stay in family cabins to enjoy the mountain breezes, by the 1970s and 1980s couples frolicked in Cove Haven's champagne glass whirlpool bathtub. But that shift in resort attractions merely reflects a larger shift in the culture of the middle class. When middle-class Philadelphians first started vacationing in the Poconos, they used their vacations to underscore a set of Victorian sensibilities. In the postwar period, middle-class identity no longer depended on maintaining those facades of domesticity and respectability—at least not all the time.

It also isn't clear how the Poconos will continue to survive as "Pennsylvania's Vacationland" in an era when family vacations for the middle class are increasingly taken at theme parks and other places of preprogrammed fun and when more and more middle-class Americans are consumers of pornography of one kind or another. Heart-shaped tubs may simply not titillate the way they once did.

The housing crisis immediately after World War II created a "push" out of the city, but the allure of the suburbs exerted an equally powerful "pull." Trees and quiet and more space certainly appealed to many, as did the promise of safety, security, and a segregated environment. In this, metropolitan Philadelphia experienced nothing different from New York, Cleveland, or Chicago. In the postwar years, Philadelphia continued to exercise some role in shaping middle-class sensibilities. As the television replaced the radio as the center of domestic entertainment, Americans turned to *TV Guide*, published by Walter Annenberg in Philadelphia, to find out what was on.[36] Each week the kids might have tuned in to Dick Clark's *American Bandstand,* broadcast from a studio in West Philadelphia, for the latest teen music or dance craze. They might have done the twist with South Philly's own Chubby Checker. Or if they were feeling more sedentary, American families might have gathered around the tube to peel back the foil from the pre-frozen bounty of a TV dinner, a 1955 invention of Gerry Thomas of Ardmore, who worked for Campbell's. For his pioneering work altering the nation's eating habits, Thomas was inducted into the Frozen Food Industry Hall of Fame in 1998.

But the very ubiquity of the middle class—the triumph of its values—in the mid-century suburbs also meant that Greater Philadelphia no longer played the same role in shaping that culture as it once did. We are all middle class now, and in that sense we all trace our roots back to the Delaware Valley.

The promises of suburbia have proved illusory. Fifty years after they began, suburbanites have recapitulated most of the urban problems they sought to escape in the first place—choking traffic, the disappearence of green space, rising taxes, strained municipal services. Vacancy rates in the older shopping centers in the suburban counties around Philadelphia, and elsewhere, are rising dramatically, and poverty rates are rising too—up a whopping 48 percent in Montgomery County during the 1990s. And, of course, no one can maintain any longer that the suburbs are immune from the problems of drugs and violence. Many of the suburbs, especially those in the inner ring, have not aged well.

The response to the deterioration of the inner-ring suburbs has been to build even further out. In this sense, suburban sprawl can be defined as the continuing pursuit of a dream that can never come true. The idyll lasts only as long as no one else encroaches on it. And people invariably do.

We are all middle class now. But it isn't as simple as that. The middle class in the postwar period has retreated, from the city and from civic life more generally. The future of the region that invented the middle class lies in whether the middle class will stop its retreat, physically into an ever receding horizon of exurban sprawl, and socially from the civic life that the city once represented.

Indeed, the future of the nation depends on it.

Two Rivers Run Through It

Sitting at his window in 1789 the Reverend Dr. Duche, a visitor from England to the new nation of the United States, wrote a "Description of Philadelphia" for readers of the *American Museum*. He looked out over the "majestic Delaware" to the woods on the "opposite shore of New Jersey . . . clothed in their brightest verdure," which afforded his eyes "a pleasing rest and refreshment . . . after it has glanced across the watry mirror." While the good reverend doctor found the city only extended about half a mile from the shore of the Delaware, he told readers that it would some day extend all the way to the "beautiful river Schuylkill."

Two centuries later, even the region's most enthusiastic boosters, I suspect, would not begin an introduction to the area by extolling the Delaware and Schuylkill Rivers—and certainly that "brightest verdure" over on the Jersey side of the Delaware is long gone.

We don't generally think of Philadelphia as a river city—St. Louis, yes; New Orleans too; maybe even Cincinnati. But the Delaware gave the region its economic life well into the nineteenth century. As he surveyed the majestic Delaware from his window, Dr. Duche marveled that "the voice of industry perpetually resounds along the shore; and every wharf within my view is surrounded with groves of masts, and heaped with commodities of every kind, from almost every quarter of the globe."

Dr. Duche's little essay also reminds us of just how central the two rivers have been to the shaping of the entire region. The story of the colony's very founding puts its two rivers at the center. William Penn, having crossed the Atlantic, floated his boat into the Delaware Bay and tentatively up river. He looked at the site of present-day New Castle as a possible location for Philadelphia, then Chester. Neither suited. His surveyor Thomas Holme went further on and found the broad, largely flat plain between two rivers. Penn's utopian experiment had found its home.

Though the Delaware was the larger of the two, and already known as a waterway of potential importance, both rivers were navigable. With the grid laid out between the two, Penn imagined not simply a port city, but a two-port city, one on each river, and city growth moving from each bank toward the center.

It didn't turn out that way, of course. As Dr. Duche's description underscores, the city itself, and the regional economy tied to it, hugged the Delaware for its first century and beyond. By the time the city grew to reach the Schuylkill in the mid-nineteenth century, the age of boats and docks was on the wane, replaced by the age of railroads and factories.

The purpose of this chapter, then, is to look at these two rivers—or more properly, the regional watershed—to see how the region has been shaped by them. Across more than three hundred years of the region's European history, these two rivers have been threads that both transect the region and tie it together. We don't think much about our rivers these days—not like Bostonians think about their harbor, or Chicagoans their lakefront—but as people in the Delaware Valley contemplate a regional future, we ought to.

* * *

Let's begin with the physical facts. They are, generally speaking, easygoing rivers, not given to much of the roiling drama of the Snake, or the Colorado, or the Russian. During the warm months Philadelphians go "tubing" on big inflated inner tubes down the Delaware, not white water rafting.

Which is another way of saying that neither river drops quickly or spectacularly during its course. The Delaware begins its journey in two branches—a west and east branch, each rising in New York state. The two branches meet at Hancock, New York, and from there the Delaware proper meanders south. Along the way it flows through the one genuinely dramatic natural feature along its path: the Delaware Water Gap. For most of its run the Delaware forms the boundary between New Jersey and Pennsylvania and here at the gap the river has cut a gorge through the Kittatinny Mountains, Mount Minsi on the Jersey side, Mount Tammany on the Pennsylvania side. The gorge is roughly two miles long and the cliffs rise about twelve hundred feet on both sides. In 1965 the federal government designated the gap a national recreation area, which now encompasses about thirty-five miles of river and about seventy-two thousand surrounding acres. Three hundred miles or thereabouts after the east and west branches join in Hancock, the river reaches the mouth of the Delaware Bay.

The river is fed by over two hundred tributaries during its run. Several of the important ones include the Lehigh, the Neversink, and the Maurice. All told, the Delaware system drains roughly thirteen thousand square miles. And while there might not be much of riverine drama along the Delaware, those three hundred miles constitute the longest undammed river east of the Mississippi, which is all the more remarkable given that the Delaware watershed includes some of the most densely populated areas anywhere in the nation.

The Schuylkill, of course, is the largest of the tributaries that

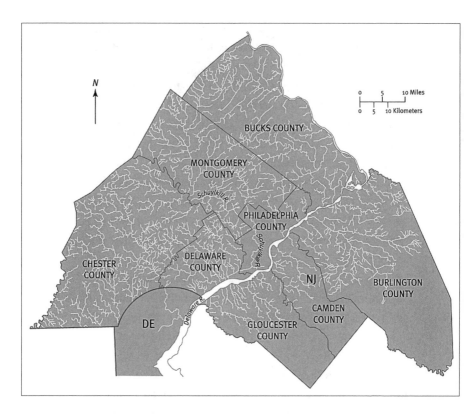

Fig. 20. Stripped of roads and human settlements, the map of Greater Philadelphia demonstrates the arterial nature of the region's two rivers. Data from the *Philadelphia Inquirer*.

feeds the Delaware. When it joins the Delaware it defines the southern edge of Philadelphia. It too starts in two branches, also designated east and west. The eastern, the larger of the two, begins as a series of springs near the town of Tamaqua; the two branches join at the town of Schuylkill Haven. From there the trip to South Philadelphia covers about 125 miles, moving mostly southeast, then almost entirely south once the river enters the city proper. All told, the Schuylkill's watershed covers over 2,100 square miles, small compared with the Delaware but significant nonetheless.

The rivers do not interest us purely for their own sake, of

course, but rather because of their relationship to human activity, and there has been human activity on both rivers for nearly as long as there have been humans on the continent. Archaeologists tell us that Paleo-Indians were making use of the rivers, particularly their food resources, as early as 8000 B.C.E. Their successors in historic times, the Lenape, followed shad upriver during the summer spawning season. The pleasant views of New Jersey weren't really the reason Penn signed his treaty with the Lenape on the banks of the Delaware. For both Native and European Americans, the river was a central aspect of their lives.

The Delaware, and the docks, wharves, and warehouses that clustered on its banks, provided Philadelphia with its link to the rest of the world. The sailing ships that came and went out of the port connected the city with the rest of the Eastern Seaboard, with the Caribbean, with Europe, and eventually with India and China. In 1784, ships left Philadelphia bound for each destination, helping to break the trade monopoly of the British East India Company. As one colonial era writer put it: "in a very little space, everything in the country proved a staple commodity . . . wheat, rye, oats . . . timber, masts, tar, sope, plankboard, frames of houses, clapboard, and pipestave." A marvel, really, "that this Wilderness should turn a mart for Merchants in so short a space."[1]

Eighteenth-century ships could make it all the way up the river to the falls at Trenton. But no other Delaware River port emerged during the eighteenth or nineteenth centuries to compete seriously with Philadelphia, and no other city of any consequence grew along the river between Philadelphia/Camden and Trenton.

In terms of regional settlement patterns during the eighteenth and nineteenth centuries, therefore, the Schuylkill, smaller though it is, proved more important. Moving upstream from the city, Manayunk—the rough transliteration of the Lenape name for the place—was a bustling settlement by 1825; further inland, Norristown eventually became the seat of Montgomery County; upriver further, Reading was founded in 1748 by two sons of William Penn, Richard and Thomas. George Washington crossed the Delaware to launch his surprise attack on the British, but he spent the winter in Valley Forge, along the banks of the Schuylkill.

The reason for this is that while the Delaware was the region's great watery thoroughfare, the smaller, more manageable Schuylkill could be more easily harnessed. The power of the river was exploited through a variety of human shapings—dams, locks, channels, races. And in that harnessing, in that reshaping of the river's contours, the Schuylkill Valley emerged as among the very first industrial landscapes in the nation by the second quarter of the nineteenth century.

Norristown used water power to become a milling center—forty thousand barrels of flour a year by the 1830s. Mill races along Schuylkill tributaries powered the furnace at Hopewell, which began producing iron in 1771 and continued until 1883. Over a dozen mills sited on Mill Creek in Lower Merion Township, Montgomery County, milled grain, sawed lumber and pounded paper pulp, making that two-mile stretch a water-powered industrial park. At Manayunk, water provided the power for a booming textile industry. By 1828, the city boasted over one hundred warping mills and nearly ten thousand people employed in manufacturing textiles. Much of that production was centered in Manayunk. Water power began the region's transformation from an agricultural trading center into a manufacturing giant.

More than anything else, however, canal building constituted the most significant human reshaping of the region's water resources in the antebellum period. Philadelphians had been looking at canal projects since the late eighteenth century. A canal to connect the Delaware with the Chesapeake had been proposed as early as 1767; Robert Morris hoped to connect the Delaware and Schuylkill rivers after the Revolution but never secured adequate funding. David Rittenhouse twice undertook a survey to assess the feasibility of linking the Delaware with the Susquehanna, but by 1796 that project too had never made it out of the planning stages. It wasn't until the early nineteenth century that Philadelphians, like others around the country, began to dig canals with real gusto. Nationally, the canal-building boom lasted a scant twenty years, from 1815 to 1835, when roughly three thousand miles of canals were dug out of the ground, filled with water, controlled by locks, and navigated along graded towpaths.

Philadelphia's foray into canal building took place on the Schuylkill when the Schuylkill Navigation Company was established. The first stage of that canal opened in Manayunk in 1818, and by 1819 the first mill there had opened. Water moving through a canal made Manayunk's industrial revolution possible.

Pennsylvania, prodded mostly by Philadelphians, embarked on canal projects largely out of a sense of panic. After the War of 1812, it was becoming obvious and distressing that the port of Philadelphia was losing its primacy as the funnel through which the agricultural production of the hinterland flowed. By 1820, for example, Philadelphia had fallen behind Baltimore in the amount of milled flour exported out of the port. By 1825, it had fallen behind New York as well. As the agricultural frontier continued to move west, canals, linking Philadelphia's waterways all the way to Lake Erie perhaps, were seen as the only way for Philadelphia to compete with New York and Baltimore. The Pennsylvania Society for the Promotion of Internal Improvements sounded an urgent note when it petitioned the state legislature to begin digging: "A large proportion of the western trade has been withdrawn from this city and the present exertions are calculated not merely to regain what is lost. The struggle assumes a more serious aspect. It is to retain what is left."[2]

By 1825, the Schuylkill Canal was largely complete and the first through traffic commenced. Canal barges could now carry freight between Manayunk at one end to a small town just above

Fig. 21. Canal traffic made the Schuylkill boom and connected the city with its hinterland. Courtesy of the Library Company of Philadelphia.

Reading at the other. That town was Port Carbon and its very name hints at the enormous change taking place in the relationship between Greater Philadelphia and its natural resources. Though the canal systems of the Delaware and Schuylkill were imagined as a way to keep agricultural products flowing into the city from the hinterland, coal, not corn, become the most important export product to make its way from the countryside into the city.

If Metropolitan Philadelphia first boomed in part thanks to its rich soils and congenial growing conditions, then it boomed again because of the hard coal—anthracite—that could be found in great abundance underneath the ground in the area around the upper Schuylkill.

Soft coal—bituminous—had been known as a fuel source for some time. It burns easily, quickly, and inefficiently. Only in 1815, however, did the Philadelphian Josiah White figure out how to ignite and burn anthracite. He ran a series of expensive experiments to burn the coal, all of which failed. Accidentally, as the story goes, his workers tossed a bunch of the "black stones" into

CHAPTER 4

a furnace and closed the door in disgust. When one of them returned to retrieve his coat, he found an enormous fire and the furnace itself red with heat. Workers then "ran through the rolls three separate heats of iron with that one fire."[3] The anthracite age was on.

Coal from Pennsylvania's anthracite fields, 365 tons worth, had come to Philadelphia for the first time in 1820, traveling down the Lehigh River to get there; it came from Port Carbon for the first time in 1823, even before the canal was completed. By the time it was 1825, a contemporary reported that the coal trade was "increasing with great rapidity; the demand for coal being, just now, much beyond the means of transporting it from the mines."[4] In its first full year of operation, the Schuylkill Canal handled 32,000 tons of freight, half of which was anthracite coal. By 1840, 658,000 tons of freight came through the system, over 450,000 tons of which came out of Schuylkill County coal mines.

Coal also filled up the canal system of the Delaware as well. The Lehigh Canal, completed in 1829, the Morris Canal in 1832, and the Delaware Canal in 1833, all converged on the town of Easton. Because of canals, Easton became a port where once it made no sense to have one. And in all three cases, the possibility of coal profits drove the construction.

The Carboniferous Period was good to Pennsylvania. During a 65-million-year span, roughly 354 to 290 million years ago, almost unimaginable quantities of organic matter were deposited in the swampy, low-lying area that would become known as Pennsylvania. In fact, geologists subdivide the period into a Lower and Upper Carboniferous, the latter referred to as the Pennsylvanian. Over time and under pressure that carboniferous—carbon bearing—material was transformed into anthracite coal.

Pennsylvania's hard coal fields came to cover almost five hundred square miles stretching across seven counties in the northeastern part of the state. As it would turn out, the three great coal veins of this area—a North Seam running from Forest City to

Shichshinny; an East Seam running from White Haven to Maca-doo; and a South Seam reaching from Shenandoah to Williams-town—contained a staggering 75 percent of the world's anthracite coal. One is hard pressed to come up with another example of such a central natural resource concentrated in so small a place.

All that coal transformed the city of Philadelphia in a number of ways. One hundred and fifty years or so after Penn imagined a two-port city, the banks of the Schuylkill itself finally became busy and active with docks, warehouses, and the coming and going of coal barges. The Delaware still connected Philadelphia's ships with the rest of the world, but the Schuylkill linked the city with the coal mines of Pennsylvania's interior.

Coal also served as the fuel for the city's transformation into an industrial giant. Philadelphia's industrial revolution depended on any number of technological innovations, the reorganization of capital, and the regimentation and exploitation of labor. But factory production could not have grown and proliferated by rely-ing solely on water wheels and wood stoves. In 1829, an anony-mous essayist writing in the *Saturday Bulletin* advocated the substitution of coal for wood in the furnaces of steamboats and other steam engines, warning that without that substitution all of New Jersey's pine barrens would be stripped of trees within a generation. "How vast the changes which the discoveries of steam and anthracite have made!" the writer trumpeted. "How mighty the effects which they are yet destined to produce."[5] Sim-ply put, coal powered industrial Philadelphia, and the city's prox-imity to the coal fields of the upper Schuylkill made Philadelphia the nation's first great industrial center.

Even on a domestic scale, coal changed the lives of city dwell-ers. Coal quickly proved a cheaper and more reliable source of heat than wood for the growing number of city households. As early as the 1820s coal-fired central heating had been installed by some forward-looking Philadelphia home owners, and by mid-century coal had eclipsed wood as the fuel of city homes. The wood hearth, around which middle-class Victorian families were supposed to gather, might have been a potent symbol, but chances are that those families actually stayed warm through the winter thanks to coal.

The city's insatiable appetite for coal transformed the landscape of coal country in ways at least as dramatic. In 1863, perhaps as a way of offering something of a diversion from the grim news of the Civil War, the writer H. M. Alden took readers of *Harper's New Monthly Magazine* on a tourist excursion through the anthracite country. "There are few trips so delightful," he began his travelogue, "as that through the great Coal Fields of Pennsylvania. . . . For the time, one can hardly choose amiss, from May, when the region puts on its robe of greenery, till November, when it assumes its gorgeous autumnal attire." With the trip over, Alden cheerily concluded: "There are few regions in which a summer vacation can be more pleasantly passed."[6]

In fairness, Alden took his trip at the beginning of the coal boom. Still, it is hard to imagine how he missed what coal mining was doing both to the landscape and the people who worked it. For most of the coal age, hard coal was mined in the same way: tunnels, deeper and deeper as the coal became scarcer and scarcer, dug into the seam; the exposed faced packed with explosives; detonation; and then the removal of the now-loosened coal to the surface. After the blasting, most of the work was done by hand by men swinging five foot, fifteen-pound steel picks. On uneventful days, coal mining was merely claustrophobic, dirty, and back-breaking. On others, of course, it killed.

Alden took his readers down into a coal shaft. As he breathlessly described it, "The rock here is mined by blasting. . . . You smell gunpowder—your guide hails out ahead—it is all right—you come up just in time to hear of an accident which, not five minutes ago—indeed in the last blasting—came near to proving fatal to a miner in the vicinity who mistook the signal! You tremble for your fate. . . ."[7] The light, almost chirpy way Alden relays the scene belies the difficulty in extracting coal, and the real danger involved in doing so. Between the Carboniferous era and the present, tectonic shifts folded the region like an accordion, creating the hills and valleys, and locking the coal into these folded layers. This meant that shafts had to be dug often at precarious angles, virtually straight down in some cases, in order to get at the coal. For some miners, the work took arms or legs or eyes or posture. And years. Long after the coal played out, miners in northeastern Pennsylvania suffered with black lung and a host of other ailments associated with coal dust. Some still do. Others went to work one day and never came back. Between 1870 and 1968, when the coal had virtually disappeared, Pennsylvania recorded over thirty-one thousand deaths in the anthracite mines—nearly one dead miner each day for one hundred years.

In 1917, with World War I raging and the United States joining the conflict, the coal age in northeastern Pennsylvania hit its peak when over 100 million tons of anthracite came out of the ground and roughly 180,000 men worked in the mines. It was the last moment when virtually everything that required power, from factory motors to railroad locomotives to Navy ships to home heating systems, burned coal, and Pennsylvania's hard coal was the best to burn.

The coal economy created several secondary urban centers in the late nineteenth century. Reading and Pottsville grew from small towns into small cities because of their role in moving coal. Further north, coal made Scranton and Wilkes-Barre booming, prosperous places as well, so much so that each developed a more diversified manufacturing economy by the early years of the twentieth century. Scranton, for example, produced more steel track than any other city in the nation save Chicago. On the Delaware side, Bethlehem, which had been founded in the eighteenth century as a Moravian community, emerged as a steel-making giant.

By the time the coal boom was over, in the years after World War II, however, it had broken the region as much as it had broken the miners. Those small industrial cities experienced the same deindustrialization as big cities such as Detroit, St. Louis, and Philadelphia—the economic implosion resulting from the loss of jobs and the closing of plants. Except those smaller places were less equipped to rebound from industrial decline, and the effects of deindustrialization have proved more concentrated and in some ways more profound.

In the fields themselves, and in the small settlements closer to them, the end of the coal age has left something more infernal. Coal mining is just as brutal to the land as it is to the people who do the mining. While billions of tons of coal came out of the ground and left in freight cars, billions more tons of slag and culm remained, blown from the original geologic formations and left in unceremonious heaps. Erosion marks the hills around coal mines and clear streams, which eventually wind up in the Delaware or Schuylkill waterways, often run foul with pollution. The little mining town of Centralia is famous because it is permanently on fire—a slow but utterly tenacious smoldering in the coal underneath the town.

As the writer Frank Macshane has put it: "It would be hard to imagine a landscape more ravaged than the countryside that runs through the Schuylkill Valley of Pennsylvania." The poet Karen Blomain, who grew up in the mining town of Archbald, describes the landscape even more starkly: "I was not to read Dante for twelve years, but at the age of six I had a perfect image of the landscape of the *Inferno* and knew the hopelessness and terror of its inhabitants, those grim faces cast in red shadows of flame and obscured by smoke. I saw it the first time in a mine cave and recognized that same terror in the tales of my neighbors and the episodes in the family history book throughout my childhood. . . ."[8]
Hard coal in every conceivable way.

Canals first brought the coal out of the mines of the upper Schuyl-kill and beyond, transforming both the hills and valleys at one end of the system and the city at the other. But the canal age didn't last much beyond the Civil War. The Schuylkill Canal recorded its most profitable year in 1859, but even that fact is a bit deceptive. In 1842, the Philadelphia and Reading Railroad opened, designed to compete directly with the canal. Most of the vast wealth produced by the Carboniferous deposits in Pennsylvania left in rail cars, not canal barges.

The Reading wasn't the first rail line in the region. That distinction belongs to the Philadelphia, Germantown, and Norristown Railroad, which began operation in June of 1832. Those who built the Reading, however, understood the profitable potential of linking the city with the coal fields by train. On January 10, 1842, amid great pomp and ceremony, an enormous train of seventy-five passenger cars brought 2,150 riders from Pottsville to Philadelphia. Right behind came another train hauling 180 tons of coal.

Not content merely to compete with the canal along its own route down the Schuylkill, the Reading brought the Delaware back into the coal business. The railroad had purchased land along the Delaware at Port Richmond and established coal wharves there. It also built a branch line running from the main line, across Philadelphia County to those wharves, and on May 17, 1842 the first load of coal arrived.

The numbers are remarkable: in 1842 the Reading carried nearly 50,000 tons of freight; in 1843 almost 220,000; the next year 475,000. The figures doubled again after 1845, when the railroad opened several short new feeder lines. By 1847 the Reading was regarded as the greatest freight railroad in the United States, carrying more tons than the mighty Erie Canal and at half the cost per mile. In 1852 the wharves at Port Richmond recorded 1.23

million tons of coal shipped from a newly expanded facility where one hundred ships could be loaded at a time. When the Civil War broke out, the Reading stood as among the very earliest examples of a vertically integrated operation. It controlled mines to ensure a steady supply of coal; loading facilities, trains, tracks, bridges; dock facilities at Port Richmond; and its own fleet of coal boats moving from the Delaware up and down the Eastern Seaboard. The port of Philadelphia had ceded its primacy to New York by then, but the Reading's ability to tie coal resources to water resources with railroad track made Philadelphia the greatest coal shipper in the nation.

Philadelphia's railroads began by hugging the Schuylkill and moving the freight of the larger region. In this sense, they merely improved upon the region's existing transportation network. Quickly, however, railroad builders realized that they need not be tied to existing waterways that had always been the most efficient form of transportation. They could also compete with the turnpikes and other roads that moved westward out of the city, and eventually they could go anywhere they wanted to, provided the financing and the engineering worked. Railroads, in other words, obliterated the natural landscape, making its contours less and less relevant to human movement.

The men who built the Pennsylvania Railroad, the greatest railroad of them all in the nineteenth century, understood this. By 1854 the Pennsylvania had laid track all the way to Pittsburgh, a connection no canal could reasonably have made, and by 1858 trains went through Pittsburgh on to Chicago, the greatest arriviste city of the nineteenth century. Philadelphia was once again connected to the American West in a way that it had not been since the opening of the Erie Canal.

Chicago, more than any other American city, was the creation of the railroad. But the Railroad, as the Pennsylvania was often simply called, grew to become the nation's largest corporation by

Fig. 22. The Reading Railroad created a vertically integrated coal operation, with the Port Richmond terminal at its center. Courtesy of the Library Company of Philadelphia.

the end of the nineteenth century, and Philadelphia was its center. By 1894, when the Pennsy's Broad Street Station was enlarged by Frank Furness, its arched glass shed was the largest in the world, and it covered over five hundred trains and sixty thousand passengers coming and going each day.

Moving westward, the Pennsylvania consolidated and then controlled the railroad operations of what constituted the industrial heartland of the country—from Philadelphia's busy hive of manufacturers, through the coal and oil fields of Pennsylvania, through the steel center of Pittsburgh, through the Great Lakes industrial centers to Chicago. Most of this expansion was done under the leadership of two presidents, Tom Scott and George Roberts, who between the two of them ran the Railroad from 1874 to 1897.

Under the tenure of Alexander Cassatt, the Pennsylvania expanded north and south, moving passengers between Washington and New York through Philadelphia. Though he did not live to
see it, Cassatt's greatest triumph came in 1910 when Pennsylvania Station, arguably the greatest railroad station ever built in
this country, and without argument the greatest victim of vandalism when it was torn down early in the 1960s, opened on Seventh
Avenue in midtown Manhattan.

The way in which the railroads reshaped Philadelphians' use of
landscape during the half century or so of their most rapid growth
underscores that the rivers were no longer central to the region's
life. Whereas the first generation of Philadelphia's wealthy estate
builders erected stately country homes along the banks and bluffs
of the Schuylkill—many of which are now incorporated into Fair-

mount Park—the Pennsy's main line west allowed a newer generation of elites to build their estates along the railroad line running from the city to Overbrook, Merion, Bryn Mawr, and as far out as Paoli, and in so doing created the social shorthand "the Main Line." In order for trains to reach Pennsylvania Station on Seventh Avenue, they had to travel under the Hudson River in a tunnel built by the Pennsylvania which constituted an engineering marvel at least as dazzling as the station itself. In the railroad age, rivers, once the most important transportation routes, were either irrelevant, or they were things to be bridged and tunneled.

Just as railroads eclipsed boats, so too trains were eclipsed by cars and trucks as the major form of transportation in the postwar period. Interestingly, or perhaps ironically, when Philadelphians built their pieces of the high-speed interstate highway system, however, they came back to their rivers. Interesting or ironic, the choice to do so has had terrible consequences.

The report issued by the Philadelphia Planning Commission in 1950 reads now as a poignant artifact of a very different time. Recognizing the congested condition of Philadelphia's streets, the commission concluded that a system of limited-access, high-speed highways ought to be built to "relieve Philadelphia's traffic congestion" and to "provide the necessary links in the internal circulation system of the city . . . thereby adding to the convenience and efficiency of the city structure." That search for "convenience and efficiency" resulted in the construction of the Schuylkill Expressway.

Words fail. Except perhaps for the obscene ones that drivers scream at each other while racing down this twenty-five-mile automotive nightmare. Is it the worst road in America? It must surely be a contender. Is it more dangerous than most? We don't call it the "Sure Kill Expressway" for nothing. Even its designing engineer, Bill Allen, can only offer this by way of a rousing defense of the expressway: "If you don't like it, don't drive it."[9]

The Schuylkill Expressway is a pure product of the 1950s, begun in 1949 as a project of the Commonwealth of Pennsylvania, jump-started again after the passage of the Federal Interstate Highway Act of 1956—that pork-barrel bonanza of highway construction money—and finished in 1959. It stands—or lays—as a monument to a modernist age of heroically big urban renewal projects, to an autocentric age when all other forms of human interaction were subordinated to the acts of merging and yielding, of a time when parking was regarded as far more important to the human condition than parks. It was built largely during the term of Mayor Richardson Dilworth. He cut the ribbon at the ceremonial opening and several years later called the expressway "the worst mistake in my administration."

Given that a road of this size, carrying as much traffic as it does, has no business being where it is, the expressway is indeed a remarkable engineering feat. As its lanes snake alongside the river from Valley Forge/King of Prussia through Center City, dumping cars finally onto the Walt Whitman Bridge, the expressway squeezes between railroad tracks, steep geologic features, and crowded urban environments. At Thirtieth Street Station, the right of way was so tight that engineers had to move the south bank of the river eight feet to accommodate the west-bound lanes, creating a grand total of two feet of clearance on both sides. As the engineer Bill Allen describes it, again sounding as much defensive as proud: "That's right. Just two feet. That's how close you are to the corner of the concrete abutment as you travel through that underpass. . . ."

And it has proved inadequate almost from the start. Because it was retroactively declared an interstate it did not conform to the engineering standards expected of other interstates. As one engineer told the *Philadelphia Inquirer* in 1969, "In retrospect, it might have been wiser to wait for those [federal] funds. At least then the expressway would have incorporated all the higher engineering standards required. . . ." In 1950, planners predicted that daily traffic volume would reach thirty-five thousand vehicles by 1970. They got that badly, badly wrong: within a year of its opening, seventy thousand trucks and cars were using the expressway each day.

The most ironic thing about the grand plans for the Schuylkill Expressway, the reason I called the 1950 commission report poignant, is the way those planners seemed really to see only one-way traffic on the expressway. It was planned and built to make city life better, to reinvigorate the city by making the cars move more smoothly—no one seems to have noticed that it would allow people to leave the city at sixty miles per hour. Many had no intention of returning.

In addition, by linking Center City with King of Prussia, the Schuylkill Expressway turned an otherwise inconsequential point on the map, named after an eighteenth-century German monarch, into a virtual synonym for the suburban shopping mall. Planners might have believed that the expressway would bring shoppers effortlessly into the Center City retail hub, but as it turned out, more and more of the region's shoppers used the expressway to get to the mall.

The expressway has also made possible the development of the Route 202 corridor, mile after aching mile of strip malls, office "parks," and banal residential subdevelopments, arcing across the region's suburbs from Chester County all the way to New Jersey. Once the expressway linked with the Walt Whitman Bridge, one set of new, booming suburbs was connected with another. The city thus became, in a quite literal sense, something to drive through. In this way, the Schuylkill Expressway facilitated, perhaps more than any other single project in the region, the flight of people, money, and jobs from the city to the suburbs and created the sprawl of the region in the postwar period.

Call it the Sprawlkill Expressway.

When planners wanted to connect Philadelphia with Interstate 95, the major north-south artery on the East Coast, they chose to run the highway along William Penn's Delaware. It was originally conceived to be part of the Pennsylvania Turnpike system, but nothing much of what we know now as I-95 got built before 1956; once the federal money came along, I-95 through Greater Philadelphia would be entirely part of the interstate system.

It was built piecemeal, however, a section here, an exit there, and it wasn't fully completed until 1985. It grew toward the city from both ends, the final section being the one that runs through Center City at Penn's Landing. To build this final piece of I-95 meant tearing out much of the city's oldest waterfront and lowering it to allow the original streets to cross over it at grade.

As it runs north from Center City, it becomes an elevated highway for several miles, literally casting dark, forbidding shadows over the several city neighborhoods it blows through. Port Richmond, one of those neighborhoods, got its revenge on I-95 in 1996 when an illegal tire dump caught fire underneath the road, causing three spans of the road to buckle. If you had stood in one of the those dark, dank places underneath I-95 in Philadelphia when it was finished, you could have almost heard people's real estate values falling over the incessant din of traffic.

Having been finished in 1985, however, it still stands incomplete, or rather uncompleted. The great promise of the interstate system was to create fast, efficient, vehicular connections between major destinations. In Metropolitan Philadelphia, I-95 fails. Coming north from Washington, drivers encounter a scant handful of signs for Philadelphia (there are dozens for New York), leaving the novice with the impression that this road might not actually go there. The experienced driver knows that to continue north through the Northeast Corridor means leaving I-95 well south of Philadelphia and connecting with the bottom of the New Jersey Turnpike.

Stay on I-95 and you discover that as it runs north through Greater Philadelphia, it does not connect to anything—not the Pennsylvania Turnpike, not the New Jersey Turnpike, not the rest of I-95. It is a road to nowhere. The Age of the Interstate has not been kind to Philadelphia. It has left the city girdled, cut off from parts of itself, and isolated to some extent from the flow of people and goods moving through the Northeast Corridor. Allowing the Schuylkill Expressway to be built straight through the heart of Fairmount Park, ruining its continuity and cohesion, was an act of vandalism that would have made the Visigoths proud.

Just as sadly, however, the highways have cut the people of this region off from their own rivers, making them unpleasant in some stretches—it is hard to enjoy the tranquility of the water flowing by over the belch and fart of eighteen-wheelers—and downright inaccessible in other places.

Philadelphia is surely not unique in this dilemma. Lots of big road projects built through lots of cities big and small severed people from their waterfronts: New York lost contact with much of the East River because of the FDR Drive; New Haven's harbor disappeared from the city, hidden by the junction of I-95 and I-91, to name just two. People are drawn almost atavistically to the water, and there is no greater measure of the inhumanness of the urban renewal projects of the mid-twentieth century than that they separated people from the water. The result in Philadelphia has been that what began, as the architect Alan Greenberger has written, as a city between two rivers became a city between two highways, which happened to be located next to two rivers.[10]

The Delaware Valley will probably not see any more massive road projects anytime soon. Perhaps a new off-ramp here, a reconfiguration of traffic patterns there, an interchange, finally, to connect I-95 to something. The region is simply too crowded with people and real estate developments to imagine large swaths being appropriated by eminent domain. I-476—the Blue Route—which connects I-95 with the expressway through parts of Delaware and Montgomery Counties probably stands as the last monument to the age of the interstate. And that road took years and years of fighting, negotiation, and litigation to complete. But it isn't merely the logistics and the money that make big new roads unlikely. More and more people have come to this conclusion: big roads simply haven't lived up to their promise. Built to revitalize the city, they have been a major contributor to suburban sprawl; designed to alleviate traffic congestion, they, especially the expressway, are now the most congested roads in the region; promoted as a way to ease the dense crowding of the city, the big roads are now where most of the region's smog gets generated, as more and more cars sit for longer and longer in traffic that does not move.

Call it auto-Malthusianism. Thomas Malthus, an eighteenth-century English scientist, posited that any individual species would increase in number to a point just beyond the carrying capacity of the environment it inhabited, using up resources at an unsustainable rate. (Malthus's work was an important influence on the young Charles Darwin.)

So too, in the second half of the twentieth century, new road projects have only stimulated, rather than reduced, car traffic. Cars on the road always multiply to beyond the capacity of the roads designed to carry them. All of which I could summarize by saying: Los Angeles. Yet there is no better example of the principle of auto-Malthusianism than the Schuylkill Expressway. It stands now not as part of the solution to the traffic problem, but as part of the problem itself.

And so planners in the region have come back to an older idea, and they have returned to the rivers to realize it. They have planned two new train lines to handle the flow of people in the region, one along the Delaware in New Jersey from Camden to

Fig. 23. Following the path of the Delaware, the River Line connects two of the region's poorest cities—Trenton and Camden—with the goal of reviving them and the string of depressed smaller towns along the way. Author's photo.

Trenton, the other along the Schuylkill between Philadelphia and Reading.

The former, of course, is done and open for business. At a cost of nearly one billion dollars New Jersey Transit has built the River Line, an electric tram of such comfort and convenience as to feel practically European.

When it opened, in March of 2004, it was roundly criticized as a boondoggle project. Too expensive to build. Too subsidized by the rest of the Jersey Transit system to be able to survive. The wrong project, in the wrong part of the state. How many people actually go between Trenton and Camden?! And these were among the kindest things said about it, even by people who described themselves as advocates of mass transit.[11]

These criticisms risk missing the point. The River Line is as much an economic development project as it is a transit project. The line links a whole set of small industrial towns along the Delaware, most of which have experienced all the problems of deindustrialization, albeit on a smaller scale. The River Line, so the hope goes, will stimulate reinvestment in these towns. Unlike the surrounding sprawl, whose blandness is generally pretty numbing, towns such as Riverside and Bordentown have some real character and distinctive architecture. Charm even. Or rather, they could have these things once people start to live, work, and play in them.

With the River Line running through, these towns will undoubtedly revive. They will become little downtown centers, stretched one after the other along the river. The town of Riverside was once home to the Keystone Watch Case Co., the largest manufacturer of timepieces in the world, and its marvelous building has been underutilized for years. Not six months after the River Line opened, a developer bought the empty building, announcing plans to turn it into condominiums.

Mass transit hubs tend to concentrate development, while cars tend to promote centrifugal patterns of development. The River Line, therefore, doesn't so much alleviate a problem as anticipate it, doesn't react to the present so much as shape the future. When developers and residents discover these towns, with their proximity to the Delaware, there will already be a mass transit line in place to serve them. In the most heavily suburbanized state in the nation, this is decidedly forward-thinking urban planning.

By contrast, the need for the line between Reading and Philadelphia is already there, but its future is much less certain. Everyone agrees that the proposed sixty-two-mile project would alleviate traffic and fuel the revitalization of many of the towns along the route. It is a good idea waiting for the political will to make it happen. The wait thus far has been agonizing.

The different fates of these two rail projects provide an instructive lesson in regional cooperation. In New Jersey, the project was handled entirely by the state, through the state transit agency, New Jersey Transit. The Reading-Philadelphia line would be a project of SEPTA, a regional body without the same pull in the Pennsylvania legislature. Further, SEPTA's board has historically not provided particularly strong leadership for the agency, making it hard to run the system it has, much less plan ambitiously for the future. So while life begins to stir on the Delaware along the River Line, Pennsylvanians on the Schuylkill Expressway are still stuck in traffic, sucking fumes.

Before we use it for transport, before we harness its power to turn mill wheels, we need water every day for the very fundamentals of maintaining life. While Native Americans had used the waters of Greater Philadelphia for millennia, it took a scant one hundred years for Europeans who made Philadelphia their home to poison their own water supply. The wells, dug primarily in low-lying parts of the city, filled with all manner of nasty detritus; the small creeks that fed the Delaware served as open sewers for city residents; and the river itself quickly grew unusable and disreputable.

In looking for a new, reliable, but above all clean source of water, eighteenth-century Philadelphians looked west again to the Schuylkill. Under the design of the engineer and architect Benjamin Latrobe, the city built a water system through which water was pumped by steam engines from the Schuylkill along a viaduct to Center Square, at Broad and Market Streets. At that point, steam pumped the water again into a storage tank where gravity would lead it through a network of pipes. Fresh water from that river began flowing into Philadelphia households in January of 1801. Within a year, Schuylkill water was being delivered to sixty-three houses, four breweries, one sugar refinery, and thirty-seven fire hydrants.

Latrobe's water system stands as the first municipal water system in the nation and, if we pause over it for a moment, as something just short of miraculous. Clean water brought dependably into a dense city and into people's homes. By contrast, New York's Croton system wouldn't be built until 1842 and Boston's until 1848. When those cities finally did get around to building their municipal water systems they turned to Philadelphia for advice and expertise.

The person those cities brought in for the job wasn't Benjamin Latrobe, but Frederick Graff. Graff had been put in charge of Philadelphia's water system in 1805 and had concluded fairly quickly that it would not work adequately. He thus convinced the city to move its entire water plant up river a half-mile or so and to build an enormous reservoir on the top of Fairmount. The reservoir would be filled with water by large steam engines—which were soon replaced, fittingly enough, with an ingenious set of water-powered pumps—and from this lofty spot gravity would take the water directly into a plumbing network. Work on the reservoir began in 1812 and the system was complete by 1822.

All this remarkable engineering was housed in an equally remarkable set of elegantly spare neoclassical buildings adorned with the sculpture of Benjamin Rush. The resulting Water Works immediately became a major tourist attraction, the must-see stop especially for European travelers. The Water Works at Fairmount probably got portrayed in paintings, prints, and other reproductions more than any other city view across the nineteenth century. The Water Works seemed to demonstrate at the dawn of the industrial age that art and science could coexist happily, that engineering and aesthetics could walk hand in hand. The Water Works on the Schuylkill River, perhaps more than any single construction, gave Philadelphia its antebellum nickname: The Athens of America.

This great municipal improvement led to another later in the century. Beginning in 1855, prompted by the city's incorporation and expansion, the City Council began to acquire a set of country estates on both sides of the Schuylkill, all above the Water Works, to be held in trust for public use. From these purchases, Fairmount Park grew, and while plans for the park stalled during the Civil War period, it played the triumphant role of host to the 1876 centennial celebration.

To be more precise, of course, it wasn't the Water Works themselves that prompted the creation of the park, but rather the water itself. Fairmount Park was envisioned, first and foremost, as a buffer around the city's water supply. In the process of creating that buffer Philadelphians built a remarkable urban playground and one of the most beautiful stretches to be found anywhere in urban America. The beauty of the Schuylkill flowing through the city inspired one M. K. C. to publish a great—and I refer only to its length—ode to the river in time for the centennial. Celebrating scenes of "undulating charm," the poet declaims: "With Christ the Jordan's banks I rove, / With Horace, tawny Tiber love; / With Scott, abide by Teviot's tide, / With stricken Grey, by Luggie's side; / But garlanded by pleasures flown, / Endeared by recollections sweet, / The Schuylkill's name I most repeat / With accent fond and tender tone; / Beyond all streams that lands can boast, / I most repeat, and love the most."[12] And so it goes for over thirty pages. Perhaps "inspired" is not quite the right word.

The creation of Fairmount Park as a way to preserve the drinking water of the Schuylkill took place during exactly the same years that the coal fields of the upper reaches of the river opened up. In a historical coincidence heavy with symbolism, the year after the nation gathered in Fairmount Park to celebrate the centennial along the banks of the lower Schuylkill, coal-miner labor activists known as the Molly Maguires launched one of the first violent labor uprisings in the nation in those coal fields. Members of the Mollys were hanged in Pottsville along the Schuylkill in 1877.

Nineteenth-century Philadelphians seem to have imagined that they could use the Schuylkill in two very different ways simultaneously—that there were, in fact, two different Schuylkills. The governing assumption of people at the time seems to have been that the industrial use of the river upstream would have no bearing on the quality of drinking water downstream. Water doesn't work that way; whatever goes in it at one point must come out of it somewhere else. By the late nineteenth century the industrial uses of the Schuylkill system upriver overwhelmed the domestic use of the water downriver. By World War I industrial pollution of varying sorts had killed the river, and the Water Works at Fairmount shut down. The beautiful and the useful, the industrial and the natural, proved to be less compatible than people had assumed in 1822.

When George Washington famously crossed the Delaware from the Pennsylvania side to the Jersey side to lead a sneak attack on the British, he did so in a Durham boat, a shallow draft barge designed to carry pig iron.

As I reread it, the preceding discussion about the Schuykill strikes me as perhaps misleading. The Schuylkill watershed did indeed develop into a great industrial center across the years of the nineteenth century. But the Durham boats that Washington used on Christmas Night, 1776 remind us that the Delaware was also a working river and that it too would grow into a thriving industrial valley. At its peak, the scale, concentration, and diversity of manufacturing on both sides of the Delaware were probably unequaled anywhere else in the world.

Washington crossed the river at Trenton. No happenstance about that. Trenton marks the fall line of the Delaware, the furthest point upriver navigable by boats coming from the south. This fact is purely a function of the region's ancient geology. The Delaware Valley sits where two great geologic formations abut one another. On the western side, the Piedmont is left over from the formation of the Appalachian chain; on the other side, the coastal plain is more sand than rock. Both formations date from the age of the dinosaurs—indeed, the very first dinosaur ever discovered in the United States was a hadrosaurus unearthed from the "green sands" of south Jersey in the 1840s. Whenever these two geologic structures meet, rivers drop, and one of those places is at the falls at Trenton.

Thus, in a pattern opposite that of the Schuylkill, the lower portion of the Delaware, from Trenton in the north to Wilmington in the south, became industrialized in the nineteenth century. Like the Schuylkill, the Delaware's first industrial use was as a great highway moving raw materials into market. Rafts of timber began trips downriver to Philadelphia as early as the 1760s; in the spring of 1828 alone roughly one thousand rafts made the trip, bringing 50 million feet of lumber into the city.[13]

But the extractive, raw material economy was quickly eclipsed along the Delaware by the manufacturing economy, and the names of the firms located on both banks read like a directory of America's industrial age. In Trenton, the Roeblings built their steel cable empire and Lenox produced fine china; toward Wilmington the Duponts made gunpowder first and a wide array of chemicals later. In between, Henry Diston built the largest steel saw plant in the country, Jack Frost sugar was refined, Cramp's built ships, RCA recorded Caruso, Campbell's canned soup, and Sun refined oil.

Shipbuilding emerged as the first important manufacturing done on the Delaware—that raft of timber that floated down to the city in 1764 consisted of tall, straight pine logs intended for ship masts. One hundred fifty years later, as part of the emergency mobilization for World War I, the navy built an enormous shipyard at the bottom of the city on Hog Island.

Everything about it was astonishing. Built on nine hundred acres of marsh, the Hog Island yard sprang to life in just ten months. It included fifty shipways and employed thirty-five thousand people. In a space of two years, those thirty-five thousand built a fleet of 122 flat-bottomed ships each weighing 7,500 deadweight tons. Sixty-one boats each year. Five each month. Astonishing. And the Italians who worked at the Hog Island yard brought sandwiches built on long, hard rolls, which were stuffed with vegetables and deli meats and which continue to be eaten by the millions by Philadelphians who know that the proper name for such a sandwich is "hoagie."

All of this industrial activity from Trenton to Wilmington over decades and decades took a predictable toll on the river itself. In its industrial stretch, the Delaware is a freshwater, tidal river. Which means that it feels the ocean tides, changing as much as six feet up and down, twice a day. Those tides, in turn, created tidal mud flats and marshes all along this run of the river, and along the many feeders that empty into it.

Before it was an industrial powerhouse, this part of the Delaware was amazingly productive biologically. Plant life—wild rice, sweetflag, pickerelweed, cattails, over seven hundred species by anyone's best count—bird life, fish, and mollusks so abundant that people named towns in South Jersey after them: Shellpile and Bivalve. Oyster beds once lined the bottom of the river as far north as the city itself and dolphins were not an uncommon sight from the banks of the river near the city. A few years before William Penn came up the Delaware, in 1679, Jacob Daenckaerts gazed out on the river in this vicinity and observed: "I have nowhere seen so many ducks together. The water was so black with them that it seemed when you looked from the land below upon the water, as if it were a mass of filth or turf, and when they flew up there was a rushing and vibration of the air like a great storm coming through the trees, and even like the rumbling of distant thunder."[14]

If shipbuilding constituted the first large-scale manufacturing on the Delaware, commercial fishing operations came close be-

Fig. 24. Coal came down from the upper reaches of the Schuylkill, and oil was refined and stored at its bottom. Courtesy of the Library Company of Philadelphia.

hind. Herring, alewife, striped bass, sturgeon—all of these came up from the ocean to spawn in the Delaware. But shad most of all. In 1896, 15 million tons of shad were caught along the Delaware. Shad fisheries lined the Delaware's tidal section.

And then the river—or at least the tidal river—died.

Untold, unknowable volumes of industrial waste of every conceivable kind got dumped into the Delaware during the heyday of the manufacturing economy. Two hundred years after Jacob Daenckaerts saw a river blackened by vast numbers of ducks, the river ran black again, this time from coal, oil, tanning by-products, and who knows what else. By World War II, 500 million gallons of raw sewage alone flowed into the Delaware. There was enough grease in the river to clog ships' cooling systems and enough oil residue to corrode their hulls. It all stank. As the age of commercial aviation dawned, ground controllers told pilots coming into Philadelphia that the smell at five thousand feet was the Delaware.[15] The Delaware Valley stood as one of the greatest industrial concentrations in the world. The river had become its sewer.

The fish felt it first. After that remarkable harvest in 1896, shad became harder and harder to find. From 15 million pounds, to 5 in

1904, to a scant quarter of a million pounds in 1921. By then the commercial fisheries along the river were dying and doomed, the first casualties of the industrial decline that would eventually sweep the whole region.

The cause of this decline appeared obvious to anyone who paused to consider it, obvious enough to be tasted in the fish itself. According to an 1895 report by the Pennsylvania Fish Commission, "The river below Philadelphia is so impregnated with coal oil that its peculiar flavor can be detected in the shad."[16] Fishermen knew that "the obnoxious poisons and gasses . . . all turned into the river" killed the fish.

The fishermen were right, even if they didn't understand the ecology of the river entirely. Anadromous fish—shad, striped bass, and the rest that filled the Delaware—strike us as almost heroic. Hatched in fresh water, the fry make their way to the ocean where they mature, often migrating seasonally from winter to summer grounds and back. Then, upon reaching sexual maturity, they return, fighting their way against currents back into fresh water to lay their eggs, and the cycle begins again. In that 1895 report, the Fish Commission wrote that this return to the spawning grounds was driven by "instincts of nativity and procreation—impulses so overmastering that nothing but death or impassable barriers will restrain them."[17]

When humans have interfered with the cycles of anadromous fish, they have usually done so by erecting "impassable barriers," like dams. Think of the sockeye salmon of the Pacific Northwest, for example, which have disappeared from the Columbia River because dams prevented them from spawning. The tragic, oily irony of the Delaware fishery is that no such barriers were ever built. The filth that emptied into the river—and the bacteria that grew in it—robbed the river of any oxygen. The fish returning to spawn literally suffocated for their troubles.

By the early nineteenth century, the Delaware's waters had

become too polluted for Philadelphians to drink. By the early twentieth, even the fish couldn't live in them anymore.

Just as Philadelphians used the Schuylkill in two very different ways, creating, in a sense, two very different rivers, so too the Delaware was turned into two different rivers, divided by the falls at Trenton. In many ways, it still is two different rivers. The contrast is striking. As Carol Collier, the executive director of the Delaware River Basin Commission, puts it, "It's such a diverse river that it's difficult for people to get their arms around it."[18]

Moving upriver from Trenton, the Delaware quickly begins to look and feel more natural. Up here it is easy to use words like "free flowing," "pristine," even "wild." Up here, the fishing, especially for trout, is good.

Of course, there is no such thing as a purely "natural" environment. As the historian William Cronon has astutely observed, everything about our experience with the "wilderness" is conditioned by our urban, technologically based civilization—from the vehicles that bring us to the wilderness, to the equipment we use to hike, camp, and fish in it, to the very expectations we bring with us in the first place. Even when we aren't logging, mining, or farming it, we use the landscape as a resource to satisfy our own desires.[19]

In the upper half of the Delaware, the pristine half, the human use of the river is no less intense, though it is largely hidden from the view of hikers and fishermen. Each and every day 800 million gallons of Delaware water are siphoned from the upper half of the river and sent to New York City. Even more astounding than the sheer volume of water being pumped into the city is the fact that the water from the Delaware is so clean that it passes untreated into New York faucets.

With this human use of the river's upper half, the purity of the water itself is not likely to be poisoned by industrialism. Because of the geology, there never was much industry north of the Trenton falls and in a postindustrial age it is hard to imagine a new generation of toxin-belching factories being built there.

But at the beginning of the twenty-first century, the water is no less threatened. This time the danger comes from the suburban sprawl, ever metastasizing across the metropolitan landscape. As more and more of the affluent want homes with river views, or at least homes farther and farther out from the crowding of the last generation of suburban sprawlers, the water resources of the upper Delaware are increasingly strained. More water comes out, more sewage goes in. More than that, the protective buffer around the river, which helps keep the water pure in the first place, shrinks and shrinks. Given that the upper Delaware traverses three states—New York, New Jersey, and Pennsylvania—there is no effective mechanism through which to control this sprawl and protect this vital resource.

If industrial indifference killed the lower Delaware half a century ago, the upper Delaware may be killed by suburbanites chasing the illusion that they can have their piece of country living and a pristine river without spoiling both in the process. It is not inconceivable that the upper Delaware could be loved to death.

It has always been a hard-working river, increasingly so as European American uses of it accelerated during the last two hundred years. It still is. While billions of gallons of water above Trenton go to slake the collective thirst of New York City, over twenty-five hundred commercial ships continue to ply the lower half each year. Ninety thousand jobs, by anyone's best guess, are connected to the industrial uses of the river, this even after the heyday of industrialism has long passed. Many of those ships carry oil—a million barrels a day—and many of those workers are employed by the river's six refineries. Between them, they process 70 percent of the gasoline and home heating oil used on the east coast.[20] And shipbuilding is back, after a hiatus of several years when the Philadelphia Naval Ship Yard was closed. On a portion of that huge site, container ships are being assembled in the most state-of-the-art facility in North America. Because of its upstream-downstream dynamics, the Schuylkill could not sustain its two uses simultaneously. Amazingly, the Delaware manages to do just that.

In the end, the water always wins.

The physical separation of people and rivers in Greater Philadelphia mirrors a psychological separation as well. We don't think about our rivers too much, and usually only when something bad happens.

The condition of the Delaware became national news in the cold winter of 1993–94. For the first time in a very long time the river froze hard enough to keep ships from docking. Many of those were oil tankers and all of sudden supplies of gas and heating oil were threatened. The river landed on the front pages again ten years later when a single-hulled tanker spilled half a million gallons of crude oil just before Thanksgiving, 2004. Because of an almost perverse set of river conditions, the huge spill actually moved upstream for a while, bringing it up to Penn's Landing, the heart of original Philadelphia.

But the watershed is a great deal more than its two big rivers, its workings a great deal more complicated. Many—most perhaps—of the small arterials that form the watershed in the region have disappeared from our view and thus from our experience. Small streams and creeks, culverts that run only after heavy rain or snow melt, marshes and swamps have all been covered, buried, redirected, or filled in.

Sharf and Wescott, in their 1884 history of Philadelphia, noticed as much:

There have been great changes in the face of the country, in its levels and contours, and in the direction and beds of its watercourses. . . . Some streams

have disappeared, some have changed their direction, nearly all have been reduced in volume and depth by natural silt, the annual washing down of hills, by the demands of industry for water-power, the construction of mill-dams and mill-races and bridges, the emptying of manufacturing refuse from factories, saw-pits, and tan-yards, and by the grading and sewerage necessary in the building of a great city. In this process, old landmarks and ancient contours are not respected. . . .[21]

The two historians were remarkably observant, identifying virtually all the problems attendant upon unregulated growth and expansion, from erosion to effluent. And they couldn't know the half of it. In the twentieth century, the building boom went on without heeding the warning implicit in those 1884 observations. Almost without exception, nothing about the "direction and beds of its watercourses" was respected in Greater Philadelphia. And for the most part those watercourses have been forgotten.

Until the rains come heavy. Then residents from across the region—from working-class city neighborhoods such as Wissonoming, to working-class parts of Delaware County, to toney sections of Montgomery County, to newly sprawled areas of Burlington County—all discover they have something in common: flooded basements.

Or worse. In certain now flood-prone areas houses have been ruined by flooding. Sinkholes have opened up in streets. Flood waters have caused secondary fuel spills from oil tanks in homes and businesses. In the summer of 2004, flood waters after a heavy rain may have permanently ruined five hundred homes in Upper Darby and Darby Township, Delaware County. David Stanko, the director of the Pennsylvania Emergency Management Agency, summed up the situation bluntly: "Ultimately the best way of helping these homeowners is to get them out of harm's way."[22]

They aren't natural disasters, these floods that seem to be hitting the region with more regularity and causing more damage than in years past. They are the perfectly predictable, inevitable result of careless, untrammeled development that chooses to ignore natural watercourses. It is a problem in many places across suburban America. The water must have some place to go, after all, and eventually it will find it, even if your basement is in the way. The difference in the Delaware Valley, as Messrs. Sharf and Wescott remind us, is that people in this region have been covering up and forgetting about watercourses longer than most.

Covered up or not, recollected however dimly, the watercourses continue to shape the region.

Take a walk with the landscape architect Michael Nairn along Mill Creek in West Philadelphia. The area is rough in some blocks, merely shabby in others, struggling in most places, still wrestling with depopulation and the loss of its economic vitality over the last forty years. Dick Clark once broadcast American Bandstand from this neighborhood, but you can't imagine that he's stopped by anytime recently. Mill Creek, of course, isn't there anymore and so a walk along it, through this very real city neighborhood, requires the work of the imagination.

Michael tells you first to notice the contour of the land. And once you start looking, you realize that there is a stream bed here, a gentle slope on two sides, cutting across the rectilinear grid and moving generally south and east. Eventually Mill Creek follows Forty-third Street, into Clark Park, emptying finally into the Schuylkill.

Once your eye has picked up this natural feature, or what remains of it, he tells you to look at the human accretion that sits on top. As we follow the course of Mill Creek, zigzagging on a grid, trying to follow a diagonal, you begin to realize that the worst examples of decay and abandonment seem to be located in the bottom of the bed, or near to it. Upslope, the buildings seem to be faring better.

Michael offers his explanation: the buildings, businesses, and homes sitting at the bottom probably suffered the worst effects of the water over the years. In some cases, that damage, mold, and rot may have gotten too expensive for people to fix, and so when they left, no one wanted to buy the house. In other cases, the damage became serious enough to cause structural damage. In either case, the result was abandonment. And like a pebble tossed in a pond, one abandoned building creates a ripple of blight up and down the block.

For landscape architects like Michael, there is an obvious solution to flooding and blight both. Restore at least some of the original watercourses. Doing this would create green corridors, crisscrossing not only the city but perhaps larger sections of the region. Those green corridors, in turn, would do a better job of dealing with the flow of water, and areas that once dreaded flooding would now have an extraordinary neighborhood asset. People would be reconnected to the water.

Michael has been involved with a larger group studying and creating such a plan for Mill Creek and to talk about it is to get excited by it. Once you pause to consider it, the idea seems so simply and absolutely right: by restoring the ecological health of some of our watercourses, we might very well restore some of the balance to the human ecology as well.

The alternative, of course, is more of the same. More attempts to divert, contain, reengineer the natural flow of water through the region's watershed. And, almost inevitably, more of the same problems of runoff and flooding. In the end, the water always wins.

You can fish now in the Schuylkill, and plenty of people do, though you still probably shouldn't eat what you catch (though plenty of people do). The river has cleaned up quite a bit over the last generation. Shad, which fed George Washington's troops at

Valley Forge, are running again. Walleye too, and they are particularly sensitive to pollution. The fish are back also in the tidal Delaware, not in huge quantities but in growing numbers paralleling the efforts to clean up the river. Amazing, really, given how toxic the river was as recently as the 1970s and how much industry still hugs its banks.

There are two ways to look at those returning fish. On the one hand, they have only come back because the industrial activity along the rivers has left, taking with it jobs and whole communities that depended on them. On the other, those fish are harbingers of an incredible ecological recovery that few could have predicted.

It is not a region of spectacular natural features. And yet the Delaware Valley concentrates more ecological areas into a small space than almost anywhere else in the nation. A two-hour drive from City Hall can bring you into almost any kind of habitat—from ocean, tidal basin, and salt marsh to deciduous and coniferous forests to mountains.

The two rivers, the Delaware and the Schuylkill, are surely the most significant natural features that traverse Greater Philadelphia. As the architect Alan Greenberger notes, great cities are usually built upon a combination of a great street pattern and natural features. Philadelphia surely has the first of those requisites, but it has largely squandered the second: its waterfronts.[23] The city itself has nearly forty miles of river front, and the region as a whole probably has hundreds.

The rivers don't take much interest in state boundaries, county lines, and differing municipal jurisdictions. So to reconnect people in the Delaware Valley to the rivers is one way to imagine a greater regional cohesion and identity. We all share and depend on our rivers, however else we might differ. And in using the rivers as a thread to tie Greater Philadelphia together, the Schuylkill, not the Delaware, leads the way.

Fig. 25. The beautiful and the industrial. A view from the Schuylkill Canal towpath. Author's photo.

It is now possible to bike or walk along the Schuylkill from Center City all the way to Valley Forge, and from there to continue on even further into the Schuylkill watershed. The route takes you through Fairmount Park, along what remains of the old Schuylkill Canal towpath through the thoroughly gentrified Manayunk, and past Norristown and Conshohocken.

It's a great ride and the water is almost always in sight. At that speed you can genuinely appreciate the features of the river and, depending on the time of year, stop to admire the wild flowers, the turtles sunning themselves, the goldfinches flashing brilliantly from one tree to another. There are also reminders along the way of the river's earlier use as an industrial avenue. Perhaps the most remarkable aspect of the Schuylkill's recent transformation is how these remnants have blended into the scenery.

Bringing people back to the river in this way has helped make it possible to imagine the revitalization of the small, struggling towns that bloomed during the industrial era and have wilted since. Norristown, the seat of Montgomery County, one of the nation's wealthiest counties, is itself a poor, depressed town. But the town's underutilized and underappreciated river frontage may prove to be one key in Norristown's rebirth.

A town of thirty thousand and slipping, Norristown has deep problems that have been festering for years. But a number of developers see the town's Schuylkill waterfront as a tremendous opportunity. Already, artists have moved into a few old factory buildings, and they have river views.[24]

There are other towns along the river with similar problems and with similar promise. When one is tooling along on a bike, it isn't easy to imagine the Schuylkill as a necklace, dotted with newly vibrant, interesting towns, each one embracing the river in its own way rather than turning their collective backs on it.

Downriver, back in the city, the Schuylkill River Development Corporation (SRDC) has plans no less ambitious. For starters, it intends to extend that path (it calls it a greenway) further south. All the way south, jumping from the eastern bank to the western, down to Bartram's Garden and beyond to the eighteenth-century Fort Mifflin.

Not content with this, the SRDC has envisioned turning the river itself into a great civic space, creating spaces for concerts and other events, boat launches, and ferry service up and down the river. The Schuylkill above the dam at the Water Works has long been the center of American rowing. Each year there are nearly three dozen regattas on the Schuylkill, more than twice that held on any other American river, and they attract thousands of rowers and fans each year. Now the Schuylkill "Navy," the coalition of rowing clubs that occupy Boathouse Row, is planning a few races in the lower portion of the Schuylkill as a way to help draw more attention to this still-neglected waterway.

The SRDC's master plan, entitled appropriately enough "Rediscovering Philadelphia's Hidden River," is filled with dazzling ideas. The plan also imagines the river not merely as a recreational facility but as an engine to drive the revitalization of struggling neighborhoods and old industrial sites that line the Schuylkill as it nears its confluence with the Delaware.

It will be difficult to make these dreams come to life and expensive to be sure. Smartly, the SRDC has approached the whole project as a series of smaller, discrete ones, each one of which is achievable and whose achievement will create momentum for the next one. Reading through "Rediscovering Philadelphia's Hidden River," one can't help but start to cheer. This is what a great river through a great city ought to be.

Over on the tidal Delaware, the reimagining hasn't come nearly so far. There is no path along the region's major waterway, nor, so far as I'm aware, any serious plans to connect the public with it. It is still a patchwork of docks, working industrial sites, and abandoned ones. Recent development on the Philadelphia side has either been entirely for private use or worse has ignored the river altogether. As one indication of the indifference with which people treat the river, Camden used several acres of prime, waterfront real estate to build a prison.

But more recently, those who control Camden have been very aggressive about redeveloping their side of the river as an ensemble of tourist attractions. The wholesale redevelopment occurring on the Camden waterfront reflects, at one level, the level of utter abandonment and decay that it had reached. That prison may even be relocated sometime soon.[25]

The renaissance of Center City has begun to spread up the Delaware now. Several large-scale residential and mixed-use projects are being planned along the river in neighborhoods such as Fishtown and Bridesburg. Yet even as these towers rise there has been little planning to ensure that the river itself will be a public asset. In fact, one of the first of these developments will be a high-rise, luxury, gated community.

Upriver you can get to the river more easily because it was

never cut off to quite the same extent. No big industry, no big road projects. And because of that, many in the region see this section of the Delaware as a real tourist attraction, especially during the summer months. Fittingly enough, the postindustrial tourist economy of this area will be built around what remains of its early industrial history: the Delaware Canal.

The canal was opened in 1832 and carried barges for almost exactly a century. The last one came down in 1931. Delaware Canal State Park stretches for sixty miles, hugging the Pennsylvania side of the river, from Bristol to Easton. The towpath is still there, making it possible and very pleasant to walk or ride along its length. There is one lock—number 11—still there and when it is finally repaired and made operable, barges will again run the canal, this time carrying tourists.[26]

By and large, the vision for the Delaware in and around Philadelphia does not extend much beyond creating a tourist destination. The Delaware River Port Authority, which operates the bridges that span the river among other things, announced a marketing strategy for the waterfront, beginning with a somewhat contrived renaming: Independence Harbor. The idea is to promote the variety of attractions on and near the water to the 28 million people who live within a day trip of the river. The goal seems to be to compete with Baltimore's Inner Harbor. The project consultant, Michael Rubin, believes that the tourist attractions in Philadelphia/Camden are simply more in number and greater in quality than those in Baltimore. "Our ships are more historically significant than theirs," Rubin said in 2002. "Our Old City dwarfs their Fell's Point."[27]

Put this way, the claim—and thus the whole plan—seems small. Too small for such a great river. Surely there are plenty of reasons for tourists to come to the Delaware, and I hope they do, dropping their dollars along the way. But marketing the river as a theme park for out-of-towners misses the point. It misses the river itself.

Penn's holy experiment began on the Delaware, and his city grew alongside it. The Delaware, and the Schuylkill, played central roles in the development of the region. Only in the last half century have people in the Delaware Valley forgotten their waterways. As the region emerges from the industrial age into the post-industrial age, one way to make the area a lively, attractive place to live will be to put the rivers back onto the center stage of our civic and public lives.

The rivers, after all, have been here from the beginning. They have seen it all.

In the Mind's Eye: Imagining the Philadelphia Region

Boathouse Row with the lights on. The Liberty Bell. The Art Museum. Independence Hall. William Penn on top of City Hall's tower.

All of these symbolize Philadelphia. They function visually as instantly recognizable shorthand for the city, and as such tend to get used whenever quick visual cues are necessary: ad campaigns, promo shots on TV, filler during broadcasts of Philadelphia sporting events.

They serve their purpose well because they are visually compelling and because they are, each of them, distinctive. In the blink of an eye, they signal "Philadelphia" and no place else. After all, most important American cities have art museums, but none has our Parthenon of Art sitting atop an acropolis.

These symbols also serve to remind us that while all cities and their regions constitute real places, with measurable populations, economic activity, political dynamics, and so forth, they also exist imaginatively. Indeed, I think it does not go too far to say that cities and their surroundings are defined through the production of cultural material—the work of artists, photographers, writers, architects, musicians, and others—at least as much as in any other way.

We may live, work in, or travel to the Delaware Valley, but if we pause to ask what the place *means*, if we are asked to describe it for someone else, we do so, I suspect, by drawing on some cultural metaphor. "It's still Rocky's town," wrote Gary Thompson not long ago, alluding to one of the most important cultural products that fixed a certain Philadelphia identity in the imagination. This is as it should be. While human beings may have first assembled in the congregations called cities as a way of fostering economic activity and of protecting themselves from other groups, cities quickly became the places where all the things we associate with civilization developed and grew: math and writing, art and music, politics and government. City and civilization, after all, share the same root word.

This is just as true of American cities as it is of cities found in Europe, Asia, or Africa. American cities, the important ones anyway, have been and remain sites of cultural dynamism. What makes Greater Philadelphia a bit different from the nation's other large metropolitan centers is the extent to which the whole region, not just the city itself, has given shape to cultural production, and how that production, in turn, has given specific parts of the region a specific identity.

Take, for example, the Main Line. We all know what we mean by that phrase: old money, suburban in the toney rather than banal sense, WASPy. We mean, in other words, Katherine Hepburn in *The Philadelphia Story*. That 1940 movie created for the Main Line an image that has endured to this day, regardless of whether or not it was or is in any way faithful. People around the country who have never been anywhere near Gladwyne or Merion "know" the Main Line because they have seen that movie.

In the twentieth century, Philadelphia has gotten a reputation for being culturally conservative, staid, stodgy. Case in point: the Pennsylvania Academy of the Fine Arts. As a training ground for painters and sculptors it has remained, well, academic. In the twentieth century the Academy did not seem much interested in modernism or any of its descendants. After World War II, when New York replaced Paris as the center of gravity in the art world, with abstraction at its center, the Academy, which still clung to its traditions of representational and figurative work, seem hopelessly out of step and stuck, like its flagship building, in the nineteenth century.

In fact, this reputation simply ignores many of the region's cultural products. Take, for example, architecture. Frank Furness stands now as easily the most innovative, wildly imaginative architect of the late nineteenth century. A generation later, the firm of Howe and Lescaze put up the PSFS Building in 1932, the first skyscraper done in the international modern style in the nation. A generation after that a Philadelphia school coalesced around the brilliant Louis Kahn, who grew up in Northern Liberties. And even as Kahn was developing his brand of modernism, a young Robert Venturi, from South Philadelphia, was conceiving of his book *Complexity and Contradiction in Architecture*, which many feel helped usher in postmodernism.

Even at the venerable Academy what was once dismissed as stodginess now strikes some as a kind of wisdom. When a group of trendy New York artists, including Will Cotton, Delia Brown, and Guy Richards Smits, gathered to do—of all things—figure drawing, one of them exhorted the others to go to the Pennsylvania Academy. "You gotta go," he said, "It's the only place in America that didn't throw out their [nineteenth-century] plaster casts."[1]

The charge of cultural conservativism may also be ever so slightly racist, given that it ignores Philadelphia's centrality for black culture. Philadelphia was home to the nation's first black intelligentsia in the late eighteenth century and the early nineteenth. In the twentieth century, to take the example of music, the city has been the home of musicians as varied as the Dixie Hummingbirds, who redefined the gospel quartet, John Coltrane, and the Roots.

Still, to counter the charge with a litany of the Delaware Valley's rich contributions to our cultural life misses the point, I suspect. What those who dismiss Philadelphia's culture as stodgy really mean is that the city never developed a self-conscious avant-garde, proclaiming itself as new, oppositional, and deliberately set apart. Philadelphia never grew a Bohemia. True enough. But Philadelphia's artists, writers, musicians have been shaped by a slightly different set of concerns, which come out of the history and traditions of the region, and which in turn shape the identity of the place itself.

We can see in the region's cultural productions some of the themes we have already covered—the interplay between history and the present, the utopian impulses of tolerance and plurality, the particularities of a subtle landscape and the way humans have interacted with it, and perhaps most of all the intersections between highbrow and lowbrow. Remember, after all, that *The Philadelphia Story* is decidedly not a "lifestyles of the wealthy and WASPy" tale. It is a comedy through which the seemingly imperious Katherine Hepburn made fun of herself. *The Philadelphia Story* has allowed audiences to laugh at Hepburn, not with her, and by extension for us lowbrows to poke fun at the highbrows.

It is still Rocky's town in some ways, because that movie captured a sense of this place where a working-class bum from South Philly can be embraced as a hero despite the fact that he loses the big fight. And the iconic moment in that film comes when Rocky runs up the steps of the Philadelphia Museum of Art and raises his arms in a gesture almost of conquest. Never did highbrow meet lowbrow more dramatically.[2]

This chapter, then, will look at how a number of Philadelphians have imagined this region and presented their vision to the rest of us.

*   *   *

In the early republic Philadelphia served as the nation's cultural capital just as it served as its political and financial capital. It was home to the nation's first important cultural institution, Peale's Museum. Charles Willson Peale was both a member of the founding generation and their painter. He, and members of his remarkable family, painted the portraits of many of the luminaries who came through Philadelphia in the late eighteenth century.

Peale believed earnestly that the new nation needed a museum, and he took it upon himself to organize one. The museum that came to bear his name housed a wonderful collection of natural history specimens, including eventually a skeleton of a mastodon, demonstrating the natural wonders of the United States, and a collection of portraits whose sitters represented the human accomplishments of the fledgling nation.

Creating a museum collection served a nationalistic function for Peale, highlighting that the United States did indeed have both science and art, whatever the Europeans might say of us. But he also believed a museum would serve an important educational role in a republic whose virtue depended on the wisdom of its citizens. In a lecture he explained why a collection of natural history specimens was of such importance to the nation: "The farmer ought to know that snakes feed on field mice and moles, which would otherwise destroy whole fields of corn. . . . To the merchant, the study of nature is scarcely less interesting, whose traffic lies altogether in material either raw from the stores of nature or *wrought* by the hand of ingenious art. . . . The mechanic ought to possess an accurate knowledge of many of the qualities of those materials with which his art is connected."[3]

Farmer, merchant, mechanic. A cross-section of American society in the late eighteenth century, and Peale thought his museum would be of use to all of them.

Peale's museum did not survive the first few decades of the nineteenth century, but his democratic, educational impulse did.

Nineteenth-century Philadelphia became the cradle of American institution building, and almost all of those institutions took as their task democratic education in order to create republican citizens.

The Academy of Natural Sciences, for example, the successor to Peale's Museum in some ways, stands as the oldest continuously operating natural history museum in the nation. Founded in 1812 by a collection of Philadelphia gentlemen, the academy opened its museum to the public in 1826. It was a popular attraction in the city, a place where visitors saw a dazzling variety of natural specimens all labeled and arranged in an order that reflected the Creator's design for the natural world. And this marvelous museum was opened for free. In 1867 the Academy scored another first when it put the hadrosaurus on display. Discovered in New Jersey, the hadrosaurus was the first dinosaur found in the United States and it created an enormous sensation. At that point, the academy began to charge an admission fee as a way of trying to keep the crowds under control (some feared that the building itself was in danger of collapse under the weight of all those visitors). It didn't work. In 1869 nearly one hundred thousand people trooped through the halls of the Academy, and they weren't coming to see the stuffed birds and the insects impaled on pins.

Two years before the galleries of the Academy were opened to the public, in 1824, W. H. Keating and Samuel Vaughn Merrick, two young Philadelphia mechanics, founded the Franklin Institute and opened its membership "to all men and women of intelligence, character and ambition who are interested in science."[4] Before it evolved into a museum of science and technology, which happened in the 1920s and 1930s, the Franklin Institute sponsored lectures, offered classes, and published a journal, all with the goal of "the promotion of the mechanic arts." In an age before engineering schools and vocational training programs, the Franklin Institute provided that kind of education to countless Philadelphia mechanics, and they in turn contributed to making the city a leading center of industrial innovation.

Even the Philadelphia Museum of Art, lofty and elite as it now looks, began its life as an institution where art and industry, the beautiful and the useful, intersected. The Pennsylvania Museum (as it was called until the 1930s) was founded in the wake of the 1876 centennial celebrations in Fairmount Park and housed in Memorial Hall until it relocated to the "new" building at the end of the Benjamin Franklin Parkway in 1928.

As the Pennsylvania Museum it also ran the School of Industrial Arts. Working in tandem, the museum and the school were charged with displaying and teaching all branches of art "applied to industry." As a leading center for industrial art education, the museum and the school hoped to contribute to Philadelphia's industrial economy in tangible, useful ways. The museum's intended audience, therefore, was not only, or even primarily, the wealthy and privileged, "those whose aesthetic tastes have already been developed by study or travel," but rather "that vast majority of our citizens, the artisans and mechanics, for whom it is the only resort of the kind accessible."[5] At the very moment when working men were being denied access to New York's Metropolitan Museum of Art—a palace of elitism if ever there was one—the Pennsylvania Museum welcomed them in. The line separating highbrow and lowbrow in Philadelphia's cultural world has always been more fluid.

While Philadelphia has a remarkable collection of institutions that date their origins back to the nineteenth or even eighteenth centuries—the American Philosophical Society, the Library Company, the Historical Society of Pennsylvania, in addition to those we have just discussed—they have all of necessity grown, evolved, changed to meet new demands, new constituencies, and new circumstances.

Except one.

West of Broad Street, at the corner of Seventeenth and Montgomery Streets, in a rough North Philadelphia neighborhood sits the Wagner Free Institute of Science. The building is imposing in this neighborhood, filled largely now with late nineteenth-century row houses, most of which have seen better days. But it isn't grand or in any way pretentious. Big windows, plain neoclassical pediments—the Wagner looks like a simple nineteenth-century Presbyterian church more than anything else.

To step inside, however, is to be transported almost magically back to the nineteenth century.

In 1855, William and Louisa Wagner opened their Free Institute to provide scientific courses and lectures to the general public. William Wagner had made his fortune as a lieutenant to Stephen Girard, whose own institutional contribution to the mission of democratic education was to establish and endow a college for orphaned boys, which still bears his name.

The Wagner's building included a lecture hall, complete with scientific apparatus for demonstrations, and a reference library, both on the first floor. On the top floor, in a large barnlike space, Wagner installed a magnificent museum gallery of natural history. The gallery contains, if not all, then at least many creatures great and small, from fossil clams to pickled fish to the type specimen for the saber-toothed tiger.

Remarkably, it is all still there, virtually unchanged, just as it was at the end of the nineteenth century. More remarkable still because so much around the Wagner has changed so dramatically. Certainly the world of science barely resembles the carefully arranged and lovingly labeled specimens in the Wagner's glass cases. And science museums have transformed into very different places as well, filled now with technological enhancements, kid-friendly activities, and all manner of things designed to make science fun.

The Wagner's neighborhood too has experienced the full cycle of economic prosperity and decline, of population growth and contraction, and of racial succession and racial violence. Just a few blocks away Philadelphia's worst race riot of the 1960s exploded in 1964, shortly after the Wagner celebrated its one hundredth birthday. Yet the Wagner continues to do what it has always done. Over one hundred and fifty years after its founding, it stands in its North Philadelphia neighborhood as the oldest continuously operating adult education program in the nation.

The Wagner is surely the finest example of a nineteenth-century museum in the United States and I confess that it is one of my favorite institutions in the region. It is by no means well endowed or well funded and so I find its stubborn refusal to change too much admirable, its continuing commitment to its mission almost heroic. I also do not think there is a better place to see—to feel—the particular impulses that drove Philadelphians to build cultural institutions in the nineteenth century than the Wagner Free Institute of Science.

In the nineteenth century, especially in the years before the Civil War, Philadelphia nurtured many of the nation's artists. Some gravitated to the Pennsylvania Academy, while others came through the city to partake in varying degrees of the city's cultural and intellectual life.

Despite this, however, it wasn't until after the Civil War that the city produced an artist who could properly be called a Philadelphia painter, who drew his work from the life of the city itself and whose images, in turn, helped to fix that life in our imagination. That painter, of course, was Thomas Eakins.

Eakins was a Philadelphian born and bred. One of the many illustrious graduates of the city's Central High School (still among the top five high schools in the state), he studied at the Pennsylvania Academy. He spent some time studying in Paris as well, but other than that sojourn he rarely left the region and never for significant lengths of time.

Fig. 26. Heroes for their time. Thomas Eakins painted those Philadelphians who triumphed in the new industrial city, such as the champion rower Max Schmitt. Thomas Eakins, *The Champion Single Scull (Max Schmitt in a Single Scull)*. The Metropolitan Museum of Art, Purchase, The Alfred N. Punnett Endowment Fund and George D. Pratt Gift, 1934. (34.92.) All rights reserved, The Metropolitan Museum of Art.

Eakins arrived on the art scene in the 1870s with stunning depictions of rowers on the Schuylkill River and with powerful portraits of prominent Philadelphians. These remain his best-known works. Through both, Eakins set out to capture what he felt to be the spirit and essence of modern Philadelphia, a place full of dynamism and energy.

As the art historian Elizabeth Johns has wonderfully demonstrated, Eakins gravitated toward rowing because he admired the way it demanded fine conditioning of its participants and a mastery of balance, coordination, and timing.[6] The boats themselves—the sculls—were new, marvellous pieces of industrial design and engineering that enabled rowers to knife sleekly through the water, leaving barely a ripple or wake. Done right, and there was the trick, the new sport of rowing combined the very latest technological innovations with athletic grace. And Philadelphia quickly became the nation's leading center for rowing. The artistic and the mechanical were harmonious again.

It wasn't only champion rowers whom Eakins captured in those paintings—Max Schmitt and the Biglin brothers—but the river itself. As I discussed in Chapter 5, the stretch of the Schuylkill above the dam at the Water Works was surrounded on both sides by Fairmount Park. In creating the park, the city unwittingly created the most picturesque rowing venue in the country—a broad, easygoing river rolling for several miles through landscaped greenery. Eakins captured that river along with the rowers.

These elements all come together in *Max Schmitt in a Single Scull*. Eakins has caught Schmitt at a moment of pause or rest. He looks back at us, hands still on the oars, relaxed but commanding. Eakins has put us in the rower's world further by placing us almost on Schmitt's level, quite literally in the river, as if Eakins had set up his easel in a nearby boat. But he teases us about that because there he is, in another scull, farther down the river. By inserting himself autobiographically in this painting Eakins also asserted that he too was part of this world of rowers and rowing. He knew whereof he painted.

In addition to the river and its banks, Eakins also shows us that the river has been traversed by several bridges. Here too is the evidence of engineering and industrial accomplishment. Eakins makes no attempt to hide the industrial city by creating a fake pastoral scene but rather shows us a harmonious visual interplay between the human and the natural, between the industrial and the bucolic.

The Gross Clinic would seem, on its surface, to be an altogether different kind of painting. Now we are inside, rather than out, and looking at a scene heavy with shadow and darkness rather than suffused with light. There is no missing or mistaking Dr. Gross—he looms up at us, occupying the center stage of this composition. And "stage" is not a bad word because we are in a theater. Dr. Gross lectures to a class of medical students while performing surgery in an operating theater. And Eakins is here too, having sketched himself in as one of the students watching the performance.

The scene strikes us first for its graphicness. The retracted incision and the exposed thigh and buttock of the patient are unavoidable (as is the patient's poor mother, who cringes at the sight). Most dramatically of all, Eakins paints Dr. Gross's hand holding the scalpel and covered in blood. Nothing euphemistic or sugar-coated about this scene. This is a surgeon at work, a teacher in front of his class, and the work and subject matter is flesh and blood and bone.

Despite the apparent differences between the two paintings, *The Gross Clinic* shares with *Max Schmitt* a concern with presenting modern, progressive Philadelphia and the men who make it possible. Philadelphia had already become an international center of medicine and medical research (it still is) and Dr. Gross was among the leading lights of that world. Eakins paints him, in a palpable way, at the height of his powers. But Eakins is also showing us an almost miraculous medical innovation as well. Look carefully across the foreshortened length of the patient's body and you will see that his head is being covered with cloth. The cloth, we realize, is soaked in chloroform and the man holding it is an anesthesiologist. This is new—just ten years earlier, during the Civil War, surgical patients were still biting bullets and downing whiskey to ease the pain. Now, Eakins shows us, we have entered an entirely new era in surgical procedure. Despite our uneasiness with the blood and gore, this patient feels no pain.

The doctor and the athlete share something else as well. Both achieved their fame and reputation entirely because of their meritorious accomplishments. Neither enjoyed his status because of some unearned privilege or merely because he was rich. In fact, though Eakins was as brilliant a portrait painter as this nation has ever produced, he was never much interested in immortalizing Philadelphia's blue bloods and old money elites. That testy relationship with Philadelphia's aristocracy, as much as the scandal he created when he permitted female students at the Pennsylvania Academy to draw from live male nude models, cost Eakins his job at the Pennsylvania Academy. Eakins was drawn to those whose talents and hard work alone enabled them to triumph in the modern city. He never had the chance to paint Benjamin Franklin, that most emblematic of Philadelphians, but he did paint the most memorable portrait of the aged Walt Whitman, the unschooled proletariat's poet, who by the time Eakins painted him lived across the river on Mickle Street in Camden.

More people come to the Schuylkill River each year to row and to watch boat races than any other place in the country. But they don't precisely come to the Schuylkill, at least those who have ever seen Eakins's rowing paintings. Making a picture of someplace changes that place forever, and thus we come to the place Eakins painted to watch the boats glide through the water, and we see it through his eyes as much through our own.

Eakins's studio is gone now, demolished as part of the construction of the Kimmel Center, the new home of the Philadelphia Orchestra, but his house is still there on Mt. Vernon Street, and it is still a hub of artistic activity. Fittingly enough, the place where Philadelphia's greatest classically trained painter lived is now the headquarters of the nation's most vibrant ongoing public art project, the Mural Arts Program. Highbrow and lowbrow, past and present intersect everyday at 1729 Mt. Vernon.

The Mural Arts Program began in 1984 as a part of the Philadelphia Anti-Graffiti Network's effort to deal with what was at the time a proliferating problem of graffiti in many city neighborhoods. The network hired the mural artist Jane Golden and gave her the task of persuading graffiti writers to switch genres and become muralists instead.

The project worked extraordinarily well. Graffiti, by no means eliminated, started to wane dramatically and murals started to pop up everywhere across the city. By 1996, Golden was directing the free-standing Mural Arts Program. Its educational programs reach over one thousand young people annually. Employing roughly three hundred artists each year, the Mural Arts Program may well be the single largest employer of visual artists in the whole region. The program has, in turn, created its own nonprofit arm, the Mural Arts Advocates, whose mission is to work with youth and foster neighborhood revitalization.

The idea is straightforward and almost utilitarian. Given the large number of vacant structures, especially in the old industrial neighborhoods around the city, there are countless surfaces that might attract graffiti. Graffiti, in turn, contributes to a sense within a neighborhood that the neighborhood is in decline, that it is neglected, that no one cares.

Golden and her squads of young muralists, working with neighborhood leaders, take one of those surfaces—often the side of a building facing a vacant lot—and cover it with a mural. The early efforts of the MAP looked homemade and amateurish. And they were, at least by comparison. As the project grew, developed, and matured so did the murals themselves. Coordinated now by professional artists, they are liable to include multiple figures, employ fractured perspective, range from representation to abstraction. And they are liable to be three or four storeys high. Most importantly of all these murals represent Philadelphia—they can be found in virtually every city neighborhood, and the faces and figures that inhabit them are all the faces and figures of the city.

There are, I think, two primary joys about public art. First are the unexpected ways public art can turn the city spaces and streetscapes into whimsical stage sets, creating juxtapositions that make us see both the art and the city in different ways. Second, public art has the capacity to break through our day, to make us pause, if only briefly, to think about something other than what we had been occupied with just a moment before. All art, of course, serves that purpose, but public art does it by surprise. And in this sense, the murals that now cover thousands of square feet all over Philadelphia are terrific public art. They are extraordinary things found in all sorts of ordinary places, and when you come across one of these creations it can take your breath away. Go visit the mural of Philadelphia's own Patti La-Belle, all thirty feet of her, facing Thirty-fourth Street by the zoo and see if your day isn't just a little bit better for the trip. In October, now designated Mural Arts Month in Philadelphia, roughly five thousand people, locals and out-of-towners, participate in mural tours, lectures, and workshops. Around the country Philadelphia has become known as the City of Murals.

The run-away success of the Mural Arts Program, and the way in which it has been embraced by Philadelphians of all stripes, has created its own irony. Murals were never really the goal of the program. Engaging kids in productive activities, employing artists, giving neighborhoods things to be proud of—these have always been the real objectives of the Mural Arts Program. The murals themselves have simply been the vehicle through which to achieve them.

The murals, however, have become much beloved. In sections of town that are now experiencing a rebirth, the murals sometimes find themselves threatened by new construction. Having helped a neighborhood, in some small way, turn around, the murals become victims of that very success. In several instances this has created a real dilemma for neighborhoods that want revitalization but don't want to lose their murals. When the Red Cross built a new building on an empty West Philadelphia lot, it covered up one of my favorite murals. It depicted a young black boy, five years old maybe, one arm raised over his head, with the caption

Fig. 27. Walt Whitman spent the end of his life on Mickle Avenue in Camden. His spirit lives on Powelton Avenue in West Philadelphia. This version of the mural shown here replaced an earlier version on the side of a house. Mural after a painting by Sydney Goodman. Courtesy of the Mural Arts Program.

"I am large. I contain multitudes." The line is from Walt Whitman, Camden's poet of the people, and I can't help but believe he would have been delighted to see it used on this mural. The Red Cross also recognized how wonderfully perfect it was and the organization had the painting re-created on the facade of its new facility.

As with so many things about Philadelphia, public art too has a long history, dating back at least as far as 1792, when a toga-clad Benjamin Franklin carved in marble was hoisted over the main entrance to the Library Company. (The building is gone, but the sculpture remains at the entrance to the Library Company on Locust Street.) Philadelphians have been putting up public art ever since. The result is a collection of sculpture, monuments, installations, even lighting designs that is the envy of any city in the nation. Taking an easy stroll through town, one can come across works by Claus Oldenberg, Jacques Lipshitz, three generations of Calders, George Segal, Louise Nevelson without even breaking a sweat. There is no major sculpture garden in the Delaware Valley, but in a sense, the city itself—especially Center City—is a great outdoor art installation. More so than in just about any other American city, public art is part of the daily experience of Philadelphians.

Charles Sheeler had a different kind of modernity on his mind from Thomas Eakins when he began his career as a painter. Sheeler belongs to the generation of painters who came after Eakins. Eakins was at the end of his life and long past his tenure at the Academy when Sheeler came there to study. He came of artistic age not so much in the modern world but in the Modern world—that moment early in the twentieth century when the currents of modernism in art and literature swirled excitingly.

Sheeler went to Paris with his friend, the painter Morton Schaumberg, just after World War I to experience this moment at its epicenter. He returned somewhat unsure how to wed his Academy training, still rooted in the realist traditions of the nineteenth century, with his exposure to the radical departures of European modernism. In his confusion, he began spending time in Doylestown, Bucks County.

Sheeler would mature into one of America's most interesting modernist painters, his work exhibiting a clean, sharp realism some have called "precisionist." His best-known paintings may

Fig. 28. Eighteenth-century modernism. Charles Sheeler developed his modernist vision by spending time looking at the eighteenth-century landscapes and buildings of Bucks County. Charles Sheeler, *Bucks County Barn*. Collection of the Whitney Museum of American Art. Gift of Gertrude Vanderbilt Whitney. Photograph copyright © 1997: Whitney Museum of American Art, New York.

be those of American industry, like *Rolling Power*, and the series of images of Henry Ford's River Rouge plant, which began as a photographic series commissioned by Ford himself.

Sheeler began to develop his vision in Doylestown. He was drawn to the agricultural landscape that still existed in Bucks County and in particular to the vernacular architecture of eighteenth- and nineteenth-century barns and of farm houses, one of which Sheeler rented as his Bucks County studio.

It is easy to see what Sheeler found appealing about the Bucks County buildings—the stark simplicity, the purely functional geometry, the integrity of the building materials. Some of his sketches of barns have the building itself floating, disconnected from any landscape, a pure object considered entirely for its own sake. His first biographer, Constance Rourke, wrote in 1938 of the house Sheeler rented in Doylestown, "Within were strong beams, simple panels, deep embrasures. . . . All was clarity: the walls were of that peculiar white which only freshly burned lime seems able to create."

The title of Rourke's biography captures Sheeler's achievement nicely. She called it *Artist in the American Tradition*. What she recognized was Sheeler's ability to combine modernist aesthetics with the vernacular material of American history. Painting in Doylestown shortly after his return from Europe, Sheeler was, in Rourke's assessment, "tapping into the main source by his use of architectural forms in Bucks County and likewise by his more or less conscious study of the handicrafts he found thereabouts."[7]

In order to create an American modernism, Sheeler looked to the forms of the past, and formatively to the past shaped by the farmers of Bucks County. For Sheeler in his Bucks County work, the connection between past and present was seamless. In this sense, he was, in the way I discussed in Chapter 3, thoroughly a Philadelphian.

In the passage I just quoted, Rourke mentions not only Bucks County architecture but also its "handicrafts" as playing an important role in Sheeler's work. She does not mention that during his time in Doylestown Sheeler had a remarkable introduction to those handicrafts through the person of Henry Mercer.

Mercer was near the end of his life by the time Sheeler rented the farmhouse next door. He came from an old Doylestown family and had the means to live independently. After graduating from Harvard, he dabbled in law and became an archaeologist—he was among the first curators of the University of Pennsylvania's Museum of Archaeology and Anthropology—and by the 1890s settled into what became his life's work.

Mercer became a collector, and he prowled the Bucks County countryside relentlessly looking to buy the "handicrafts" of the preindustrial small town and agricultural life that had thrived there through the eighteenth century and the early nineteenth. Looking back on it, Mercer remembered this shift from archaeology to collecting in an almost epiphanic way:

It was probably one day in February or March of the spring of 1897 that I went to the premises of one of our fellow-citizens, who had been in the habit of going to country sales and at the last moment buying what they called "penny lots," that is to say valueless masses of obsolete utensils or objects which were regarded as useless. . . . The particular object of the visit above mentioned, was to buy a pair of tongs for an old fashioned fireplace, but when I came to hunt out the tongs from the midst of a disordered pile of old wagons, gum-tree salt-boxes, flax-brakes, straw beehives, tin dinner horns, rope-machines and spinning wheels . . . I was seized with a new enthusiasm and hurried over the country, rummaging the bake-ovens, wagon-houses, cellars, hay-lofts, smoke-houses, garrets, and chimney-corners, on this side of the Delaware valley.[8]

Eventually Mercer's enthusiasm would yield a collection numbering in the tens of thousands, housed in a museum he built for it in the center of Doylestown, a wonderfully, whimsically bizarre Rhine castle made entirely out of poured concrete. There is—and I can say this with a great deal of confidence—nothing like the Mercer Museum anywhere in the United States, and if you haven't been there yet, watch your chin when you enter, for your jaw will undoubtedly hit the floor.

Mercer did not gallop across Bucks County driven by mere antiquarianism, or whatever it is that infects people to collect compulsively. There was a method to his madness, or at least he thought there was. Mercer firmly believed the objects he collected—of the sort he litanied in that recollection—illustrated the history of Pennsylvania. In turn, he believed just as firmly that the history of Pennsylvania represented the history of the nation. In the catalogue to his first public exhibition he wrote: "In the largest sense the story of Eastern Pennsylvania and of its Bucks County is that of the whole nation. As often the founders of Indiana, Kansas and Missouri have returned to the shore of the Delaware to look with affectionate curiosity upon the birthplace of their ancestors."[9] Not for nothing did Mercer call this exhibit "Tools of the Nation Maker."

Mercer also wanted to use his collection to reorient how Americans understood their own history. Rather than focusing on the great men and big events, Mercer wanted history to consider ordinary people and their ordinary work as central to the history of the nation. In a lecture, he picked up one of the axes in his collection and posed this contrast: "You may go down to Independence Hall in Philadelphia, and stand in the room in which the Declaration of Independence was signed and there look upon the portraits of the signers. But do you think you are any nearer the essence of the matter there than you are here when you realize that ten thousand arms, seizing upon axes of this type, with an immense amount of labor and effort made it worth while to have a Declaration of Independence by cutting down one of the greatest forests in the North Temperate Zone?"[10] His museum, then, stands as a monument to Bucks County's settlers and farmers, to everyday people doing everyday things. And in those activities, Mercer believed, resided the real history of the nation.

We can't know to what extent Mercer and Sheeler chatted and shared ideas when the painter stayed in Doylestown, though they surely did to some extent. Both drew an immense cultural significance from the landscape of Bucks County and the way human forces shaped it. Sheeler saw the promise of modernism, and Mercer found the significance of history, both exploring simple Bucks County barns and the handicrafts of their builders.

Though Philadelphia has produced a prodigious number of painters and sculptors, though it has given rise to some of the most important architects of the nineteenth and twentieth centuries, though it has produced musicians of almost every variety, it has not been the home to an indigenous literary tradition, certainly not to the extent that Chicago and Boston have been.

Bucks County, on the other hand, has. Since the end of the nineteenth century, a few painters have made their reputations in Bucks County, but writers even more prominently. Never quite a colony, the writers who came to Bucks County during the twentieth century constituted more of a loose association. The journalist Josephine Herbst, who covered the Spanish Civil War in the 1930s and was blacklisted by McCarthyites for her work in the 1950s, was among the first prominent writers to buy a Bucks County retreat. She was followed by S. J. Perelman, the screenwriter and humorist, and his brother-in-law Nathanael West. He, in turn, so the story goes, persuaded Dorothy Parker and her husband Alan Campbell—another screenwriter—to move to Bucks County in 1936. At roughly the same moment, the poet Jean Toomer, a leading figure of the Harlem Renaissance, moved to Bucks County and stayed until his death in 1967.

The playwright George Kaufman set up house in a place called Barley Sheaf Farm, now a bed and breakfast operation, and he hosted John Steinbeck and the Marx Brothers among others. Kaufman collaborated with fellow writer and neighbor Moss Hart to write *George Washington Slept Here*, which became the basis some years later for the television series *Green Acres*.

James Michener, who grew up in Doylestown, certainly became the most successful of the Bucks County writers in the second half of the twentieth century. Before he went on to create the big epics for which he is best remembered, he won the Pulitzer Prize in 1948 for a collection of short stories titled *Tales of the South*

Pacific. Michener worked with Oscar Hammerstein, who had also moved to Bucks County, to turn those short stories into the musical *South Pacific*. Hammerstein, one half of the most successful Broadway musical duo of all time, never made it to Oklahoma as far as I know. The corn that grew as high as an elephant's eye actually grew in a field not too far from Doylestown.

It is, frankly, an astonishing roster of talent and accomplishment and yet it does not include Bucks County's most internationally famous, most celebrated writer. That honor belongs to Pearl Buck, who moved into a nineteenth-century farmhouse in Perkasie in 1935.

Born in 1892, Buck had grown up with missionary parents in China—speaking Chinese and English—and she spent most of her early life there. She and her family had to evacuate to Shanghai during the Boxer Rebellion of 1900, and she spent a terrifying day in hiding during the infamous Nanking Incident in 1927. She finally left the deteriorating conditions in China in 1934 and found her way to Bucks County.

By the time she arrived she had already established her literary celebrity. She had published a few short stories and one novel (*East Wind, West Wind*) in the 1920s and followed these in 1931 with *The Good Earth*. It was an astonishing blockbuster. It was the best-selling American novel of 1931 *and* 1932; it earned her a Pulitzer Prize and the Howells Medal. In 1937 MGM turned it into the most expensive film the studio had ever made. It led, in 1938, to the Nobel Prize in literature, making Buck only the second American, and the first woman, to win it.

That would suffice as a rich and successful career for anyone, but for Buck it proved merely a prelude. *The Good Earth* both defined Buck's career as a writer and stands as a metaphor for the work she did until her death in 1973. Through *The Good Earth* more Americans—more westerners—had their introduction to China. *The Good Earth* and Buck's other books about China have been translated into more languages than the work of any other American author according to statistics kept by the United Nations. Buck presented not an exoticized, remote, inscrutable China, but a China of hard-working peasants, struggling farmers, women who bear children while in the fields working. A deeply human China.

Buck spent her American life championing the causes of social justice and racial equality, and she acted as a bridge between cultures. She worked alongside Eleanor Roosevelt, wrote for the NAACP's magazine *The Crisis*, and served on the board of trustees of Howard University for twenty years. She was a feminist a generation early—the first edition of Betty Friedan's *The Feminine Mystique* carried an endorsement from Buck. Outraged that American adoption agencies refused to place Asian or mixed-race children, in 1949 she founded Welcome House, the first international, interracial adoption agency in the world. While she won a Nobel Prize in literature, she deserved the Nobel Peace Prize as well.

And in the middle of all this—the meetings, the organizations, the travel, the constant lobbying and speechmaking—she found some time to write. Over seventy books, in fact, by the time she died, in almost every genre—novels, biographies, autobiography, children's stories, poetry, plays, and translations from Chinese. It was one of the most remarkable lives of the twentieth century, and when it came to an end, Buck had herself buried at her farm in Bucks County, which operates now as a museum and as the headquarters of Pearl S. Buck International, carrying on the work she started.[11]

These writers, and the painters who also developed in Bucks County, undoubtedly came for a variety of reasons. Cheap real estate, perhaps, and the proximity to two great urban centers. But I suspect that they also found a distinctive sense of place in the agricultural landscapes of Bucks County, dotted with farm houses and punctuated with tidy towns, that helped nurture the work they did. Even the corn proved inspiring.

Most of that landscape is gone now, bulldozed under, paved over, as the tide of suburban sprawl has washed over much of Bucks County. I was struck by the poignancy of that several years ago as I was reading about a small controversy in Newtown Township. Township officials had granted permission to a developer to put up some McMansions on a tract of farmland only after the developer promised to preserve the eighteenth-century barn that still stood there. And then—surprise, surprise—the barn was torn down anyway. Construction was halted, at least for a bit, while township officials fumed.

They were too late, of course, and not just on that site. The landscape of Bucks County has disappeared, farm by farm, road-widening by road-widening, development by development over the last fifty years. That sense of place has disappeared along with it. Twentieth-century American culture owes an enormous debt to the writers and artists of Bucks County, but one wonders whether Michener, or Hammerstein, or Buck would have been able to find their inspiration there now.

There are few barns left for Charles Sheeler to paint.

There have only been two family dynasties in the history of American painting, and they have both been Philadelphian: the Peales in the late eighteenth century and early nineteenth, and the Wyeths in the twentieth century and twenty-first.

N. C. Wyeth, the founder of the family, had an enormously successful career as an illustrator of children's books, among other things, early in the twentieth century. His illustrations for the Scribner's editions of children's classics remain well loved and a kind of standard. Flush from his success with *Treasure Island*, in 1911 he moved his family to the tiny eighteenth-century settlement of Chadds Ford, in Chester County. There he raised his remarkably creative children in a remarkable compound of eighteenth-century buildings.

N. C.'s illustrations take viewers on any number of adventures through time and around the world. His work is filled with pirates and Revolutionary War soldiers and frontier adventures. His son Andrew, however, the most famous and successful of his artist children, never left home, artistically speaking. He has painted almost nothing but the landscapes and people of Chadds Ford (and the landscapes and people of the family's summer home in Cushman, Maine) over the course of his very long career.

If we have an image in our mind's eye of Chester County, it is because of Andrew Wyeth's paintings. To say "Brandywine" is to call Wyeth to mind. It is an image of rolling hills, small copses of trees, old farm buildings, the etched and weathered faces of country folk, and above all, these scenes soaked in his characteristically muted palette—grays, browns, sepias. And then there is the light, that slanting, cold light, which makes so many of Wyeth's paintings look like November or perhaps March. The moviemaker M. Night Shyamalan, who has also done a great deal to burn a particular vision of the Delaware Valley in the popular imagination, recognized the extent to which Andrew Wyeth has shaped our view of Chester County. Shyamalan's film *The Village* is set in nineteenth-century Chester County, and Shyamalan deliberately set out to make the movie look like an Andrew Wyeth painting. "Andrew was the main inspiration for the look of the movie," Shyamalan told an interviewer. "The grays and the minimalism, and the light—that's all from Andrew." Shyamalan finds Wyeth's work, particularly his paintings of interiors, to have a "creepy" beauty, and for Shyamalan, Wyeth's vision of Chester County became "our religion."[12]

Wyeth "officially" began his career in 1932 when his father invited him into his studio as an apprentice. In the 1930s the tradition of American realism and representation was still quite strong, but almost immediately the rest of the American art world began moving in a different direction. By the end of the 1940s, with abstract expressionism all the rage and "action painting" in vogue, Wyeth's quiet scenes of Chadds Ford seemed at the very least out of step, if not downright old-fashioned. As he told a *Life* magazine interviewer in 1965: "In the art world today, I'm so conservative I'm radical." None of that ever interested Wyeth very much, so he claims, and now that our ardor for abstraction, and for the "pop art" trivialities that followed it, has cooled, Wyeth's commitment to his particular vision looks like a remarkable artistic independence and integrity.

In his work as a whole, Wyeth has painted an extraordinary history, an intimate story of a particular place populated by characters we watch change, age, and finally—when they disappear from Wyeth's canvases—die. (Actually, Wyeth has created two histories, one set in Chadds Ford, the other in Maine.) His creation, this intense study of a place and its people over a long period of time has no parallel in American painting that I can think of. Perhaps the closest analogy, and I don't mean to draw it too tightly, is Faulkner's fictitious Yoknapatawpha County. In painting after painting we watch the seasons change, the Kuerners, Karl and his wife Anna, the old black man Tom Clark, and of course Helga, the German nurse who attended to Karl Kuerner when he was dying and then in turn became Wyeth's model.

Despite whatever critical chilliness blew his way, Wyeth has never labored in obscurity. He had his first show in 1936 at the Art Alliance of Philadelphia. Almost twenty years later, Harvard awarded him an honorary doctorate. Less than ten years after that, in 1963, he received the Presidential Medal of Freedom from President John Kennedy (though presented to him by President Johnson). And so it has gone throughout his career. He was even elected to the Soviet Academy of the Arts in Leningrad in 1978, back when there was a Soviet Academy and a Leningrad. In 1953, when the New York art world fell in love with Jackson Pollack, Wyeth had a big show in Tokyo. And all the while his paintings have sold well, in large part because his career has been skillfully managed by his wife, Betsy.

Not obscure then, but certainly alone or nearly so. Wyeth has famously steered away from art circles and from public celebrity. He has worked privately, jealously so, and independently. The characters who populate his canvases over and over again are his neighbors, his friends, and his family. And he has made it clear in interviews and in his work that he prefers the company of these country people—farmers, laborers, drifters. The internationally famous artist and the country folk in his neighborhood—highbrow and lowbrow sitting on the porch drinking beer.

Creepy may not be quite the right word to describe Wyeth's work, but the paintings do have a haunted quality to them. They are still, almost preternaturally so, and the angles, perspective, and light convey a sense both of tranquility and of foreboding. In some of his portraits, the intimacy—the sensuality—of the figures is so intense, we feel as viewers as if we have intruded on a very personal, private moment.

Wyeth's accomplishment, then, is to have captured a world simultaneously real and entirely of his own making. His paintings have a timeless quality and yet they are deeply time-bound as well. While the characters who populate Wyeth's world age and change—we watch them over the years—their settings do not. Very little of the twentieth century intrudes on these scenes, certainly almost nothing from the latter half of that century. The buildings all date from the eighteenth century or early nineteenth; the landscapes surrounding those buildings also appear unchanged. Not even the interiors of those buildings betray any evidence of the modern world—no telephones or big-screen TVs or dishwashers. Likewise, agriculture isn't practiced the way it is portrayed in Wyeth's paintings anymore. Horse drawn carts, wooden barrels used to ferment apple cider, these are anachronisms now. Just as Henry Mercer furiously collected the artifacts of a disappearing nineteenth-century agricultural world, Andrew Wyeth has created a world left behind by the march of technological change. There is nothing in any of Wyeth's paintings to hint at the fact that Rt. 202, as overbuilt, as overcongested as any road anywhere in suburban America, is literally just down the road from Chadds Ford.

That sense of anachronism adds a feeling of poignancy to many of these paintings, because agriculture of any kind is disappearing from Chester County as farm fields yield to subdevelopments and country lanes morph into strips. In this sense, by so resolutely ignoring it, these paintings document the loss of one of the nation's distinctive landscapes. To say "Brandywine," then, is to call to mind an Andrew Wyeth image because the place itself has largely disappeared. Whether he intended it or not, what Wyeth's paintings do finally is preserve a record of what was once there, and recently enough that we feel we still might be able to find it.

There were two blockbuster events in the American art world in 2004. The first was the much anticipated, much hyped reopening of the Museum of Modern Art in its expanded and transformed building. The second was a court ruling by an otherwise obscure Montgomery County Orphans Court judge who decided that the Barnes Foundation, and more to the point, the paintings owned by the foundation, could move from Merion to Philadelphia.

The two events make an interesting counterpoint. The Museum of Modern Art, which started as a small institution dedicated to promoting a certain vision of the twentieth-century avant-garde, found itself wrestling with the consequences of its own success. The avant-garde art at the center of MOMA's collections is now thoroughly mainstream, indeed canonical. An institution that once thought of itself as cutting edge, esoteric, and reserved for that small group of initiates who understood modern art has now become a major tourist destination. All this, and more no doubt, was on the minds of MOMA's custodians as they undertook the museum's expansion and renovation.

The Barnes Foundation, in contrast, found itself in court because of its systemic institutional failures. Its tiny endowment generated negligible revenues, and its gate receipts, restricted by another court order in response to the concerns of Merion residents about too much tourist traffic through their expensive neighborhood, did not pay the bills either. In a word, the Barnes was broke, choked nearly to death by a combination of bad management, difficult neighbors, and the almost baroque dictates of Albert Barnes's will. And so it came to pass that the foundation's director, backed by some of the largest philanthropic players in the region, filed papers in Montgomery County Orphans Court asking that the foundation be permitted to expand its governing board and move its collection to a new venue in the city.

What is unarguable is that Albert Barnes had an extraordinary eye for painting. One might quibble with a few of his choices, but taken as a whole there is probably no finer collection of impressionism, postimpressionism, and early modernism anywhere in the country, and certainly none assembled by a single person. What is equally unarguable is that Barnes was a lousy institution builder. Some of that ineptitude surely resulted from Barnes's particularly perverse and irascible personality. Yet, there is something thoroughly Philadelphian about the tortured history of the Barnes Foundation, and it exemplifies perhaps better than any other institution in the region both the promise and the difficulties that result from the particular way highbrow and lowbrow, elite and popular have intersected in the Delaware Valley's cultural life.

Barnes himself grew up as part of Philadelphia's middle class, attended Central High School (Eakins's alma mater), and then made a fortune—fittingly enough—in pharmaceuticals. His product Argyrol was probably the most widely used antiseptic of its time. His fortune made, he turned to art.

Many other wealthy collectors of the late nineteenth century and early twentieth, Isabella Stewart Gardner, Henry Clay Frick for example, relied on the taste and judgment of others when buying their paintings. Not so Barnes, whose confidence in his own eye never wavered. And an extraordinary confidence it must have been given that Cezanne, Matisse, Picasso, Renoir, and the rest were still regarded as outré by much of the art world. Barnes got a taste of that public opinion when he put his paintings on public display at the Pennsylvania Academy in 1923. The critical reception was less than warm, and Barnes never recovered or forgave. The critics were philistines, he cried, and, in this at least, it turns out he was right. Denouncing the elite, inbred Philadelphia art and cultural world, he took his paintings to Merion and built himself a beaux arts jewel box, designed by Paul Cret, to put them in.

In this location, Barnes undertook to create a museum, a school of art appreciation, and a program in horticulture besides. In the course of his collecting Barnes developed his own ideas about aesthetics and the school was his attempt to turn those ideas into a philosophy and a curriculum. It has always relied heavily on the paintings in the Barnes collection, making the endeavor a bit intellectually self-referential. Still, the courses were interesting enough to attract the attention of the noted philosopher John Dewey, who worked with Barnes for a while until their relationship, like almost every other one in Barnes's life, soured.

Barnes conceived his foundation, then, with its tripartite purpose, in part as a great nose-thumbing gesture toward Philadelphia society, its veins running blue with old money and its institutions reeking with the stench of a provincial elitism. Barnes underscored his populist commitments by championing folk art and "negro" art as well as the art of avant-garde Europe. Tucked in among the Modiglianis and Matisses are several paintings by the West Chester native Horace Pippin. No one had heard of Pippin when Barnes started buying his work. Now he is recognized as one of the important African American painters of the mid-twentieth century. Barnes's eye was almost unfailing.

Barnes was well known enough as an advocate of African American painting that he contributed an essay to Alain Locke's epochal volume *The New Negro*. There might have been some alma mater loyalty at work there, since Locke too was a graduate of Philadelphia's Central High.

By the time Barnes died, none of the foundation's constituent parts were running particularly well. The school catered to small groups of devotees and while Barnes had claimed that his building on Latches Lane was a museum, he was never much interested in letting too many people see the paintings. It took a court case—what else—to open the front door just a little bit to the public. At his death, Barnes restricted the way endowment monies could be handled, relying heavily on railroad bonds, which proved not to be such a wise investment, and he granted majority control of the foundation to Lincoln University, a small, traditionally black college in Chester County. When the Philadelphia cultural world learned of that, you could almost hear Barnes cackling from the grave.

Lincoln University probably never had the resources to support the multibillion-dollar collection, well away from its campus, it now found on its hands. In addition, Barnes had thoroughly alienated those people who might have donated large sums of money to the place. So the foundation struggled on until a critical mass came together with a bailout plan.

Those who opposed the foundation's request to break Barnes's will, no pun intended, tried to turn the legal fight into a morality play. Moving the paintings out of Merion and into Philadelphia amounted to nothing less than a cultural anschluss, engineered by those very forces of elitism, the Pew and Lenfest Foundations among others, for which Barnes himself had contempt. Julian Bond, a veteran of the civil rights era whose father had been president of Lincoln when Barnes made his decision to put the board under Lincoln's control, charged everyone involved in pushing the move with racism.

It isn't quite so simple. While it isn't yet clear that the new manifestation of the Barnes will be financially solvent, it does seem clear that in its old incarnation it certainly wasn't going to survive. More than the financials, however, and despite Barnes's antielitist posturing, the museum was only ever enjoyed by a tiny few. In the center of Philadelphia it will certainly become a major tourist attraction, but that constitutes a kind of populism too. As a result, the Barnes will likely lose a measure of its independence, its quirky charm, and with those losses perhaps some of its identity. It will also gain an audience it has never before had. In the end, perhaps that is a compromise worth making.

It has been, as I suggested earlier, a Philadelphia-flavored fight. Philadelphians are suspicious of elitism, and the accusation that the Barnes was going to become elitist was designed to tap into that deep sentiment. By contrast, no one slings the charge of elitism around in New York because New York's cultural institutions, by and large, have always been unabashedly and unapologetically elitist. It isn't a dirty word there the way it is in Philadelphia. When it reopened, after all, MOMA announced that visitors would now be charged a whopping twenty dollars—the highest admission anywhere!—for the pleasure.

Few cities can lay claim to their own sound—Chicago and Memphis have their blues; San Francisco had rock from bands like the

Grateful Dead and Jefferson Airplane in the 1960s, but the sound didn't survive the rising real estate values in the Haight that drove the hippies out. Philadelphia, in contrast, has two distinctive sounds that define it. Sounds that are instantly recognizable to anyone who listens. Sounds that could only have come from Philadelphia and that make the city a fixture in the aural landscape of people around the world.

The first Philadelphia sound emerged in the early twentieth century. The Philadelphia Orchestra played its first public concert in November of 1900. It was founded out of the same impulses that created symphony orchestras in other cities such as Boston, New York, Chicago, and Cleveland. Orchestra music, played by professionals in formal dress in formal settings, became the epitome of highbrow culture in American cities in the early twentieth century.

Then in 1912 the orchestra hired Leopold Stokowski to be its musical director and he gave the group a slightly different identity. He was flamboyant, he loved publicity, he married Gloria Vanderbilt. In 1916 he put one thousand musicians and singers on stage at the Academy of Music to perform the American premier of Gustav Mahler's enormous Eighth Symphony. Beginning in 1933 he began to offer "youth concerts" for thirteen to twenty-five-year olds and the tickets sold out within hours of going on sale. And Philadelphia loved him for all of it.

Through the instrument of the orchestra, Stokowski helped make classical music more fun and more accessible for Philadelphia audiences. He made it, and I intend no slight by this, more middlebrow. Who else but Stokowski and the Philadelphia Orchestra could have played a starring role in Disney's 1940 animated spectacular *Fantasia*? Who else but Stokowski would get to shake Mickey's hand?

Critics, at least certain critics, looked down their noses at what they regarded as the maestro's antics. But as the music critic Jay

Nordlinger put it recently when reviewing some reissued Stokowski recordings: "His talent for publicity has always colored his reputation, but suffice it to say that he was a great—truly a great—conductor."[13]

Fittingly enough in the City of Firsts, the Philadelphia Orchestra logged a number of firsts with Stokowski, including the first commercially available recordings made with the new electrical method (Stokowski actually began recording with the orchestra in 1917 across the river at the Victor Talking Machine Company in Camden), and the first commercially sponsored radio broadcast by an orchestra in 1929. (The Fabulous Philadelphians would also be the first orchestra to appear on a national television broadcast in 1948 under Stokowski's successor, Eugene Ormandy.) Most importantly, by the time Stokowski stepped off the podium in 1938 he had created the Philadelphia Sound.

The sound is big and warm, without being loud or bombastic. Stokowski managed to impose a strict discipline on the playing without choking any of the richness. Ormandy too emphasized precise timing and skillful execution, but all in the service of an essentially romantic sound. At the center of the sound has been the orchestra's matchless string section, which despite the fact of its large size, always played with a single voice under Ormandy. Both Stokowski and Ormandy loved the big, romantic repertoire—Dvorak, Sibelius, Franck. When Vladimir Horowitz chose to play Rachmaninoff's Third Piano Concerto to celebrate the fiftieth anniversary of his Carnegie Hall debut he called Ormandy to conduct.

At the same time, and belying again Philadelphia's reputation as a culturally conservative place, both Stokowski and Ormandy embraced a great deal of contemporary music, some of it difficult and challenging, like the works of Schoenberg and Shostakovich. Ormandy, for example, premiered Walter Piston's Symphony no. 7 in Philadelphia in 1961. Composers loved to work with Ormandy.

Ormandy too has not gotten the credit he deserves as a conductor from critics, especially as those critics demanded more "scholarly" interpretations of musical scores. His enormous popularity with the public also surely made some critics sniff. But quite apart from his musical gifts, that popularity is important in and of itself. He was not imperious or aloof in the tradition of so many orchestral conductors. Some conductors attempt to awe their audiences. Ormandy, as Robert Jones has nicely put it, tried to draw listeners into the music.[14] As Duke Ellington famously said about music, if it sounds good it is good, and under Stokowski and Ormandy the Philadelphia Sound, first and foremost, always sounded good.

The Philadelphia Orchestra may well be the most recorded and most widely traveled of any symphony in the world. Over the course of a century, then, more people have probably been exposed to the Philadelphia Sound than to that of any other orchestra. It probably is what orchestral music means to a countless number of people around the world. The sound defines the city for a large number of people, especially abroad, and the orchestra is their first stop if they ever come to visit. When Christoph Eschenbach was introduced as the orchestra's new director, he confessed that as a child growing up in postwar Germany the only records he had available to him were recordings of the Philadelphia Orchestra. As the critic Jay Nordlinger wrote of the Philadelphia Orchestra on the occasion of its centenary in 2000: "Just possibly, the Philadelphia Orchestra is the most treasured musical institution in the world."[15] A statement like that is unprovable in any empirical way, of course. But it is also undeniable.

In February of 1958 four white teenagers from Bartram High in Southwest Philadelphia calling themselves Danny and the Juniors put out a single that reached the top of the charts and stayed there for seven weeks. "At the Hop," a catchy dance tune, still pops up every so often on oldies radio stations but has otherwise been lost to the trivia bin. Buried deeper in that bin is the fact that Danny and the Juniors had help on that single from one Leon Huff of Camden.[16] Less than ten years after Huff helped put "At the Hop" on the charts, he teamed up with Kenny Gamble to form one of the most successful and influential writer/producer teams in the history of American popular music. Gamble and Huff, along with Thom Bell, created music that has been called alternately soul, pop-soul, pre-disco, and crossover, to name some. None of those labels work because, put more simply, they created the Sound of Philadelphia.

Gamble and Huff found each other in the mid-1960s. They scored their first top-ten national hit in 1967 when the Soul Survivors came out with "Expressway to Your Heart." That year, the Chicago singer Jerry Butler came to town, his career stalled, and he became "The Iceman," the purveyor of cool. By 1969, Gamble and Huff had hit their stride, issuing three singles—"Only the Strong Survive," "Moody Woman," and "What's the Use of Breaking Up"—that perfected their style. In 1971 they were finally able to form their own label, Philadelphia International Records, with a distribution deal through CBS Records. They opened their offices on South Broad Street, two blocks down from the venerable Academy of Music and now directly across the street from the orchestra's new home at the Kimmel Center. The two sounds of Philadelphia stare at each other across Broad Street.

At the end of each year *Billboard* magazine publishes a ranking of records and producers based on sales and airplay and in 1974 Gamble, Huff, and Bell sat on top. Between them they had twenty-one hit singles in a single year. By the end of the 1970s, the team had collectively produced thirty-one gold or platinum singles and nearly that many gold or platinum record albums. They also eclipsed Motown as the most profitable black-owned entertainment company in the nation, at least for a time.

The songs themselves were not as important as the way they were arranged and produced. The Sound of Philadelphia is a slick, crisp sound, with an energetic but disciplined rhythm section and a generous use of strings and horns. There are also other instruments that had never been heard before in pop music—vibraphones and marimba and an electric guitar distorted to sound like a sitar. In fact, quite unlike the Motown operation in Detroit, the house band for Gamble and Huff was just as important as the front men, and it certainly didn't labor in the same kind of obscurity. Called MFSB, which, depending on who you ask, symbolized the family nature of Philadelphia International—mother, father, sister, brother—or something else a bit raunchier, the band itself issued a number of its own recordings, many of which became hits.

Philadelphia has always had a vibrant creative music scene, never mind the way some people complain about it. It was not purely an accident that Marian Anderson, Paul Robeson, and John Coltrane, to name only three, came to live in town. But it is a small, close-knit scene and as a consequence musicians don't spend all their time at home in one musical genre. As the critic Tom Moon has pointed out, there is great deal of cross-pollination in the Philadelphia musical garden, and listening to the Sound of Philadelphia songs now you can hear the shades of jazz, the beginnings of funk, and Caribbean rhythms, in addition to pop, soul, and R & B.

Those big string sounds, after all, that great rise and swell of sound was heard first on the other side of Broad Street with the Philadelphia Orchestra. It is no coincidence that some of those orchestra musicians played on the Gamble and Huff song "Love Train." The sounds that come out of Philadelphia, and there are many of them, result from this mixing of genres, races, and influences. The Sound of Philadelphia didn't happen to come from the city, according to Gamble and Huff, it came out of the city. As

Leon Huff put it, "[We] hear the town better than anybody else, we know what it sounds like sweet, and what it sounds like going bad."[17] It is dance music, first and foremost. Gamble and Huff grew up in the shadow of Dick Clark's *American Bandstand*, which in the 1950s was still playing white music, with white dancers, to white audiences exclusively. Gamble and Huff, at least in their public utterances, never betrayed any interest in discussing their music in the provincial terms of race. Nor were they particularly interested in appealing to that "crossover" (read: white) audience, though Thom Bell worked to produce several Elton John songs, David Bowie cut *Young Americans* at Sigma Sound Studios, and the Rolling Stones came to town to get some of that Philadelphia sound in the mid-1970s. Still, there is something of poetic justice that the producers of *Soul Train*, the black answer to *American Bandstand*, picked the song "TSOP," an instrumental by MFSB, as their theme.

But Gamble and Huff have always believed there was more to their music than a good dance beat. As Bell told *The New York Times* in 1973, the music appealed to "folks who want to listen as well as those who dance." Gamble, in that same interview, elaborated, "[We] work to give our audiences a number of different things to hear. It's all there, if you want to listen to it."[18]

Beyond the music itself—the strings, horns, multiple percussion line—Gamble went on to remind people that there was a message too, a Philadelphia message: "The records we make project a call for harmony and understanding. Some people think it's hip to mock that, but we're just trying to live up to what this city is supposed to symbolize."[19] In Philadelphia even the most commercially successful pop music carries the burden and possibility of the city's founding ideals. With the Sound of Philadelphia, you can dance in the peaceable kingdom.

It might have been a throw-away remark, but I think the reference to Philadelphia's founding and symbolization means something to Gamble and Huff. In 1997 Epic records released a three-CD set of Gamble and Huff songs and called it *The Philly Sound: Kenny Gamble, Leon Huff and the Story of Brotherly Love*. Both men have been out of the music business for a while, after the Sound of Philadelphia ran its course and Philadelphia International Records ceased to be the hit factory it had once been. In 1990 Gamble founded Universal Community Home, which is part of the larger Universal Companies, as a nonprofit community development project. Gamble was living a very comfortable life on the Main Line at the time but decided to move back to the city, to a row house in his old neighborhood in South Philly, which by that time had degenerated quite considerably.

He is nothing if not a shrewd businessman, and he has approached neighborhood revitalization with the same hard-nosed, unsentimental principles. His attempt to transform the neighborhood he came from has not been without controversy and complaint. It has also enjoyed some terrific success as even a cursory walk through the area reveals. You probably won't hear the O'Jays or Harold Melvin and the Blue Notes on those sidewalks today, but in a very real sense, if you listen hard enough, you will hear the Sound of Philadelphia at work.[20]

"People all over the world."

The lyrics, like much of Gamble and Huff's work, don't scan well or rise to the level of poetry.

"Join hands."

But that wasn't ever the point of the songs that came with the Sound of Philadelphia.

"Start a love train. Love train."

You recognize that one right away, and the version you know is the one that was a huge hit when the O'Jays sang it. It is a classic Sound of Philadelphia song, backed by a driving, tight rhythm section and a swelling string part. Eminently danceable. More than any other Sound of Philadelphia song, that one is the soundtrack to my own growing up. Hearing it still brings back swirled memories of hot summer nights, cars with the windows rolled down, and the alarm on my AM clock-radio.

But there is another version of the song, not as well known, done by Bunny Sigler, which is in some ways more powerful. Sigler slowed the song down—it runs to six minutes as opposed to the O'Jays' three-minute version—and the big orchestration has been replaced with a smaller group, including an organ. At the end of the song all the instruments except the organ fade away and the melody is carried by the humming of back-up singers.

The result is something you sway to rather than dance to, something more gospel than soul. Something that emphasizes the plaintive quality of the song. It isn't bitter, but it sounds more than a bit melancholic. The O'Jays sang confidently that this love train was pulling into the station any minute. Sigler isn't quite as sure when or if it's going to come at all. That, in six minutes and as succinctly as anything, is Philadelphia, the real measured against the ideal, the weight of the past and the promise of the future. When Sigler sings the song, it has the power to make me smile and cry all at once, even now.

The Naked City and the Story of Decline

For the last fifty years we have told roughly the same story about metropolitan America in the Northeast and the Midwest. In the postwar period, those suburbs have grown, proliferated, and thrived, while the cities at the centers of those regions have declined, decayed, and been eclipsed by the rising cities of the South and West.

It is hard to argue with the numbers, so let's do a quick review. America urbanized dramatically over the nineteenth century, hand in glove with the rise of the industrial economy. When the nation was founded in Philadelphia, probably over 90 percent of the population lived on the farm. In 1890, the federal census revealed that the fabled frontier had closed and that the value of things made in factories exceeded the value of farm products for the first time. In 1920, the census announced that a majority of Americans now lived in cities.

America had entered its "urban moment," when the city became the inescapable fact of American life and of the American imagination. Most of the big American cities continued to grow in terms of population, economic activity, and political clout through the Second World War. Most of the industrial powerhouses hit their peak populations between 1950 and 1960.

That moment did not last long. People—white people almost

exclusively—fled the cities for the new suburbs, taking their buy-ing power, their property taxes, and their jobs with them on the new interstate highways that sliced through cities on their way out to the new developments. As early as 1959, Wilfred Owen of the Brookings Institution wondered: "Despite all the centuries that urban concentrations have grown and prospered, we have begun to doubt that the city can survive the automotive age, or even that it should."[1] In 1980, according to the census, a majority of us now lived in the suburbs and two-thirds of American manu-facturing had moved there too. Philadelphia lost thousands of industrial jobs and one quarter of a million residents, roughly 25 percent of its 1950 high. That's worse than some cities and considerably better than others such as Detroit, St. Louis, and Cleveland.

As a consequence of what we now call somewhat bloodlessly "deindustrialization," American cities imploded. The disappear-ance of jobs and people created all of the social pathologies we associate with the inner city that I alluded to in Chapter 1—crime, drugs, violence, and a hundred different kinds of desperation caused by unremitting poverty. The inner city became a place abandoned economically and politically, literally and metaphori-cally.

Deindustrialization, and everything attendant upon it, set up the dynamics beneath the story we have told about our older met-ropolitan regions—affluent, largely white suburbs pitted against increasingly poor, increasingly black cities. Much of the writing about cities in the last twenty-five years has an almost apocalyp-tic ring to it. For Fred Siegel, cities are *Where the Future Once Happened* and the Yale scholar Ed Rae titled his magnum opus about the city of New Haven *The End of Urbanism*, to cite just two recent examples.

That is not the story I chose to tell here, and for several rea-sons. First, it is a more than twice-told tale, and much as I may find it persuasive, I didn't see any point to echoing that narrative yet again. Yes, the consequences of deindustrialization were devastating to Philadelphia in many ways, and yes, the suburban development of the region has been extraordinary. But we know that story already—we have heard it all before.

Further, I wanted to see what happened if I turned that story upside down. Recognizing that deindustrialization was a force as damaging as any flood or earthquake, I wanted to see just how resilient the city has proved to be. Like the tsunami that hit Southeast Asia in 2004, very few saw deindustrialization coming, nor could they predict what the consequences would be. It resulted from forces over which Philadelphians—or Chicagoans or Clevelanders—could exercise very little control.

In a brief, twenty-year period—roughly from 1960 to 1980—deindustrialization completely changed the economic and physical landscape of the city. Yet unlike the victims of natural disasters, those who remained in the city had to clean up the mess largely on their own, without any large-scale, comprehensive, adequately funded plan to do so. Above all, poverty is hugely expensive, and that expense is borne disproportionately by American cities. Europeans I have taken through some of Philadelphia's old industrial neighborhoods marvel that things could have been allowed to deteriorate so much. In Europe, central governments would have stepped in long ago.

And yet, the city has survived. More than that, it has taken the worst body blows of economic and political decisions and absorbed them. They hurt, to be sure, but the city never hit the mat. Urbanism, at least in Philadelphia, has certainly not come to an end.

At the same time, I wanted to invert the usual happy story of suburban development, which stresses private developers delivering for consumers a product they clearly want. Instead, I have pointed out some of the problems that have come with untrammeled suburban development. Only recently have people begun to do an accounting of some of those costs—environmental degradation, lost time stuck in commuting traffic, overburdened municipal infrastructure, and the like. But I have also been interested in those things that can't quite be toted up in a ledger book. How much does it cost all of us when natural landscapes and the human activity they reveal are erased into sameness? How do you tally the loss of a sense of community for people? What is a sense of place really worth, and how do we measure its disappearance?

These are the problems Americans face all across the suburban and now exurban landscape, but they are particularly important in this region, I have suggested, because, like the city itself, the whole Delaware Valley is saturated in history. That history, in turn, creates a connection between the past and the present, the city and the suburb that makes the daily experience of our lives richer. It creates that elusive sense of place, and it is fast disappearing.

This all leads to a third reason I chose to write this book the way I did. I believe that part of the reason we understand metropolitan history the way we do stems from the methods we use to study the problem in the first place. Over the last thirty years or so, the writing about cities has been dominated by quantitative studies, by counting those things we can count.

In urban America, the numbers certainly haven't looked good. All the things that ought to go up—like population, jobs, income—have gone down. Meanwhile, all the things that ought to go down—crime, poverty rates, homelessness—have been going up. Out in the suburbs, of course, the graphs are all going in the right direction. It is hard to argue with those numbers.

But at the same time, it seems to me that there are two problems with the quantitative approach to understanding regional dynamics. First, it largely proceeds from that most American assumption that bigger is necessarily better, that growth must always be the goal. Take, for example, the question of urban population. The high point that the older industrial cities hit just after World War II is the point from which we measure their subsequent decline. Yet I suspect that those figures represent an artificial bubble, brought on by the Great Depression, when no new housing got built and when families had to double up, and by the war itself, which saw an influx of people into city factories, now turned into defense plants. Were it not for those events, perhaps Detroit and Pittsburgh and Philadelphia would never have grown that big in the first place.

Lewis Mumford was among those mid-century writers who worried that cities such as New York and Chicago and Philadelphia had grown too big, that at those sizes they had lost their human scale and the ability to provide the kind of humane urban life that was possible when cities were smaller. By a demographic coincidence, Philadelphia began the twentieth century with just about the same number of souls as lived in it at the end of the twentieth century, 1.5 million. But by the end of the century the city was a more equitable place, a more racially tolerant place, and a much livelier cultural center than it was back before the city's alleged decline.

Second, the quantitative approach to American urban studies has meant that we only study those things that can be counted, graphed, tabled, and turned into statistics. We have paid less attention to those things that can't be counted—neighborliness, tolerance, inspiration. Those things are trickier to get a handle on, but that fact makes them no less important. So I tried to pay some attention to those things we can't quite count—the region's relationship with the past and to its utopian impulses, to cultural inspiration and middle-class aspiration. The city is, it goes almost without saying, much, much more than the sum of its countable parts. When we start to look at those more elusive things—like ethnic diversity and racial integration, like intellectual ferment and cultural vitality—Philadelphia during the last generation looks remarkable indeed, while the suburbs seem to lag well behind.[2]

Finally, I wrote this story the way I did because I believe that the way we tell stories matters a great deal. Stories—narratives—don't simply describe a reality; they condition our understanding of that reality. A history that narrates the suburbs as ascending and the city as declining not only misses much of the story; it shapes the way we think about the present and the future. It makes it easier for us to be cynical or despairing about the city, and it makes it easier to ignore the very real problems now facing suburban areas.

If we are going to imagine a different future, one in which a healthy city functions as the hub of a healthy region, one in which common problems—and they are all common problems—can be addressed cooperatively, one in which that which is unique and most special across the region can be preserved and nurtured, then we must begin by telling a different story about ourselves.

That is what I have tried to do here. Cities and the regions around them are, finally, acts of the imagination, and I only hope that my imaginings will have some resonance with you.

N O T E S

Prologue

1. Actually, the line is "There are eight million stories in the naked city," but I have taken license here.

2. Sam Bass Warner, *The Private City: Philadelphia in Three Periods of Its Growth*, 2d ed. (Philadelphia: University of Pennsylvania Press, 1987), p. xiii. Warner's study originally appeared in 1968. This quote is from the preface to a newer edition.

3. According to some police estimates, well over half the customers for illegal drugs purchased in the city come from the suburbs, as the steady stream of New Jersey and Delaware license plates through Philadelphia's badlands attests. In May 2004, to take one example, federal investigators announced indictments against twenty-seven people connected to an alleged "major" cocaine ring. Of those twenty-seven, twenty-five lived in Philadelphia's suburbs.

4. Rustin's West Chester years are considered in a new biography by historian John D'Emilio, *Lost Prophet: The Life of Bayard Rustin* (New York: Free Press, 2003).

5. Personal interview, March 2003.

6. The report is titled "Back to Prosperity, a Competitive Agenda for Renewing Pennsylvania." For an account of Toll Brothers and the way they operate, see Jon Gertner, "The Housing Industrial Complex," *New York Times*, October 16, 2005.

7. "Blight and Sprawl," *Philadelphia Inquirer*, April 21, 2002. Hylton helped found 10,000 Friends of Pennsylvania, and the organization Save Our Lands, Save Our Towns.

8. Andrew Cassel, "Phila. Acts More Like N.J. Than Like Penna.," *Philadelphia Inquirer*, April 23, 2004.

9. The problem of how we conceive of metropolitan regions is not, of course, lim-

ited to Philadelphia. The area around Chicago is now referred to generically as Chicagoland, which makes the whole place sound more like a theme park than the nation's third largest metropolitan area.

10. See Henry Glassie, "Eighteenth Century Cultural Process in Delaware Valley Folk Building," in Dell Upton and John Michael Vlach, eds., *Common Places: Readings in American Vernacular Architecture* (Athens: University of Georgia Press, 1986), pp. 394–425.

11. See Patrick Healy, "Where the Twain Meet," *New York Times*, May 23, 2004 for a nice piece on Long Beach Island.

12. Bob Fernandez, "Medications to Mouthwash, Pa. Production Leads Nation," *Philadelphia Inquirer*, August 23, 2003.

13. For a good summary of recent job and commuting trends, see "We're Going in Reverse," *Philadelphia Inquirer*, March 6, 2003.

14. Quoted in "Leaving Isn't the Problem, Relocating to Philadelphia is," *Philadelphia Inquirer*, August 8, 2003.

15. See "Brain Drain? Not So Fast," *Philadelphia Inquirer*, June 11, 2004.

16. Data from the Center City District, Philadelphia.

17. Personal interview, March 2002.

18. Thanks to Elise Schneider of the Tasty Baking Company for this information.

Chapter 1

1. Russell F. Weigley, ed., *Philadelphia: A 300-Year History* (New York: W. W. Norton, 1982), p. 1.

2. "Instructions of William Penn to the Commissioners for settling the colony, 30 7th mo. 1681," in Mary Maples Dunn and Richard Dunn, eds., *The Papers of William Penn, 1680–1684* (Philadelphia: University of Pennsylvania Press, 1982), p. 121.

3. It is, or was, a real city in what is now Turkey. I'm not sure whether people in the seventeenth century would have been aware of its existence beyond the scriptural reference.

4. Sam Bass Warner, *The Private City: Philadelphia in Three Periods of Its Growth*, 2d ed. (Philadelphia: University of Pennsylvania Press, 1987).

5. Sydney Ahlstrom, *A Religious History of the American People*, 2d ed. (New Haven, Conn.: Yale University Press, 2004), p. 213.

6. The phrase comes from Henry May, *The Enlightenment in America* (New York: Oxford University Press, 1976), p. 127.

7. See Edward T. Price, "The Central Courthouse Square in the American County Seat," in Dell Upton and John Michael Vlachs, eds., *Common Places: Readings in American Vernacular Architecture* (Athens: University of Georgia Press, 1986), 124–45, especially the map on p. 127.

8. The parkway is indeed dramatic and well-loved. But it does not function as a strolling boulevard as it was intended. Several organizations, including the Center City District and the *Daily News*, have begun to discuss what can be done to make the parkway work better as a city asset.

9. For more on Hicks, see Edna Pullinger, *A Dream of Peace* (Philadelphia: Dorrance and Company, 1973), and Carolyn Weekly, *The Kingdoms of Edward Hicks* (New York: Abby Aldrich Rockefeller Folk Art Center in association with Harry N. Abrams, Inc., 1999).

10. Personal interview with Tom Hoopes, May 2003.

11. I have taken this quote from Nathaniel Popkin's splendid book, *Song of the City: An Intimate History of the American Urban Landscape* (New York: Four Walls Eight Windows, 2002), p. 149. It is the finest book about contemporary Philadelphia I have come across.

12. Ibid., p. 148.

13. For the most complete telling of Rustin's story, see John D'Emilio, *Lost Prophet: The Life of Bayard Rustin* (New York: Free Press, 2003). Rustin is quoted there, p. 230.

14. E. Digby Baltzell, *Puritan Boston and Quaker Philadelphia* (New York: Free Press, 1979), pp. ix–x.

15. The essay appeared in 1903 in *McClure's Magazine* and was later included as a chapter in Lincoln Steffen's book *The Shame of the Cities* (1904).

16. Henry James, *The American Scene* (Bloomington: Indiana University Press, 1968), p. 283.

17. One recent example: Faced in the summer of 2004 with a small cut in the operating funds it receives from the city, the Philadelphia Museum of Art suspended

its hugely popular Wednesday-evening programming. In any other city, of course, a wealthy donor would have stepped forward immediately to keep the doors open. Not so at the PMA.

18. Gretchen Morgenson, "An 'Oops' at the Bank of 'Wow,'" *New York Times*, August 1, 2004.

19. See Greg Downs, "City's Survival Depends on All," *Philadelphia Inquirer*, June 30, 2004.

20. Personal correspondence, 2004.

21. As far as I am aware, no one has given the MNS the scholarly examination it deserves. Lakey has written a lengthy paper on the history and theory of the MNS, which was to have been included in a book project that never materialized. See George Lakey, "'Catching Up and Moving On': What Can We Learn for the Future from the Movement for a New Society?" (unpublished manuscript). My quotes come from a personal interview, August 2003.

22. John Sedgwick, *Peaceable Kingdom: A Year in the Life of America's Oldest Zoo* (New York: Morrow, 1988).

Chapter 2

1. Many historians, including Dorothy Ross and Michael Kammen, have written about the development of an American historical consciousness in the nineteenth century. My own book looks at the place of Native Americans in developing this historical sense: *History's Shadow: Native Americans and Historical Consciousness in the Nineteenth Century* (Chicago: University of Chicago Press, 2004).

2. Henry James, *The American Scene* (Bloomington: Indiana University Press), p. 280.

3. These institutions are central to Gary Nash's book *First City: Philadelphia and the Forging of Historical Memory* (Philadelphia: University of Pennsylvania Press, 2002).

4. Thanks to Stephen Hall for this information.

5. The book that resulted, *The Philadelphia Negro*, was a pioneering study in the new field of social science and it remains an important work of scholarship. It

has been reissued in a centennial edition edited by Elijah Anderson (Philadelphia: University of Pennsylvania Press, 1996).

6. Lincoln Steffens, *The Shame of the Cities* (New York: Hill and Wang, 1957), p. 136; James, p. 283.

7. In advance of Franklin's three-hundredth birthday (Franklin was born in 1706), several new biographies have appeared, including Edmund Morgan's *Benjamin Franklin* (New Haven, Conn.: Yale University Press, 2002), Gordon Wood's *The Americanization of Benjamin Franklin* (New York: Penguin Press, 2004), and Walter Isaacson's *Benjamin Franklin: An American Life* (New York: Simon & Schuster, 2003). H. W. Brugels titled his biography of Franklin *The First American* (New York: Doubleday, 2000).

8. I have taken most of this information from an essay written in 1961 by Martin H. Weik of the Aberdeen Proving Ground and posted on the web at http://ftp.ar1/~mike/comphist/enrac-story.html.

9. The story of how the park was shaped is told in Constance Greiff, *Independence: The Creation of a National Park* (Philadelphia: University of Pennsylvania Press, 1987).

10. For more on the history of historical interpretation at Williamsburg, see Richard Handler and Eric Gable, *The New History in an Old Museum* (Durham, N.C.: Duke University Press, 1997).

11. In fairness, the historical interpretation at the INHP has improved tremendously since it was first opened, and it now tells a more inclusive story about the eighteenth century.

12. Some things really don't ever change. The building trades unions in Philadelphia continue to exercise a monopoly control on construction in the city and have helped throttle a greater recovery for the city.

13. Quoted in Elizabeth Frazer, "1776–1926 at the Sesqui-Centennial," *Saturday Evening Post*, September 11, 1926, p. 65.

14. I have taken these quotes from Winterthur's website, www.winterthur.org, as it appeared in the summer of 2004.

15. Thanks to Harris Steinberg for this quote.

16. Both quotes from Stephan Salisbury, "Plan Would Cleave Independence Square," *Philadelphia Inquirer*, August 6, 2004.

17. The fights over security and design are ongoing. Thus far the Department of the Interior has been absolutely intransigent. Aesthetic questions to one side, the current security perimeter around the park is entirely ineffective, and has been shown to be so by a number of studies. It punishes those who agree to obey the rules, making a trip to the Liberty Bell and Independence Hall inconvenient, unpleasant, and over-long. It is easy enough to simply breach the fence if you feel like it; I've done it a number of times.

18. Full disclosure: Kyle is also a friend of mine and we have discussed Poor Richard's quite a bit over the years. These quotes come from a personal interview, summer 2004.

19. Thanks to Tom Sugrue for this information. He cites Keith Reed, "Ringing It up in Philadelphia," *Boston Globe*, October 21, 2003.

20. Garrison is the subject of a recent biography, from which I have drawn some of this material: Henry Mayer, *All on Fire: William Lloyd Garrison and the Abolition of Slavery* (New York: St. Martin's Press, 1998).

21. Quoted in ibid., p. 176.

22. For an excellent history of the role of Independence Hall in the national imagination, see Charlene Mires, *Independence Hall in American Memory* (Philadelphia: University of Pennsylvania Press, 2002).

23. Quoted in ibid., p. 245.

24. Among other things, Cheney fancies herself a historian, and in this self-styled role she led a scurrilous public attack on the national history standards designed by Gary Nash, this despite the fact that she readily acknowledged never having actually read them.

25. The symbolically conservative use of Valley Forge was taken to its logical, if bizarre conclusion in the summer of 2004 when the American Nazi Party— officially the National Socialist Movement—received a permit for a rally on park grounds. They believe that George Washington was both an anti-Semite and a white separatist and thus want to link their noxious agenda with him. As their spokesman Jeff Schoep put it: "Valley Forge is important to us because this is where George Washington camped out. We are patriots, and we are honoring our founding fathers." See Nancy Petersen, "Nazi Group Approved for Valley Forge Rally," *Philadelphia Inquirer* August 25, 2004.

26. Quoted in Godfrey Hodgson, *America in Our Time* (New York: Vintage Books, 1976), pp. 9–10.

27. "Federal Land Purchase Ends Development Plan in Valley Forge Park," *Bucks County Courier Times*, July 7, 2004.

28. Quoted in Edward Colimore, "Paving History and Putting up Parking Lots," *Philadelphia Inquirer*, June 27, 2004.

29. Du Bois, p. 19.

30. Mayer, p. 173

31. Stephen Mihm, "Liberty-Bell Plan Shows Freedom and Slavery," *New York Times*, April 23, 2003.

32. E-mail letter from Lawler to Bomar, November 13, 2003. Thanks to Howard Gillette for letting me use his archive of material about this controversy.

Chapter 3

1. Quoted in Stuart Blumin, *The Emergence of the Middle Class: Social Experience in the American City, 1760–1900* (New York: Cambridge University Press, 1989), p. 1.

2. For much of this discussion I have relied on James T. Lemon's *The Best Poor Man's Country: A Geographical Study of Early Southeastern Pennsylvania* (Baltimore: Johns Hopkins University Press, 1972).

3. Ibid., p. 27.

4. Ibid., p. 227.

5. Ibid., p. 223.

6. William Cronon, *Nature's Metropolis* (New York: Norton, 1991).

7. Much of Blumin's book *The Emergence of the Middle Class* takes place in Philadelphia.

8. The phrase, once again, comes from Sam Bass Warner, *Streetcar Suburbs: The Process of Growth in Boston, 1870–1900* (Cambridge: Harvard University Press, 1962).

9. Blumin, p. 220.

10. Figures from Russell Weigley, ed., *Philadelphia: A 300-Year History* (New York: W. W. Norton, 1982), p. 363.

11. Quoted in ibid.

12. I have relied on John Hepp's splendid book, *The Middle-Class City: Transforming Space and Time in Philadelphia, 1876–1926* (Philadelphia: University of Pennsylvania Press, 2003) and for this discussion especially pp. 193–94.

13. Donna Rilling, *Making Houses, Crafting Capitalism: Builders in Philadelphia, 1790–1850* (Philadelphia: University of Pennsylvania Press, 2001), p. viii.

14. See ibid., especially pp. 40–45.

15. Ibid., p. 52.

16. Both quoted in ibid.

17. Weigley, p. 421.

18. Ibid., pp. 422, 494–95.

19. I am thankful to the architect and historian Neal Hitch for this quote.

20. Quoted in Hepp, p. 168.

21. *The Levittowners: Ways of Life and Politics in a New Suburban Community* (New York: Vintage, 1967).

22. All quoted in William Benjamin Piggott, "The Geography of Exclusion: Race and Suburbanization in Postwar Philadelphia" (Master's thesis, Ohio State University, 2002), p. 20.

23. Matthew Blanshard, "A Vision of Suburban Utopia Blurs," *Philadelphia Inquirer*, October 9, 2000.

24. In his 1964 history of the Jersey Shore, Harold Wilson spends all of fifteen pages on the era before the shore resorts. See Harold Wilson, *The Story of the Jersey Shore* (Princeton, N.J.: D. Van Nostrand Company, 1964).

25. McPhee's book, *The Pine Barrens* (New York: Farrar, Straus & Giroux, 1968), came out in 1968. It is still a wonderful read.

26. Quoted in Wilson, p. 43.

27. Quoted in ibid.

28. Ibid., 106–7.

29. Quoted in ibid., p. 79.

30. This is the biggest point Nasaw makes in his book, *Going Out: The Rise and Fall of Public Amusements* (New York: Basic Books, 1993).

31. William Cronon, "The Trouble with Wilderness," in Steven Conn and Max Page, eds., *Building the Nation: Americans Write about Their Architecture, Their Cities, and Their Landscape* (Philadelphia: University of Pennsylvania Press, 2003), p. 137.

32. Lawrence Squeri, *Better in the Poconos: The Story of Pennsylvania's Vacation-land* (University Park: Penn State University Press, 2002). Squeri's is hardly a scholarly book, but it is a useful if breezy trot through the history of the region, and I have drawn some of my discussion from it.

33. Ibid., p. 71.

34. Ibid., p. 117.

35. Ibid., pp. 68–71.

36. In fact, the first public demonstration of a television broadcast took place at the Franklin Institute in 1934.

Chapter 4

1. This is quoted in Bruce Stutz's wonderful book about the Delaware River, *Natural Lives, Modern Times* (Philadelphia: University of Pennsylvania Press, 1998, 1992), p. 174, but he provides no original citation.

2. Quoted in Russell F. Weigley, ed., *Philadelphia: A 300-Year History* (New York: W. W. Norton), p. 266.

3. Quoted in ibid., p. 237.

4. Quoted in ibid., p. 239.

5. "Pine Lands of New Jersey," reprinted in Steven Conn and Max Page, eds., *Building the Nation: Americans Write about Their Architecture, Their Cities, and Their Landscape* (Philadelphia: University of Pennsylvania Press, 2003), pp. 99–100.

6. H. M. Alden, "The Pennsylvania Coal Region," in Conn and Page, pp. 112–13.

7. Ibid., p. 112.

8. Both quotes from Karen Blomain, *Coalseam* (Scranton, Pa.: University of Scranton Press, 1993), pp. 11, 13.

9. I have taken this quote from the web site www.phillyroads.com/roads/schuylkill, but I believe it comes originally from an interview Allen did with the *Philadelphia Inquirer* in 1983.

10. Alan Greenberger, "River Bred," *City Paper*, September 2, 2004.

11. See "Light Rail, with the Emphasis on Light," *New York Times*, March 13, 2004.

12. M. K. C., *The Schuylkill: A Centennial Poem* (Philadelphia: Jno. A. Haddock, 1876).

13. Stutz, p. 176.

14. Quoted in ibid., p. 198.

15. Ibid., p. 201.

16. Quoted in ibid., p. 200.

17. Quoted in ibid.

18. Quoted in "A River Pulled in Two Directions," *New York Times*, December 6, 2004.

19. Cronon's essay, "The Problem with Wilderness," appeared originally in the *New York Times Magazine*, August 13, 1995, pp. 46–47.

20. Figures from "A River Pulled in Two Directions."

21. Quoted in Stutz, p. 199.

22. Quoted in "Residents Demand Solution to Floods," *Philadelphia Inquirer*, August 4, 2004.

23. Greenberger, "River Bred."

24. "Poised for a Rebirth?" *Philadelphia Inquirer*, November 25, 2003.

25. For a thorough consideration of Camden's recent history and its ambitious and controversial plans for revival, see Howard Gillette, *Camden After the Fall: Decline and Renewal in a Post-Industrial City* (Philadelphia: University of Pennsylvania Press, 2005).

26. "Canal Work Nearing the End of the Line," *Philadelphia Inquirer* February 8, 2005.

27. "A Grand Plan for the River's Key Sites," *Philadelphia Inquirer*, November 8, 2002.

Chapter 5

1. Carol Kino, "Go Figure," *New York Times*, April 17, 2005. Of course such a comment may reveal as much about the fatuity of trendy New York artists as about the timelessness of the Academy's mission.

2. Another Philadelphia first: Rocky was the first movie to use the steady cam, technology that made filming that scene on the steps possible.

3. This is quoted in my book, *Museums and American Intellectual Life, 1876–1926* (Chicago: University of Chicago Press, 1998), p. 34.

4. Quoted in ibid., p. 248.

5. Quoted in ibid., p. 263

6. Elizabeth Johns's book, *Thomas Eakins: The Heroism of Modern Life* (Princeton,

N.J.: Princeton University Press, 1983), is in my opinion the best study of Eakins's relationship to the city.

7. I have written about Sheeler's relationship to Bucks County and to Henry Mercer in *Museums and American Intellectual Life*. Rourke is quoted on p. 185.

8. Quoted in ibid., pp. 165–66.

9. Quoted in ibid., p. 171.

10. Ibid., p. 169.

11. Full disclosure: the very best biography of Buck, *Pearl S. Buck: A Cultural Biography* (Cambridge: Cambridge University Press, 1996), was written by my father, Peter Conn. It too is an extraordinary book.

12. See "A Scene Straight out of Andrew Wyeth," *Philadelphia Inquirer*, July 25, 2004.

13. Jay Nordlinger, "The Philadelphia Sound at 100," *The New Criterion*, June 18, 2000.

14. www.eugeneormandy.com/ormandyap.htm.

15. Nordlinger, "The Philadelphia Sound."

16. See Tom Moon, "From the Hop," *Philadelphia Inquirer*, February 16, 2003 for an article that looks at the forty-five greatest Philadelphia musical moments since 1958.

17. Quoted in John A. Jackson, *A House on Fire: The Rise and Fall of Philadelphia Soul* (Oxford: Oxford University Press, 2004), p. 135. Jackson's book is encyclopedic in its detail and frustratingly short on larger social and musical analysis.

18. Quoted in ibid.

19. Ibid.

20. See Annette John-Hall, "His Music Is the Blueprint," *Philadelphia Inquirer*, August 3, 2003.

Epilogue

1. Wilfred Owen, *Cities in the Motor Age* (New York: Viking Press, 1959), p. 3.

2. According to a 2005 report, all aspects of the culture scene have exploded recently, with gross receipts at cultural venues and events across the region topping one billion dollars. See Patricia Horn, "Area Basks in $1 Billion of Culture," *Philadelphia Inquirer*, October 2, 2005.

INDEX

ACKNOWLEDGMENTS

In many ways this book began long ago, but it wasn't until Bob Lockhart of the University of Pennsylvania Press approached me to write it that it occurred to me to do so. My first thanks is to him for giving me the opportunity to collect so much of what has been floating around in my head and to make it coherent. Thanks too to series editor Judith Martin for her encouragement and suggestions, as well as to Laura Miller and Erica Ginsburg of Penn Press for their assistance.

This book provided a marvelous excuse to talk with a number of people about the city and the region. For their time, their indulgence, and their insight I thank Chris Satullo, George Lakey, Tom Hoopes, Lisa Haynes, and Michael Nairn. Joseph Becton, Kirk Hastings, Marc Stein, and the staff of the Library Company were generous with their help in researching photographs.

For the last few years I have been the token historian in Philadelphia's Design Advocacy Group. This lively, engaged group of architects, planners, designers, and others meets monthly to discuss matters of the built environment in the region, and those discussions have enriched this book immensely. Thanks in particular to Harris Steinberg, who invited me to DAG's first meeting and whose conversation have been particularly valuable to me. A number of friends and colleagues have read this book or talked about it with me and have made it better. However, I owe a particular thanks to Eric Schneider, Morrie Vogel, Howard Gillette, Mike Zuckerman, Max Page, Bruce Kuklick, Tom Sugrue, and David

Watt. My friend and colleague Wendell Pritchett, himself a son of Philadelphia, gave this a thorough critique.

My siblings, David, Alison, and Jennifer, constitute some of the smartest, sharpest, and certainly funniest people I know. The ceaseless hard time they have given their big brother over the years has not only made me laugh but has made me work harder at what I do. My parents, even in their wisdom, probably do not appreciate fully all that I owe them.

This book was written in almost equal parts in the small town of Yellow Springs, Ohio, and in the University City section of Philadelphia. On the face of it, these two places would seem a world apart. In fact, in both I have been lucky beyond measure to find a community life that has supported and nourished me, and a group of friends who understand what community truly means.

I have always prided myself on being an intrepid explorer, but I have met my match in my wife and partner, Angela Brintlinger. Though a product of the Chicago area, she has become an enthusiastic Philadelphian, and not even the arrival of our two children, Olivia and Zachary, has slowed our adventuring around the city and the region. She, and they, are the very best traveling companions.